SEEN

and

UNSEEN

SEEN

and

UNSEEN

Technology, Social Media,
and the Fight for Racial Justice

MARC LAMONT HILL
and TODD BREWSTER

ATRIA PAPERBACK

New York   London   Toronto   Sydney   New Delhi

ATRIA
PAPERBACK

An Imprint of Simon & Schuster, Inc.
1230 Avenue of the Americas
New York, NY 10020

Copyright © 2022 by Marc Lamont Hill and Todd Brewster

First Atria Paperback edition February 2023

ATRIA PAPERBACK and colophon are trademarks of Simon & Schuster, Inc.

For information about special discounts for bulk purchases, please contact Simon & Schuster Special Sales at 1-866-506-1949 or business@simonandschuster.com.

The Simon & Schuster Speakers Bureau can bring authors to your live event. For more information or to book an event, contact the Simon & Schuster Speakers Bureau at 1-866-248-3049 or visit our website at www.simonspeakers.com.

Interior design by Suet Chong

Manufactured in the United States of America

10 9 8 7 6 5 4 3 2 1

The Library of Congress has cataloged the hardcover edition as follows:

Names: Hill, Marc Lamont, author. | Brewster, Todd, author.
Title: Seen and unseen : technology, social media, and the fight for racial justice / Marc Lamont Hill and Todd Brewster.
Description: First Atria Books hardcover edition. | New York, NY : Atria Books, [2022] | Includes bibliographical references and index.
Identifiers: LCCN 2022007010 | ISBN 9781982180393 (hardcover) | ISBN 9781982180416 (ebook)
Subjects: LCSH: Social justice—United States. | Racial justice—United States. | Social media and society—United States.
Classification: LCC HM671 .H55 2022 | DDC 303.3/720973—dc23/eng/20220310
LC record available at https://lccn.loc.gov/2022007010

ISBN 978-1-9821-8039-3
ISBN 978-1-9821-8040-9 (pbk)
ISBN 978-1-9821-8041-6 (ebook)

Daily Progress photo on p. 227 by Ryan Kelly.

Massive mural memorializing George Floyd unveiled in Canarsie by artist, activist, and Brooklyn ambassador Kenny Altidor/AKART1.

To the memory of all those throughout American history who have suffered at the hands of vigilante and police violence. May seeing bring learning, and learning bring justice.

Love forces, at last, this humility: you cannot love if you cannot *be* loved, you cannot see if you cannot be seen.

—JAMES BALDWIN

Contents

Introduction

Since the end of the Civil War, America has been nagged by what was often called, as if describing a problem child, the "Negro question." And for the great majority of that time the answer was one delivered by white journalists and white academics, white politicians and white policymakers, white pastors and white businessmen, white novelists and white scientists. Some of the most commanding contributions to the discussion have come from practitioners of the communications profession, and as the tools of communication became more powerful, so, too, did their messages. Indeed, it would be no exaggeration to say that the storytelling of novelists, filmmakers, journalists, and academics was as crucial—perhaps even more crucial—to establishing Jim Crow and its era of cruel servitude as was the work of segregationist lawmakers.

It was white people who owned the cameras and white people who made the movies, white people who ran the publishing companies, edited the newspapers, and funded the research, and white people who wove tales that sentimentalized the Confederacy, adjusted the lessons of the Civil War to be more favorable to the South, and argued that Reconstruction failed because Black people, inferior by their very nature, had nonetheless been entrusted with equality and authority at the expense of the interests and feelings of the defeated white majority. In short, "Negroes" were what white people saw them to be, wished them to be, and even forced them to be. How do you answer the "Negro question"? Let white people do it for you.

Even those who counted themselves as sympathetic to the plight of Black America tended to offer pity more than understanding, to see the problem of race as secondary and not systemic, as something to be repaired rather than reenvisioned. Responding in 1890 to criticism that the "First Mohonk Conference on the Negro Question" in upstate New York had included only white participants, the progressive theologian Lyman Abbott wrote that the presence of the "negro" in discussions about "his vices and virtues, his capacities and incapacities, his ignorance and knowledge" would only inhibit free discussion. "A patient," he explained, "is not invited to the consultation of the doctors on his case."

Such misguided paternalism lasted well into the twentieth century and, indeed, persists today. Noting the entrenched nature of racism in our public institutions, the psychoanalyst and author Joel Kovel, writing in 1970, coined the term "metaracists" for those who, while not overtly racist in their behavior, "acquiesce in the larger cultural order which continues the work of racism." Much more recently, Betsy Hodges, the former mayor of Minneapolis, responding to the police killing of George Floyd, challenged American liberals for resisting systemic solutions in favor of the "illusions of change," of things that "make us feel better . . . but fundamentally change little for . . . communities," including "the hoarding of advantage by mostly white neighborhoods."

But early in the twenty-first century, Americans find themselves living at an inflexion point. Thanks to the rapid democratization of technology that is so characteristic of our time, the messages delivered by our communication tools are no longer exclusively, or even predominantly, the work of the white and the powerful. They no longer represent only the voices of those who see Black lives as inferior to white lives or, at the very least, dependent on white largesse. They are, with different degrees of influence and power, the varied voices of all of us.

This is a book about that change, about both the good

and the bad, about what social media and the ubiquity of video evidence of racism is doing to us as a society. It looks back at the history of race and technology to discover how photography and the movies were used to shape American race relations, furthering or hindering racial justice, and it looks forward to address the challenges that our new era, empowered by fresh democratic tools, poses to racial justice. To address all of this, we chose a handful of scenes of racial confrontation and violence that have taken place over the past few years, scenes that were captured on cell phone cameras, on law enforcement bodycams, on surveillance video, or on the camcorders of marauding self-sponsored videographers and then distributed across the internet and on social media. There, they were chopped into short memes, framed into social media messages, utilized as recruitment pitches, played backward and forward, sped up and slowed down, and otherwise dissected for hidden meanings.

One result has been that a more realistic, unfiltered picture of Black life is emerging. Long-held claims of racially motivated police and vigilante violence now have the evidence that they formerly lacked. Calls to action no longer need to rely solely upon the persuasiveness of the speaker, for the visuals precede them, motivating people who might otherwise not have believed that a white police officer attempting to arrest a Black man for the crime of passing a counterfeit twenty-dollar bill would subdue him with a knee on the man's neck until the life was squeezed out of him, breath by breath.

This alone is no small achievement, for it is "invisibility," as Isabel Wilkerson has written, that has long given systemic racism its "power and longevity." But the changes brought by our new technologies are not only in what we can now witness; they are also in what we can now do. Large social movements have always been at the mercy of the technology of their times, and the structure, method, language, and goals of those movements were determined in part by the nature of that technology. But today's media is infinitely more pliable. Events can be livestreamed across the world. Videos can be shot and posted on YouTube or Instagram or Facebook, where they can be watched today, tomorrow, a year from now, or ten years from now, and shared with neighbors and coworkers, with old friends from high school and strangers you just "friended" because, well, Facebook thought you should. Comments can be collected, disseminated, and then re-disseminated ad infinitum. People can be mobilized within minutes and directed in real time from their phones, with more people connected in more ways than during any other time in human history. The break with the past is nothing short of stunning. "The thing about King or Ella Baker is that they could not just wake up and sit at the breakfast table and talk to a million people," activist DeRay Mckesson said in an interview with the magazine *Wired*. "The tools that we have to organize and to resist are fundamentally different than anything that's existed before in black struggle."

In the late nineteenth century, photography helped expose the barbarity of lynching at the same time that the crusading Black journalist Ida B. Wells was uncovering the lies that condemned Black men (and some women) to the fate of the rope. By the mid twentieth century, the work of sympathetic photojournalists, both white and Black, helped drive the Civil Rights Movement, creating images of despair and injustice that seared the popular consciousness—pictures that, to this day, stand as essential iconography of America's progressive history. Marching in Montgomery in 1965, Martin Luther King Jr. declared that the movement would no longer let white men "use clubs on us in the dark corners. We are going to make them do it in the glaring light of television."

But the developments of the past few years, particularly since the cell phone and its progeny became an essential presence in everyday life, have changed the pace, tone, and character of this longstanding practice. Indeed, it sometimes feels as though the history of communications will one day be understood to be divided between everything that came before the cell phone and everything that came after it—and the story of race in America will be different for it.

Of course, we don't yet know *how* it will be different, and there are plenty of reasons to be skeptical that the outcome will be a positive one. After a bloody civil war brought an end to slavery, the nation wanted to move on, convinced that the practice of bondage was just that, a practice, and that once this stain on the American creed of equality had been removed, that would be the end of the story. In fact, slavery was only the worst manifestation of a centuries-old caste system that persisted in new forms, reenergized, in the post–Civil War era by Southerners' lust for revenge. Similarly, when Jim Crow was made illegal under the pressures brought by the freedom movement of the 1950s and 1960s, finally taking up where Emancipation had left off a hundred years earlier, the country conflated that success with the grander American story of fighting tyranny—whitening it, in a sense— before discovering more subtle ways to return to old, shameful social norms in coded calls for law and order, mass incarceration, and the dismantling of the social safety net.

The scenes we describe in this book need to be recognized for their place in that history. They also need to be understood for their place in the broader history of communications. The new imagery is just that, imagery— fleeting, ephemeral—and in our time, we are drowning in imagery, most of which we apprehend through our smartphones. Videos telling the truth about police violence are squeezed between a Twitter rant from a disgruntled Yankees fan and an Instagram influencer's demonstration of a recipe for avocado toast. The screen they occupy is the same size. It doesn't get bigger to underscore the importance of one message over another. The campaign for racial justice becomes just one more commodity, and slogans like "Black Lives Matter" assume an awkward place in corporate marketing strategies, where the next consumer trend will one day supplant them.

Still, some images, some messages have the quality of being, paradoxically, both ephemeral and enduring, both there and not there. The video of the killing of George Floyd has a lasting impact because we believed it, saw it as a faithful representation of what happened on the streets of Minneapolis that day, and because it was shared over and over again as if it were actually happening over and over again, which is of course a core part of its message. There is one George Floyd on video but many more who see the same fate away from the scrutiny of the lens.

Progress, however, is always an elusive target, and even the starkest representations of the truth can be distorted by reinterpretation or reframed to tell a completely different story. They can be discredited by distractions and innuendos that often amount to nothing more than victim shaming. That, in fact, is what happened to the story of George Floyd when Candace Owens, a Black conservative commentator, posted a video on YouTube calling Floyd "a horrible human being" and providing details of the crimes for which he was convicted earlier in his life. "White Americans are not uplifting Derek Chauvin and pretending that he is an amazing human being," she insisted, as if the story were nothing more than a competition of character. The video garnered over 100 million views. But the same thing happened to the stories of Trayvon Martin, Eric Garner, Michael Brown, and, for that matter, long before social media, the fourteen-year-old Emmett Till and every "brutish" or "beastly" lynching victim, purportedly put down because he or she was a threat to all that was good and civilized. The democratization of technology means that now there is greater access for all people, including those who use pictures and messages to stand against racial justice or to beat back progress.

The persistent rush of images that has replaced reading can also force upon us a rigid presentism. We don't stop to receive the news and react to it. We drink it in, as if from a firehose, trained by technological impulse to discard and "move on." Even the act of repetition is suspect. It can reinforce, yes, but it can also dilute. What shocks the first time becomes mere record on the second showing, and unremarkable on the third.

The danger to all of this is that we repeat the rhythm of American history, one of progress followed by regress, followed by more progress and then even more regress. Even this moment, ripe as it seems for substantive change, may well slip us by. But if so, that will be on us, both white and Black. The opposition is mobilized—but so are those who see in this moment one more opportunity to direct the eyes of the nation. "Seeing, which comes before words, and can never be quite covered by them, is not a question of mechanically reacting to stimuli," wrote the great art critic John Berger. "We only see what we look at," and "to look is an act of choice."

ONE

The Spectacle of Death

I t's a simple question: Why?

Why, after so much writing and analysis on the prevalence of police violence directed at people of color—so much data, so many first-person accounts, and, finally, so much cell phone and surveillance video—it took the video of the deadly violence used on George Floyd to trigger a broad response of sympathy and outrage about racial injustice? Historians may well ponder this long into the twenty-first century. But only, of course, if the image of the knee-in-the-neck lynching of Floyd does not recede with time, does not fade like so many other stories of unarmed Black men killed by police and vigilantes, does not evaporate into the ether like the millions of images traded on Snapchat and Instagram every day.

The accounts of others who in recent years met the same or a similar fate as George Floyd are numerous, even if we recite only some of the names of those who became widely known—Breonna Taylor, Oscar Grant, Kathryn Johnston, Trayvon Martin, Sandra Bland, Eric Garner, Rekia Boyd, Alton Sterling, Mya Hall, Walter Scott, Renisha McBride, Michael Brown, Ahmaud Arbery, Rayshard Brooks, Philando Castile. But all these victims, each of them gone from us now, share one thing: our knowledge of them was enhanced through the modern media tools available—through cell phone and surveillance video, Twitter alerts and Facebook groups, and the playing and replaying of footage, both forward and reverse, zoomed in to analyze every movement, zoomed out to determine context, dissected and repurposed, shown in courtrooms and on YouTube and spliced to form memes. Indeed, it was these tools and technologies that provided the unique ability to keep the stories of injustice not only alive—text alone can do that—but compelling and persistent, like an unattended car alarm ringing through the night.

It is cliché to say that our age speaks through pictures, both real and imagined, more than ideas: a border wall; a rogue immigrant caravan; a roaming, young Black man in a hoodie; a man with a knee in the neck of another man as he gasps, "I can't breathe." But where a photograph becomes an object, something to be held or framed or thumbtacked onto a bulletin board or published in a book—think of how our mind's eye charts the story of the Civil Rights Movement with images of Bull Connor's Birmingham firehoses, John Lewis marching bravely across the Edmund Pettus Bridge, and fifteen-year-old Elizabeth Eckford walking fearlessly to Little Rock High School while being taunted by a crowd of white students—the "pictures" of our time, millions of them, when passed through our obligatory devices, form something more like a persistent conversation, a parlor argument rendered through flash cards, one vivid image replaced by the next vivid image until the exchange drifts off like a text stream finally gone unanswered. And then, in a persistent rhythm, another irrelevant exchange begins. Maybe a TikTok of men singing sea chanteys or customers brawling at a Walmart over the few remaining pieces of sale merchandise.

In the late nineteenth century, long before pictures became a prevalent form of discourse, Black journalist Ida B. Wells boldly published investigations of American lynchings. She did so because, otherwise, the dead "had no requiem, save the night wind, no memorial service to bemoan their sad and horrible fate." Absent the effort of the chronicler, they were like the dead bodies of Union soldiers, left to decay in "an unknown and unhonored spot." By exposing lynching for what it was—not the crazed violence of a fevered few but a festive ritual central to white southerners' conceptions of white superiority—Wells helped to initiate the modern movement for civil rights.

In the cacophony of images that dominate our times, will the grisly footage of George Floyd and his executioner, Derek Chauvin, demand the kind of sustainable awakening that Wells's work did in hers? Will it inspire a new racial analysis? Will it force us to reimagine and, ultimately, reshape a society still plagued by racial injustice? Or will George Floyd, as his brother, Philonise, worried aloud in an appearance before Congress, be nothing more than "another face on a T-shirt . . . another name on a list that won't stop growing"?

———

Over and over again (twenty-two times), George Floyd calls out for "mama." Over and over again (eight times) he says, poignantly, "I am not that kind of guy." What "kind of guy" does he mean? The guy the officers assume him to be? And if so, what, exactly, does he think that is? The kind who passes a counterfeit twenty-dollar bill? Or the kind he fears lives in the recesses of Derek Chauvin's imagination? Did the two men lock eyes and pass to each other some knowing expression, some exchange that defined each for the other and became the basis for their interaction? And this is key, because there is caricature at work here. We know that the clash between Black and white in America has often navigated a canyon of misunderstanding and asymmetric power relations, one painted in broad brushstrokes throughout history. But here, between the officers and Floyd and then, finally, between Officer Chauvin and Floyd, we're witnessing the very same grotesque dynamics in miniature, all twisted and perverted, a wound with the scab torn off. It's as if video has taken us beneath the surface to go where the naked eye cannot, to a place where the relationship between Black and white is exhibited to us in infinitesimal detail. We are eye to the microscope, ears to the headphones, witnessing an interaction few get to see so up close.

FLOYD: "Why don't you all believe me, Mr. Officer?"
OFFICER KUENG: "Take a seat!"
FLOYD: "I'm not that kind of guy! I'm not that kind of guy, man!"
BYSTANDER: "You can't win, bro."
FLOYD: "I'm not trying to win."
OFFICER KUENG: "Stop moving."
FLOYD: "Mama, mama, mama, mama."

Because Floyd is in such distress, the scene feels almost too intimate, the experience prurient, like we're watching something that maybe we shouldn't be watching. And all of this, of course, is made even more difficult because we see the full pursuit of Floyd and the struggle to subdue him—both predator and prey, competition and result. At times it feels disturbingly like a nature show. It's not that we haven't all witnessed the act of killing in vivid motion-picture form before, narratively delivered. We have. But our experience with violence on film tends, of course, to be what we see in an acted form while sitting with strangers in dark theaters, or with a few others at home, or watching alone on our tablets or phones—all situations in which we greet what we see according to certain established filmic conventions, including that the violence isn't real, that we suspend disbelief in the interest of following a narrative, and that the deeper we descend into that narrative, the greater the reward of escape from our own world and its troubles we receive. But this, here, is the problem, because the George Floyd video *is* our world, and these *are* our troubles.

FLOYD: "I can't breathe, officer."
OFFICER CHAUVIN: "Then stop talking, stop yelling."
FLOYD: "You're going to kill me, man."
CHAUVIN: "Then stop talking, stop yelling. It takes a heck of a lot of oxygen to talk."

The fact that we do recognize this as "our world" is a triumph over the film. We load it on one screen and shift back and forth to others, checking our bank account balances, email accounts, texts, Twitter feeds. We click on it and reverse it, fast-forward it, or hold it in a pause. We switch to another video on TikTok—a couple dances the jitterbug in the rain, a precocious child unknowingly embarrasses their parent, an online influencer models her new workout gear or hair product, a dog bounces up and down on its hind legs to a silly soundtrack being sung by its owner— and come back to it later. But it is there, and it is undeniable. Zoomed in, it's George Floyd and Officer Chauvin; zoomed out, it's the whole story of race in America. Black and white. The world, writ small, writ large.

BYSTANDER: "He's going to choke him. Are you going to choke him like that? I'm not scared of you, bro. You're a pussy-ass dude, bro."

FLOYD: "I can't breathe."

OFFICER KUENG: "You're doing fine. You're talking fine."

FLOYD: "I can't breathe."

BYSTANDER (TO CHAUVIN): "You such a man, bro. That shit crazy."

FLOYD: "I can't breathe or nothing, man. This cold-blooded, man. Ah-ah! Ah-ah! Ah-ah!"

CHAUVIN: "You're doing a lot of talking, man."

FLOYD: "Momma, I love you. I can't do nothing."

———

By all accounts, George Perry Floyd Jr. was an unlikely candidate for martyrdom. Still, his story resonated. It resonated with whites because the cruelty inflicted on him was so undeniable, so elemental ("Momma! . . . Momma! I'm through"), and so protracted (nine minutes, twenty-nine seconds) that it could be neither ignored nor dismissed. A shooting is an instant; a lynching is a performance. Floyd's death resonated with many Black Americans for the same reasons, but also because it was so familiar. George Floyd wasn't just an individual but a Black Everyman whose murder spotlighted the underside of America's racial landscape. As Black people watched the last breaths being squeezed from Floyd's body, they could see themselves in his suffering; or an uncle, or a sister, or even a long-departed ancestor.

The life story of George Floyd, like all human stories, was shaped by the history that preceded him. Born in Fayetteville, North Carolina, in 1973, he was two when his parents separated, and he moved with his mother and four siblings to Houston's Third Ward. "Tre," as it is affectionately called, had once been one of Houston's grander residential areas. With stunning Victorian homes, it supported a white neighborhood in its southern extension and a Black population to the north. But in the years after World War II, following a familiar urban pattern in America, whites abandoned the city for the growing suburbs and Blacks moved to the areas that whites were abandoning.

Along with the growth of suburbia came the expansion of the highway system, allowing the white commuters in the new suburbs the opportunity to get into and out of the city with ease. Interstate 45 divided the old Fourth Ward, I-10 separated the Fifth, and State Highway 288 split the Third. Absent a monied class to attract investment, the social cohesion of the new urban Black neighborhoods was disrupted by the highways, and with that, the city's old neighborhoods went into a rapid decline.

Floyd grew up in the Cuney Homes, a public housing project made up of two-story brick-faced units (nicknamed "The Bricks") that was built by the Houston Public Housing Authority back in the days of the New Deal. It was named for Norris Wright Cuney, a mixed-race politician who had been born into slavery, the product of his enslaved mother and her white master. As a freedman, Cuney emerged during Reconstruction as a prominent voice in the Texas Republican party; that is, until the "Lily-White Movement," established to lure white voters back from the Democrats, ousted the "Black and Tans" from Republican ranks.

By the early twentieth century, the party of Abraham Lincoln was actively discouraging Black membership, and once-powerful politicians like Cuney and others like him were little more than a topic for memorial acknowledgment. Even the act of naming the housing project after Cuney had more to do with reinforcing the message of subordination than celebrating achievement. If there was any doubt about where racial attitudes in Houston stood, across town, in the First Ward, the hospital was named for the president of the Confederacy, Jefferson Davis. It occupied land that was once the burial place of Confederate soldiers. (Closed in 1938, the hospital was declared a historic landmark in 1987.) The naming of a housing project in the Third Ward for Norris Wright Cuney was less about championing Black people than about declaring, "This is your place. Be grateful for it. And don't come near ours."

George Floyd graduated from the segregation-era Yates High School (formerly Yates Colored High School), which was named for yet another courageous post–Civil War Black leader, the Baptist minister and former slave Jack Yates. In 1868, Yates joined Houston's Antioch Missionary Baptist Church, itself founded by seven freed slaves, and served there until 1891. During that time, he was instrumental in the establishment of Emancipation Park, a patch of land in the Third Ward celebrating the end of slavery. But like so many achievements during Reconstruction, this one was spat upon when, in 1892, the road next to it was named for Dick Dowling, a Confederate general known as the "hero" of the Battle of Sabine Pass for successfully pushing back an attempt by the Union army to invade and annex part of Texas. In 1905, the city added a marble statue of Dowling, the first piece of public art in the history of Houston, in front of City Hall. In 2017, under petition, "Dowling Avenue" became "Emancipation Avenue." In that same year, a twenty-five-year-old man was arrested on charges of attempting to blow up the Dowling statue, and it was removed in 2020. Slowly, Houston is catching up with its history.

At Yates High School, Floyd, at six feet four inches (some say six feet five, others six feet six, and the clerk at Cup Foods who reported him estimated six foot eight and muscular), was a power forward on the basketball team and a tight end on a football team that went to the state championship in 1992. He then briefly attended South Florida Community College and Texas A&M–Kingsville on a football scholarship before returning to the Third Ward. His dream of a career in professional sports gone, Floyd began hanging out with a local rapper named Robert Earl Davis Jr., better known as DJ Screw. It was the 1990s and hip-hop was still in a space where creative experimentation was more important than commercial exploitation, still playing to an audience more Black than white, still primarily the music of the streets. Screw is credited with inventing "chopped and screwed," a studio remixing technique in which tracks are slowed down ("poured molasses" is the metaphor often summoned) and overlaid with scratches and beats. "Big Floyd" joined Screw's group Screwed Up Click. After Floyd's death, his deep baritone was eerily resurrected on social media in Screw's version of "Tired of Ballin'" and "Sittin' on Top of the World Freestyle." There, Floyd takes the mic for the third verse: "On the grind, true south sider/Watch me crawl low on my motherfuckin' spiders/Welcome to the ghetto, it's Third Ward, Texas/Boys choppin' blades on their motherfuckin' Lexus."

For Floyd, it was an honor just to work with Screw, who was something of a local legend who enjoyed a cult following around East Texas. The artist's sound was gaining attention nationwide, but it was his artistic integrity, his determination to resist commercialism and work only for himself and his fans and no one else, that cemented Screw's following. At its inception, rap was never meant to be commercial; it was an underground sound, rooted in the oral traditions of African American life. The first place it was heard was in the South Bronx, a spontaneous art that filled abandoned lots, turning them into instant block parties with DJs spinning vinyl deep into the night. Like the oral tradition itself, the sound was, by definition, ephemeral, creating a spontaneous moment before evaporating into the dawn. Even the act of recording was seen by some purists to be at odds with the hip-hop aesthetic. In this sense it followed a pattern established by another Black art form, jazz, which also thrived on improvisation— and indeed, back in the 1940s if you missed Bird or Dizzy or Lester Young at the club, well, too bad; just try to be around next time, because while you could always listen to recordings, they would never be the same.

Screw not only eschewed commercialization, he was also authentic, a fixture in his basement studio where he overindulged in food, drugs, and all-night, all-day creative experimentation. He didn't seek a fortune through his work, preferring to remain loyal to the neighborhood and using what money he had to help out teenagers and send support to friends in prison. In this he followed a strain of thought in the Black community that associated commercial exploitation with white power and the "lie," as W. E. B. Du Bois called it, "an ancient lie spread by church and state, by priest and historian" that "mankind can rise only by walking on men; by cheating them and killing them." Screw's rejection of the inevitability of exploitation earned him enormous local cred, and indeed, each Wednesday, when he would prepare new tapes and sell them from his house, cars would line up around the block for the chance to grab his latest creations: ten dollars apiece for Maxell cassettes with titles scrawled on them by Screw's own hand. In the late nineties, he opened a store, selling only his own music from behind bulletproof glass. There were no displays. You came in and requested your tape from across a counter, like a drugstore prescription for amphetamines or—more appropriately, given the slowed-down rhythms that were Screw's specialty—tranquilizers. It was all in the interest of holding the work close to the chest, away from monied interests, many of them white, that might force creative compromise and otherwise take advantage of him. Screw had no interest in letting others, particularly white businessmen, define him. Even if it meant that he would earn less money, Screw would be true to himself. And he was, until he died in 2000, likely the result of an overdose—after his body was discovered next to a toilet in his studio, an autopsy revealed codeine mixed with PCP and Valium—but more than twenty years later, people are still making pilgrimages to his relocated shop. It turns out that even in death, Screw retains some of the aura of the folk hero that he was in life.

After Floyd's brief flirtation with hip-hop, his life went into decline—not that he had ever risen very far—and followed a familiar trajectory. Like many of the victims of the postindustrial urban American economy, particularly poor Black women and men, he entered a cycle of drugs, despair, and crime. The details and particulars of Floyd's struggles would be later used, if not to justify his fate, then certainly to lessen the collective white guilt surrounding his death—the notion that, sure, it's sad that he met such an awful end, but given where his life had been going and all the "bad decisions" he'd made, are we surprised? But to particularize is to miss the pattern. Floyd was just the latest, and most public, example of a well-worn racist narrative, one deeply engrained in American life long before Emancipation, in which a violent end is explained away as a failure of biology. It's the one that says that the Negro can't handle freedom, that he is preordained to a life of dependency, that he is morally vacant, that he cannot be trusted to make noble use of his "equality," or, worse, that he is all of that and also a bloodthirsty monster, more beast than human. It was used as a justification for slavery and, after the end of slavery, as a justification for Jim Crow and its many tentacles that not only gripped white Americans then but many Black Americans too, as when no less than Du Bois, the towering Black intellectual of the early twentieth century, said in an 1897 speech that "unless we conquer our present vices they will conquer us. We are diseased, we are developing criminal tendencies, and an alarmingly large percentage of our men and women are sexually impure. . . . [T]he first and greatest step toward the settlement of the present friction between the races—commonly called the Negro Problem—lies in the correction of the immorality, crime, and laziness among the Negroes themselves, which still remains as a heritage from slavery."

Caught selling one gram of cocaine, Floyd was sentenced to six months in prison. Then, shortly after his release, for refusing to provide a policeman with his name and address he got another fifteen days. A charge for drug possession and another for criminal trespassing followed, with prison time and then more prison time, before he was nabbed for armed robbery in a home invasion and incarcerated for four years. Floyd had entered the world of what Michelle Alexander referred to over a decade ago as "the new Jim Crow," an era of mass incarceration that produced punitive policies and astronomically high mandatory sentencing guidelines, an era that forced Black men and women from their families and communities, wreaking havoc on Black lives. As Alexander put it, the criminal justice system was "no longer concerned primarily with the prevention and punishment of crime, but rather with the management and control of the dispossessed."

———

The particular downward cycle that gripped the life of George Floyd began shortly after the end of slavery and the failure of Reconstruction. Among the first people to record it honestly was Ida B. Wells. Like Norris Cuney, Wells was born into slavery, in Mississippi. Her mother was an enslaved Black woman named "Lizzie," and her father was "Jim," the offspring of his white master, Morgan Wells, and an enslaved woman named "Peggy." (Until Emancipation, enslaved Blacks commonly had no surnames; after Emancipation, they generally claimed the names of their former masters, in what retrospectively looks like a form of branding.) But Ida Wells was an infant when Abraham Lincoln issued the Emancipation Proclamation and three years old when the Thirteenth Amendment banning slavery was ratified, meaning that her time in bondage was short, and her early childhood was lived out in relative comfort. Harder days followed. In 1878, at age sixteen, Wells lost both parents and a brother to a yellow fever epidemic that raged throughout the region, and by the time she had established herself as a young journalist—no small feat for a woman, much less a Black woman, in that time—the climate had shifted from the initial promise of Reconstruction to the brutality and injustice of Jim Crow. "The slave went free; stood a brief moment in the sun," wrote W. E. B. Du Bois of this time, "then moved back again toward slavery."

After the death of her parents, Wells left Mississippi to teach and live with relatives in Memphis, Tennessee, a city with its own painful racial scars. What is today known as the "Memphis Massacre" occurred just one year after the end of the Civil War when recently freed slaves roamed the streets reveling in their new status, and Black businesses thrived. After an altercation between two horse-drawn hacks, violence erupted, with white mobs targeting the shantytown in which Black veterans and their families lived. The men were stationed at Fort Pickering, a Confederate garrison captured by Union forces in 1862. Forty-eight people perished, forty-six of them Black, and the South Memphis neighborhood that housed Black churches, homes, and schools was burned to the ground.

Shortly after her arrival in Memphis, Wells was recruited to write for a local Black newspaper, the *Free Speech*. Her approach to the issues of the day was to condemn those who committed violence on Black people and at the same time condemn Black self-hatred and any subservience that made them kowtow to the white man's demands. She was particularly opposed to the accommodationist philosophy of Booker T. Washington, who believed in acquiescence to white society as a defensive position, at least until the Black community could learn enough trades and make enough money to stand on its own.

Not surprisingly, Washington was every southern, and many northern, white's favorite Black leader, and he later became the first African American to be invited to dine with the president at the White House. But Wells saw anyone who followed Washington's logic—and, as dreams of a real Reconstruction faded, there were many who did—to be on a fool's errand.

There were things that appealed to Wells about Washington, most significantly the notion that Black people needed to trust only other Black people. "Let the Afro-American depend upon no party, but on himself for his salvation," she wrote in 1892. But she found him blind to the physical threats that continued to blunt African American progress and, through his silence, an accomplice to the steady erosion of the rights that had been achieved in the decade after the Civil War. To Wells, there were two images that demanded to be considered in what was now post-Reconstruction America. One was the path to Black achievement; the other was the hangman's noose that awaited them there.

Washington believed that when white people saw that Blacks had achieved economic success, they would respect them and treat them as equals. But Wells knew this was folly, and in this she was prescient; white people had no tolerance for Black success, and were in fact threatened by it. Wells had firsthand experience watching Black enterprises thrive in Memphis only to engender violence from white mobs who saw them as taking profits from their own businesses. Indeed, the gruesome lynching of the proprietors of the People's Grocery, a successful Black business in Memphis run by friends of Wells's, was a turning point for her. When it came to fending off such attacks, the law offered no refuge. Indeed, Wells declared that "a Winchester rifle should have a place of honor in every black home, and it be used for that protection which the law refuses to give," arguing that only when the white man runs as much risk of losing his own life as the one whom he pursues will he begin to show the necessary respect for the African American. "The more the Afro-American yields and cringes and begs . . . the more he is insulted, outraged, and lynched."

Wells spoke from a place of righteous anger, but her work was more revelatory than polemical. Disturbed by the barbaric and repugnant nature of lynching, she began her own investigation into the practice and discovered inconsistencies and outright falsehoods in dozens of cases, particularly when it came to charges of rape. Two months after the People's Grocery lynchings, Wells published an editorial in the *Free Speech* arguing that the "old thread-bare lie that Negro men rape White women" was in fact a ruse to cover up consensual relations that could well be "damaging to the moral reputation of their women." For the white population, the subjugation of the African American was deeply tied up with fears of sexual conquest, and so at the time these were incendiary words. Within days, the offices of the *Free Speech* were ransacked and burned to the ground by a white mob. There were calls to lynch Wells herself. In fact, a local white paper ran an editorial demanding that "the wretch who utters these calumnies" be tied to a stake, "brand[ed] . . . in the forehead with a hot iron," and (thinking that it was her male partner at the *Free Speech* who had written it), his genitals removed "with tailor's shears." Undeterred, Wells, in exile, simply began writing elsewhere. "Somebody must show that the Afro-American race is more sinned against than sinning, and it seems to have fallen upon me to do so."

In her pamphlet *Southern Horrors* and, later, in another she titled *Red Record*, Wells critiqued lynching and investigated accusations ranging from rape, murder, and burglary to simple "insubordination" and "uppitiness." Regardless of the "crime," the punishment for any of these was death at the stake. In addition to calling the charges against Black victims into question, Wells also reframed the act of lynching itself, and it may be this that is her most significant legacy. In the American South of the Jim Crow era, Ida B. Wells exposed lynching for what it was, a festival sport with deep psychological and historical overtones, cloaked in the rituals of the courtroom as if to give state to what was nothing more than a vigilante act. To understand the context, you have to situate the moment: only a few decades from the end of slavery and from the "science" of Harvard zoologist Louis Agassiz, who saw African Americans, with their "fat lips and grimacing teeth, the wool on their heads, their bent knees, their elongated hands," as members of a "degraded and degenerate race." Untethered from the chains that once bound them, removed from a hierarchy that forced an etiquette of nodding respect, unschooled in the written and unwritten rules of white supremacist society, and, perhaps most critically, a constant reminder of the Confederacy's humiliating defeat and the economic devastation that resulted from it, the New Negro was seen by white southerners as a people that needed to be annihilated, and to be annihilated they had to first be demonized and caricatured.

No matter the nature of the "crime," mere prosecution would offer little satisfaction in this context, and maybe none, since it could potentially lay bare the lie at the heart of the white community's charges. Turning the fate of the accused over to the legitimate institutions of justice would also have the undesirable effect of acknowledging the freedmen's equal standing before the law. In the perverse logic of the white supremacist, there was no law on which to try a "fiend" or a "brute," only extralegal means to eradicate the problem, and lynching was the one that both punished the accused and laid out a public threat to Black people everywhere.

Like many, Wells had originally thought that lynching was an aberration, punishment by exaggeration, a momentary bit of insanity driven by a frothing desire to safeguard the white woman. This was, in fact, the "excuse" routinely put forward by southern apologists—that in order to "protect their women from Black monsters" the "human nature" of the lynchers gave way to mob rule, and therefore, while lynching was something to be condemned for its barbarity, the mob "must be pitied as well as condemned." Wells found that even among African Americans "the crime of rape is so revolting" that they would believe the charge to be legitimate and never even think to challenge it nor the harsh punishment meted out in response. Wells took a different point of view. She argued that "a concession of the right to lynch a man for a certain crime, not only concedes the right to lynch any person for any crime, but (so frequently is the cry of rape now raised) it is in a fair way to stamp us a race of rapists and desperadoes."

Through her research, Wells showed just how widespread lynching was, and how it was a deliberate, not a spontaneous or instinctive, act. Its aim was not justice, not even "frontier justice," but merely "an excuse to get rid of Negroes who were acquiring wealth and property and thus keep the race terrorized and 'keep the nigger down.'" The lies were numerous and spelled out in a complicit press. The "eight-year-old daughter" of a Mississippi sheriff "raped" by a "big, black burly brute" turned out to be an eighteen-year-old who had made her own way voluntarily to the cabin of the man, seeking relations with him. In Texarkana, Arkansas, a man accused of raping a white woman had in fact been engaging in a consensual relationship with her for over a year. Indeed, she had been a "willing partner" whose miscegenation, once discovered, became a source of shame to her and her family and had, therefore, to be stamped out. Under threat of violence, the woman branded the Black man a rapist, and "after coal oil was poured over him . . . gladly set fire to him" as fifteen thousand people watched.

It was not only that so many of these charges were flat-out wrong; it was that the truth challenged the culture's doctrine of white superiority. Wells concluded that to the southern mind, any voluntary relations between the white woman and the Black man were deemed to be not just criminal or wrong but "impossible." They constituted a "mésalliance," a word that literally means a union of people from two different stations (as when marriage to a com-

moner spoils the monarchical line), but which has overtones suggesting the contamination of the superior blood.
Since it "could not happen," the statement of an alliance
was, prima facie, "a proof of force." Lynching, then, was not
only retribution for the crime; it was a way to cleanse the
race of the stain caused by exposure to inferior genes, and
since it wasn't just the woman who had been exposed but
by extension the race itself, the community must join the
ritual of public execution, dismemberment, and extermination.

"Extermination" was key, because there had to be no
evidence remaining of the abomination, no memorial to
the life they were taking, nothing that could be lowered
into a grave and marked for posterity lest the "impossible"
be recognized as having happened. If there was any resi-
due to a lynching, it had to be in the form of souvenirs, the
bits of clothing and charred body parts that were rescued
like relics from a big game hunt and secreted away in attics
and closets for showing on special occasions. That, and
the psychological scar that lynching was intended to leave
in the Black mind, and did. In his 1912 novel *The Autobiography of an Ex-Colored Man*, the Black writer James
Weldon Johnson writes that a critical part of the horror of
lynching was the persistence of images that one could not
bear to see but could forever "hear." For it was not only the
victim of the lynching who suffered; it was those of every
succeeding generation who, in the telling and retelling that

marked Black folk memory, learned of the fate that could await them, too.

In one notorious Paris, Texas, episode, a "harmless, weak-minded fellow" named Henry Smith, Ida Wells wrote, was charged with the murder of a child, a crime that she acknowledged would have been horrific enough to send him to the gallows. But it was not sufficient to try Smith for simple murder; the details of the murder had to be exaggerated and falsified to include rape and mutilation of the body so as to turn Smith into a monster worthy of a fate worse than death. A tale of bloated innocence was concocted, with the child reported to have been "last seen singing 'Jesus Lover of My Soul' in her childish treble voice," whereafter the attacker, a "brawny, muscular" brute possessed of "animal passions and appetites" and "devoid of any humanizing sensibilities . . . outraged" raped her and then, grabbing her by the heels, ripped her body apart in "the mad wantonness of gorilla ferocity." How could it be otherwise than that the "vengeance of an outraged God" would work his ways "through the instrumentality of the people"? Naturally, the "energy of an entire city and country" had to be "turned toward the apprehension of the demon who had devastated a home and polluted"—the verb here was carefully chosen—"an innocent life."

If, in fact, the act of lynching represented a moment of mob insanity, white supremacist rage unchecked, it nonetheless had no shortage of enthusiasts justifying it in the very deliberate profession of the mainstream press. Both southern and northern newspapers reporting on the events fed the hysteria with incendiary language ("Criminal Calendar: Two Murderous and Thieving Negroes Lynched by a Kentucky Mob" and "Deserved It All: A Brutal Negro Lynched by Indignant Farmers," to offer just two examples), with imagery in the form of illustrations of bloodthirsty Black brutes and, once again, the language of victim shaming. In one instance, the *Atlanta Constitution* offered a $500 reward for the capture of one accused victim who was later lynched. In another, it addressed a recent lynching with a headline that read "An Eye for an Eye." It then described how the body of the man was riddled with bullets and that his ears were cut off. No effort was made to question the man's guilt or to object to his extrajudicial fate in a country that claimed to believe in the rule of law. Instead, the editorialist appealed to "sensible" Negroes by saying that the way to end lynching was for Negroes to stop doing the kinds of crimes that "provoke it." His advice: "If a Negro wants to escape the danger of lynching, let him keep his hands off white women."

Culling data and making careful use of illustrations and photographs, Wells and other members of the Black press fought back. One newspaper, the *Indianapolis Freeman*, known as "the colored *Harper's Weekly*," became a pioneer in elaborate drawings that not only showed the act of lynching in excruciating detail but included symbolic figures like Uncle Sam and the robed Ethiopia as witnesses. "See how my people are murdered, maltreated, and outraged in the South," Ethiopia says, "and you, with a great army and navy, are taking no measures to prevent it." These appeared next to articles documenting the factual errors reported by the white press under titles like "America's Pastime" and "The Record of Shame."

Republishing statistics gathered by the *Chicago Tribune*, Wells (whom many today see as a pioneer of "data journalism") showed how charges of "wife beating," "barn burning," "well poisoning," "burglary," "incendiarism," and the issuing of insults to whites all resulted in death by lynching. When the stepson of Henry Smith offered no information on the whereabouts of Smith, he was lynched for the crime of "not cooperating." Wells also showed that when white men were charged with the crime of raping Black women, they received relatively light sentences. Indeed, one observer commenting on the lynching of Henry Smith noted the number of "superior white men" in the audience who "are the reputed fathers of mulatto children."

While Wells raised persistent questions about the veracity of the charges against lynching victims, she also provided copious detail on the events themselves, laying bare the bestial nature of lynching and those who reveled in it. In fact, it was this attention she paid to the "spectacle" of death—death and mutilation as entertainment— that brought a new awareness of the act. In addition to detailed descriptions, she published morbid photographs and drawings of men hanging by the noose or burned alive, gruesome pictures that risked charges of voyeurism. Yet in fact they were a triumph of repurposing, for these were the same pictures of lynchings that had been published in white newspapers with screaming headlines, and adopted as images for postcards, celebrating the triumph of white honor over the Black beast. If Wells had one message, it was not that crime should go unpunished but that the criminally accused had rights before the law, and that no one, not even the convicted, should face the torture and inhumanity of a lynching. There could simply be no tolerance for it in a civilized society.

It's important to understand just how inspired Wells's work was in her day. She wrote without vindictiveness, offering not only the first detailed accounting of the practice of lynching and holding up the horror of it to challenge the conscience of the nation but also urging others to do the same—to "keep up the agitation and take the necessary steps to get the facts," believing, as she put it, "that there is still a sense of justice in the American people and that it will yet assert itself in the condemnation of outlawry and in defense of oppressed and persecuted humanity."

Wells went on to be a force in the establishment of the NAACP. Being more militant than her times, she frequently clashed with Du Bois, the organization's leader, and eventually drifted toward the more radical views of the uncompromising Boston editor Monroe Trotter and of the pan-Africanist Marcus Garvey. Still, there is no doubt that her campaign against lynching triggered the NAACP's own, including its 1918 study *Thirty Years of Lynching in the United States* and, before that, the July 1916 publication of its magazine, the *Crisis*, which laid out in extended photographic detail the Waco, Texas, castration and barbecue of a mentally deficient seventeen-year-old named Jesse Washington. There, as in Wells's earlier work, pictures sold as celebratory mementoes of a grisly display of white supremacy became evidence, instead, of an unspeakable shame, raising awareness around the country.

Why, then, over a hundred years later, is our moral slumber still being stirred by stories of Black men being throttled by white men until their last desperate breath expires? Why hasn't the spectacle of death forced us into a state of permanent outrage and vigilance?

———

In 2013, when Floyd was granted his release from Diboll Correctional Center, he returned to the Third Ward and the Cuney Homes; fathered a daughter, Gianna, with his girlfriend, Roxie Washington; and turned his attention to God. The church, of course, has been a persistent refuge for Black Americans, and Floyd, haunted by addiction and a sense of hopelessness, was no different from millions of other Black men who, like a young James Baldwin, supposed that "God and safety were synonymous." He volunteered for Resurrection Houston, a local church. Patrick Ngwolo, Resurrection's charismatic leader, saw Floyd as critical to neighborhood outreach, in particular Resurrection's "Church in the Bricks," which brought the word of the Holy Gospel to the Homes by way of the basketball court. It was Ngwolo's idea, one he had carried over from his days at nearby Good Hope Baptist: if you can't get people to the chapel, bring the chapel to them. And so there was "Big Floyd," a new father, fresh out of a Texas prison where he experienced things we can only imagine, working closely with Ngwolo, carrying the baptism pool, setting up chairs and tables and a provisional altar, inviting parishioners into a make-believe sanctuary that, because it was so make-believe, had, perhaps, the quality of being more real. A friend, the Christian rapper Ronnie Lillard, aka Reconcile, told the Minneapolis *Star Tribune* that back then Floyd had told him, "I'm not just going to flex from a church pew standpoint, but I'm going to try to be as Jesus as I can from a street standpoint." That meant calling on the cred he had built with DJ Screw to confront Third Ward youth drifting into drugs and crime and getting them to give it up for prayer.

Resurrection's official mission is "to raise followers of Jesus for the city," but Ngwolo knows something about the community his church serves and, so, in addition to worship, he has adopted the pursuit of justice as an equally important ministerial goal. The pastor is not only seminary-trained; he's also a lawyer, a former associate at the distinguished Houston firm of Akin Gump Strauss Hauer & Feld. These days, in addition to running Resurrection, Ngwolo has his own law firm, C. Patrick Ngwolo & Associates, specializing in criminal defense, DWI, and drug charges. It turns out that there are a lot of people facing time in the Third Ward, and there are a lot of people being nabbed for drug crimes.

Floyd spent two years back in Houston, but God alone couldn't set his life straight; at least not there in Texas, where he continued to struggle with the ghosts of his past, with the aimlessness that results from self-degradation and the drugs that provide an escape, however temporary, from it. Frustrated by the state budget cuts to rehab facilities, another Houston pastor, Johnnie Riles III, had begun urging addicts to relocate to other cities, in particular Minneapolis, where a Salvation Army program had been successful. And so, prompted by this advice from a man of God, Floyd borrowed money for a bus ticket and headed 1,200 miles north to embark on a new life.

To many in Floyd's Houston crowd, Minnesota was an odd choice. They told him to be careful, that there were "no Black people there"—and that certainly had long been Minneapolis's reputation, one bolstered by the comments of Calvin Griffith describing why he had uprooted Major

League Baseball's Washington Senators in 1960 and made them the Minnesota Twins. "I'll tell you why we came to Minnesota," he said to an admiring audience, unaware that a reporter was in the room. "It was when I found out you only had fifteen thousand Blacks here. Black people don't go to ball games, but they'll fill up a rassling ring and put up such a chant it'll scare you to death. It's unbelievable. We came here because you've got good, hardworking white people here."

Whatever those racist comments revealed about Griffith, having a small African American population did not de facto mean that *Minnesotans* were racist, but if Floyd comforted himself with that thought, he entered into a familiar deception. Minnesota was in the North, after all, and while there are historical examples of northern states that openly embraced white supremacist values—particularly Indiana, where the Ku Klux Klan effectively ran the state government in the early 1920s, and others, like Michigan and Ohio, where the Black Legion, a violent Klan offshoot that targeted Blacks, Jews, and Catholics, thrived—the racism above the Mason-Dixon line has always tended to be more whisper than shout, more covert and less codified.

The traditional characterization was to say that the South practiced de jure segregation and the North de facto, a distinction that Robert Penn Warren once described, mockingly, as "inherent inferiority" versus "accidental inferiority." But the more we learn, the less sufficient those terms seem to be to describe life as it is lived. The demarcations between Black life and white life were so firmly drawn down South and so impervious to those who were divided by them that there was never any question as to what one could and couldn't do even if it all represented one big dystopian carnival of unrelenting injustice. But in the North, racism, especially the racism of white liberal society, lurked in the dark recesses of real estate covenants, mortgage barriers, social custom, and legislative dealmaking, where its shape was ill-defined and often invisible to the naked eye. At least with Jim Crow, Black people could have some semblance of their own institutions. In the North, Black people were left to float in the white world, drifting without a tether. Ralph Ellison noticed this long ago when he wrote that "the cultural history of Negroes in the North reads like the legend of some tragic people out of mythology, a people which aspired to escape from its own unhappy homeland to the apparent peace of a distant mountain; but which, in migrating, made some fatal error of judgment and fell into a great chasm of mazelike passages that promise ever to lead to the mountain but end ever against a wall."

To Ellison, the irony of Jim Crow was that it actually served as a force for stability, as "one of the bulwarks which men place between themselves and the constant threat of chaos." Put differently, the South was the conviviality and community of the Negro Leagues; the North was Jackie

Robinson getting spiked in the shin as he slid into second, shunned in the locker room of his own team, a lonely soldier bearing a torrent of verbal abuse from fans and players alike, and then asked to march stoically forward, and maybe even exhibit a countenance of gratitude. After he was called before the House Un-American Activities Committee (HUAC) to testify to his opposition to communism, Robinson earned a good pat on the head. "Quite a man, this Jackie Robinson," an editorial in the *New York Daily News* read, as if it were praising a show horse. And more than a decade later, when the Boston Red Sox became the last team to integrate, pitcher Earl Wilson arrived with a scouting report that read "well-mannered 'colored' boy, not too black, pleasant to talk to, well educated, very good appearance." That was how the North accepted Black life, when Black people exhibited deference and stayed out of sight.

When compared with Jim Crow, Ellison's description of the dilemma posed by the racism of the North recalled the warnings of Booker T. Washington—not the submissive, pull-yourselves-up-by-the-bootstraps ones, but the calls to Black nationalism that appealed, ironically, to more militant leaders like Ida B. Wells. Washington's particular embrace, of course, was not a belligerent one. He believed, along with the white southerner, that the Black race was not ready to stand on its own. But for Wells and others, it wasn't that Black people weren't ready for freedom; it was *white* people who weren't ready for *Black* freedom, and even those who might speak as if they were couldn't be trusted.

This racial pessimism is a strain of Black thought that you can still find today in the language of hip-hop, in the move to so-called affinity housing for African Americans on college campuses, and even in Black Twitter and other social media spaces. Historically, it goes back even earlier than Washington, to the pre–Civil War arguments of the Black newspaperman and abolitionist Martin Delany, who, frustrated and cynical about the opportunities for Black people to ever share in the fruits of white American society (he himself had been thrown out of Harvard Medical School when a majority of students there objected to the "evil" represented by the presence among them of someone "we would not tolerate in our houses"), championed a Black separatism, considered the possibilities for an emigration of Black Americans to the Caribbean or even back to Africa, and emphasized Black capital, Black pride, and the establishment and maintenance of Black institutions in the face of white supremacy. "We are a nation within a nation," Delaney wrote, "as the Poles in Russia, the Hungarians in Austria, the Welsh, Irish and Scotch in the British dominions."

But if the notion of Black separatism goes backward from Washington, it also goes forward, too, to Marcus Garvey and his Universal Negro Improvement Association

(UNIA). Garvey, who counted Washington's book *Up from Slavery* among the most powerful influences of his life, arrived in America from the Caribbean in the late 1910s, embracing the black, red, and green of African culture, preaching a Delany-like gospel of self-reliance, self-respect, and a union of all Black peoples the world over. It stretches forward also to Malcolm X, whose father was an evangelist for Garveyism and who, as an adolescent, "conked" his hair, "literally burning my flesh to have it look like a white man's." Malcolm later concluded, in retrospect, that this was his "first really big step toward [the] self-degradation" demanded of Black people, and turned instead to embrace the Nation of Islam's principles of Black pride, Black self-determination, and Black separatism. "It is a very grave matter," James Baldwin once wrote, "to be forced to imitate a people for whom you know . . . you do not exist."

To these Black nationalists, segregation per se was not the problem—they, in fact, preferred to live with Black people. No, it was the effect of segregation, the message of inferiority and subjugation that it carried, and the idea that not only in sexual relations but even in real estate the Black race carried a threat of contamination to the white race, and whether it was Jim Crow laws or the "invisible barbed wire fence of the restrictive covenants," as sociologists St. Clair Drake and Horace Cayton wrote in their 1945 study of Chicago, the white race was determined to root its supremacy in an immovable soil.

Of course, that push to withdraw, to reject, to feed from one another rather than even try to gain access to the larger whole of American life always competed with its integrationist counterpart, whether it was from the writings of Du Bois or the speeches of Dr. King, or from the white liberal voices that sought reconciliation for the sins of the past, that believed progressive achievements might actually build a society of "diversity" (the twenty-first century's preferred term) where Black and white thrived together. It was in this spirit that many took comfort from Martin's words about the long arc of the moral universe bending "toward justice," even if they knew that the line wasn't original to him but borrowed from the white Boston abolitionist minister Theodore Parker, whose original quote displays a less confident vision. To Parker, who despite his anti-slavery impulses spoke to finding common cause with the Anglo-Saxon who feared "the Africanization of America" and wanted "the superior race to multiply rather than the inferior," the arc of the moral universe was indeed a "long" one that he did not "pretend to understand." In fact, his vision was such that he could not "calculate the curve and complete the figure by experience of sight" but only "divine it by conscience." And it was only there, from that distant place, that Parker concluded that "it bends toward justice."

Nonetheless, in recent years, Minnesota had shown signs of the growing racial diversity that integrationists once dreamed of. Even today, a mere 7 percent of the state's population is African American, but 20 percent is nonwhite. That number demonstrates how Minneapolis in particular became a preferred landing spot for large communities of immigrants from Southeast Asia and Africa. Indeed, modern Minnesotans have prided themselves on supporting a polyglot community of Somalians, Laotians, Ethiopians, and Cambodians, one that in turn has embraced progressive values. For instance, the state's fifth Congressional district, which includes the eastern portion of Hennepin County and all of Minneapolis, is represented by the Somali American Ilhan Omar, a Muslim. And when she was elected in 2018, she replaced Keith Ellison, now the state's attorney general, who had the distinction of being the first Muslim to serve in the US Congress and the first African American congressman from Minnesota.

Still, as with so much about America's history with racism, the past continues to shape the present. In 2016, a digital venture undertaken by the University of Minnesota did for the streets of Minneapolis what an X-ray does for the body: it illuminated otherwise invisible internal structures that predetermined outward behavior. In this case, it was real estate covenants that reached back to the early twentieth century and were later reinforced by federal lending patterns during the New Deal. In this, Minneapolis was no different from Chicago or St. Louis or literally any American city where the Home Owners' Loan Corporation (HOLC) offered banks detailed and color-coded maps advising where it was "safe" for lenders to grant mortgages to prospective buyers and where it was dangerous to do so. It was all part of the New Deal's much-heralded attempt to revive the housing industry that had collapsed with the Great Depression, and for mortgage lenders and prospective white homeowners, it worked. But one of the criteria that HOLC used was to alert underwriters to the "infiltration of inharmonious racial groups," which it saw as having a deleterious effect on property values, one comparable to the impact of "non-conforming land uses" like industrial plants, sewage facilities, or strip malls. The logic was simple: You don't want a body shop to move next to your split-level. And you sure don't want a Black family there, either.

This practice of "redlining," as it is known (since the worst areas for investment were colored in red), was a perfect foil for northerners to the South's more explicitly exclusionary Jim Crow. They wouldn't have to countenance ugly-sounding Jim Crow housing laws in their communities; the mortgage industry would just deliver the same result silently. The practice became illegal in 1968, but the deed had already been done. With no federally backed mortgages to spur development, Black and "ethnic" neighborhoods lacked substantial homeownership and were populated instead by renters who paid disinterested, often hostile white landlords possessed of little motivation for maintenance and investment. Bad neighborhoods became worse. Worse neighborhoods became slums. Slum neighborhoods became uninhabitable.

Minneapolis was one of the worst cases. There, the disparities between white neighborhoods and Black neighborhoods were striking, with consequences that continue to be far-reaching. A lack of homeownership meant that Black enclaves had little clout to pursue the government for improvements. Black neighborhoods had fewer parks, fewer trees, more asphalt; houses went into disrepair and new construction was rare. Even the climate was experienced differently. Without trees to provide shade and with large amounts of asphalt generating heat, temperatures in these neighborhoods in the summers were significantly higher than those in other parts of the city, making life even more unbearable. We know because it's all there in the data, available now to be parsed by anyone with a laptop and an internet connection.

Still, the reason to reflect on all of this is not to point the finger at Minneapolis as "racist"—that would be too easy—but, to extend the metaphor of the X-ray, to recognize the way that the nation's nervous system, bone structure, circulatory system, and subcutaneous tissue have, over generations or even centuries, been functioning and evolving in ways that reinforce and enhance a racial hierarchy that values white people over Black people, and that anything short of a full reckoning with this truth is mere sloganeering. As

Malcolm X understood more than half a century ago, the failure of American "Negroes" was baked into the system that created them. Speaking to the Northern Negro Grass Roots Leadership Conference in November 1963, Malcolm disparaged Martin Luther King's March on Washington and the nonviolent campaign for a "desegregated lunch counter, a desegregated theater, a desegregated park, and a desegregated public toilet." Mocking Martin, Malcolm said that there was no revolution in being free to "sit down next to white folks on the toilet"; no, "revolution is based on land. Land is the basis of all independence. Land is the basis of freedom, justice, and equality."

———

In Minneapolis, Floyd spent just one week in the Salvation Army program that Pastor Riles had suggested to him, then left to join a ninety-day program at Turning Point, a Black-owned, Black-run rehabilitation clinic that describes its mission as addressing chemical dependency through "culturally specific behavioral health services and training." Peter Hayden, who founded Turning Point in the 1970s after his experience as the only Black person pursuing recovery in a local Alcoholics Anonymous program, does add some of the principles of Kwanzaa to his practice, but the approach to addiction is otherwise much like the traditional twelve steps associated with AA. What makes

Hayden's work different from AA's is that he seeks to create an atmosphere that feels familiar and safe to African Americans who might find a white establishment suspicious, indifferent, ignorant, or even hostile.

Turning Point is a Black operation for Black people. It is, in a way, just a more recent manifestation of the Black nationalist impulse embraced by Washington, Garvey, and, finally, Malcolm. Even the logo announces that, and those who come there to be healed recognize that Hayden and his staff know things that white people do not know, have experienced things that white people have not experienced. They get what it is to be Black in America, to suffer the indignities, the prejudice, the degradation, the violence, and, especially, given their mission, the crippling dependency on drugs. Hayden, for instance, has not only experienced his own issues with addiction; he has also known violence. Visiting Atlanta in 2016, his daughter Taylor Hayden was caught in the path of rival gang gunfire and killed. She was just twenty-five years old.

Floyd made friends with another addict at Turning Point, Eric Cornley. Like Floyd, he was a big man. Aware, as big people can be, that they might obstruct the view in a crowded room, the two men found themselves sitting in the back during meetings, and through conversation a bond was developed. Like Floyd, Cornley had once played competitive sports and, like Floyd, he had come from far away, looking to restart a life stalled, perhaps irreparably damaged, by addiction. Floyd quickly found a girlfriend, too. While working as a security guard at the Salvation Army, he met a white woman who told Floyd of her own history with addiction. He suggested they pray together, which they did; then Floyd asked for her number. Courtney Ross was not put off by Floyd's addictions; she saw the two of them as being on a mutual journey, each struggling with their respective demons. Still, speaking to the *Washington Post* after Floyd's death, Ross noted the disparities between her life as an addict and his: "I've done drugs. I've sold drugs. I can get a job, people try to make me happy. The reason he has a record is that he's a Black man, and the reason I don't is because I'm a white woman, and that's as real as it gets."

The jobs Floyd got were all recognitions of his size and strength and race: a security guard for the Salvation Army, a bouncer at the Conga Latin Bistro dance club. There is a market for big Black men who scare people, and Cornley, who went by the nickname "Big E," also was able to find employment because of his size. He and Floyd moved in together, sharing a town house owned by Floyd's dance-club employer. The place was in a tony, overwhelmingly white Minneapolis suburb known as St. Louis Park. There were three bedrooms in the unit, but, as the *Post* reported, the two men dragged their mattresses into the living room so they could sleep near each other. People at Turning Point said they were "like brothers." Then, one night in October 2017, Floyd returned home and found Cornley dead from an overdose. Ross said that he took the loss hard, and that he receded, the pain brought on by the absence of Cornley's companionship matching the intensity of the questions his death raised. If Cornley had failed, what were his chances? What were any of their chances? Then, a few months later, came the news that Floyd's mother was dead of a stroke.

Floyd soldiered on, but friends noticed a dent in his will. He started using again; so, too, did Ross. They got clean, and then coronavirus hit, the Latin Bistro shut down, and Floyd was out of a job. He and Ross turned to opioids for comfort. To keep himself steady, Floyd made to-do lists. One obtained by the *Post* read "1. Let this be the day I claim victory over the dark situation through the Holy Spirit; 2. Always know you are wright [*sic*] here with me; 3. No matter the time you can always grab you some word. You can get + gather ya self in da morning + feed your spirit. Follow that with your workout." By 2020, Floyd had two new roommates—Alvin Manago, who had worked with Floyd at the Conga Latin Bistro, and Manago's girlfriend, Theresa Scott, whom Floyd called "Tee Tee." Among their lasting memories of Floyd is an image of him alone in his room, reciting Bible verses while weeping to himself, and another of him one morning in May 2020, when, just as he was about to depart the town house they shared, ostensibly on his way to see friends, he stopped instead and prayed with them for an hour. That was the last that Manago and Scott saw of George Floyd. Or, to be more precise, it was the last they saw him *in person*.

———

It was, ironically, Memorial Day when an image of Floyd, his body pinned to the pavement next to the right rear tire of a police cruiser, appeared on his roommates' phones. It was the same picture that appeared on the phone of Peter Hayden and every recovering addict and every relapsing addict who had passed through Turning Point, the same image on the phone of Patrick Ngwolo and every parishioner at Resurrection House, of every resident at the Norris Wright Cuney Homes and of rap-loving pilgrims on their way to pay homage to DJ Screw. It was the image that looked out from the phones of the teenagers playing basketball on playgrounds at Jack Yates High School and throughout the Third Ward. The guards at the Diboll Unit saw George Floyd in that instant; so, too, did the author Michelle Duster, great-granddaughter of Ida B. Wells. Every student at Malcolm X Shabazz High School in Newark, New Jersey, and Malcolm Shabazz City High School in Madison, Wisconsin, watched the video of Floyd gasping for breath, as did every visitor to the Marcus Mosiah Garvey Multimedia Museum in Kingston, Jamaica, and the Marcus Garvey Guest House at the W. E. B. Du Bois

Memorial Centre in Accra, Ghana, the city where Du Bois died in exile in 1963.

As the details of Floyd's encounter with the police outside Cup Foods in south Minneapolis passed halfway around the world, Palestinians recognized the name of the grocery store owner, Mahmoud Abumayyaleh, as one of their own. Five days later, when Eyad al-Hallaq, a thirty-two-year-old autistic Palestinian man, was shot and killed by Israeli police at the Lions' Gate checkpoint in the Old City in Jerusalem, mourners joined his image with the image of Floyd, two victims of an unspeakable brutality felled by power exerted from behind a uniform and a badge. Aboriginal activists in Australia and the indigenous peoples in Indonesia asserted a kinship with Floyd. Soon, marchers protesting the treatment of Floyd appeared in Lafayette Square, across from the White House; in New York City, where mourners reenacted the image of Floyd by pinning each other to the ground, knee to the neck; and in Paris, where parallels were drawn to the 2016 story of Adama Traoré, an immigrant from Mali who died of asphyxiation while in police custody in the suburb of Beaumont-sur-Oise, handcuffed and face to the ground. In an investigation, one gendarme said that Traoré, like Floyd, had told them that he couldn't breathe, but they didn't believe him.

The images of Floyd not only appeared on the newsfeeds of major newspapers; they also traveled back and forth on social media, where they were amended with headlines suggested by algorithms and matched to data sets, like-minded joined with like-minded, outrage joined with outrage, disgust joined with disgust, and, in those places where the descendants of those who long ago crowded town squares inebriated by the sight of a Black man hanging from a noose still reside, no doubt satisfaction was joined with satisfaction. In Ida B. Wells's time, it took a generation before her investigations, graphic descriptions, and published photographs of lynchings could form a movement against such barbarism. Now, here in an instant, the spectacle of death, produced at the corner of Thirty-Eighth Street and Chicago Avenue in Minneapolis, had mobilized people the world over.

TWO

"You About to Lose Yo' Job"

In February of 2020, more than three months before the murder of George Floyd, Johnniqua Charles was detained outside Diamonds Gentlemen's Club in Dillon, South Carolina. She claimed to have left her purse with the DJ and, when stopped by security guard Julius Locklear as she went back to retrieve it, she flew off in a rage. "We start arguing, and I get real disrespectful with my mouth and I say, 'Suck my dick,'" she explained later. "Other people were around and they started laughing—maybe he thought I tested his manhood or something—so he threw me up against a car." As she was being handcuffed, Charles repeatedly asked Locklear why she was under detention and challenged him: "You can't hear me? Then I'm going to sing it to you."

Recognizing the power to expose his behavior, Charles moved her body in rhythm as she chanted, "You about to lose yo' job, you about to lose yo' job—get this dance!—You about to lose yo' job, 'cause you are detaining me . . . for nothing," concluding with, "Is this shit worth you losing your job? 'Cause you are about to."

And with that, a meme was born.

The officer's bodycam was malfunctioning, but it turned out that a coworker was recording the scene. He gave the video to Locklear, who later posted it on Facebook, not to expose Charles but to celebrate her. The security guard had not lost his job at the strip club, nor his day job as a bail enforcer. In fact, far from being upset by the encounter, it turned out that Locklear, who is also Black, had rather enjoyed it. On the post accompanying the video, he wrote, "Okay "IM NOT POSTING THIS TO BE FUNNY TOWARDS THIS SUBJECT"""!!!!I'm posting it cause that rap was lit 😂😂😂😂😂 like I wish I could put a beat to it LOL." And, of course, that's exactly what someone did next. The clip was picked up by DJ Suede and iMarkkeyz, who incorporated popular video clips of Childish Gambino, Beyoncé, Bobby Shmurda, Bugs Bunny, Duke Deuce, Elmo, Future, and Tichina Arnold, turning it into a full-blown one-minute-twenty-four-second bop.

As protests over police violence toward African Americans grew over the next few months, culminating in the reaction to the killing of George Floyd, the "You About to Lose Yo' Job" rant became ubiquitous. Joined with bars from Ludacris's "Move Bitch," crowds of protesters shouted "Get out the way, bitch, get out the way" at law enforcement officers as they blocked the streets. Yet throughout, Charles remained oblivious to her random celebrity. Unhoused and suffering from addiction issues, she had been out of touch with her family for months, leaving her sister to raise her three-year-old son, Juju, while she wandered the streets, a social media spectacle disconnected from the spectacle of social media. It wasn't until June that Charles became aware of the video, reconnected with her sister, and returned home. Soon she was appearing on Instagram in a live stream, introduced as "the lose yo' job girl that the world is going crazy about." A GoFundMe page followed, raising $55,386 for her. "I'm glad this video touched many of you and made you smile," Charles wrote to her well-wishers. "Thanks for all the love." By election time, a new meme created by "Teri in New York" had been constructed, repurposing Charles's rap as a message to the defeated Donald Trump, this time featuring Joe Biden, Kamala Harris, footage of the late John Lewis, Barack Obama, and even Bernie Sanders.

Candace Owens, the Black conservative commentator, was right when she said that George Floyd is no hero. He isn't. But our digital age certainly made him a martyr. It was the cell phone video captured by seventeen-year-old high school student Darnella Frazier that served as incontrovertible evidence of Floyd's slaughter and sparked the process of converting a struggling, middle-aged addict with a prison record into a symbol, a touchstone, an icon, his name recited by children in classrooms, his face painted in colorful tribute on city walls, his soul prayed for in churches, synagogues, and mosques the world over. We almost didn't need to wait for the wheels of justice to turn. Derek Chauvin's fate, at least in the court of public opinion, was sealed the moment that Frazier aimed her camera at him, confirming the cell phone camera as society's newest surveillance tool, one capable of exposing all manner of injustice, whether that be an overzealous security guard at a strip club or a police officer committing murder on a Minneapolis street.

Once her name was known, Frazier, too, was being hailed for her courage, her own GoFundMe page raising over half a million dollars to provide "peace and healing" for the trauma brought on by what she had witnessed and for the continuing trauma from the digital age's unique form of insults and threats, which she endured long afterward. "It's been nights I stayed up apologizing and apologizing to George Floyd for not doing more," she said, "and not physically interacting and not saving his life." And what a modern thought that is, that somehow the camera was an agent to the crime. In the age of the cyberwarrior, it's hard to be a truth teller.

But let's be clear: Floyd did not act the hero here. In fact, he was brutally acted upon. And Frazier's presence at this historic moment was an accident. She was there to accompany her nine-year-old cousin, who wanted snacks from Cup Foods but was too young to go on her own. It took presence of mind for her to point her cell phone camera at the scene, while she, along with a small sidewalk crowd, scolded the police for what they were doing. And it took a steely perseverance for her to continue to point the camera while she watched a man die before her very eyes.

While it was Floyd's still image that would proliferate later, it was the video itself, posted on Facebook, that changed the world. Without the cell phone at her disposal, Frazier and the other bystanders could only have described what they saw, and memory, being at best a subjective tool for discovering the truth, too often falls victim to the dictates of power. That's because the recall of witnesses to crime must first go through a hierarchy of believability, one that enhances or discounts testimony according to cultural signals like race, gender, economic standing, authority, presentation, articulateness, and personality. Given all that, what are the chances that a hypothetical Darnella Frazier from a time before cell phones, recalling to a judge or jury the deadly assault she saw committed on a hypothetical George Floyd, would have been believed over the testimony of a white male law enforcement officer like Derek Chauvin and the blue wall of silence built to protect him?

We are greeted each day by a bombardment of imagery, much of it manipulated and distorted to make us feel certain feelings and do certain things, like spend unlimited money and believe in implausible conspiracies. But while we've grown increasingly suspicious of the truthfulness of the picture, for the moment, at least, unedited raw video still has the quality of record. Raw video shot by a mere bystander—not a professional, not an activist with an agenda—arriving at the scene by chance and recording a violent injustice committed in her presence is even more believable, more reliable, since our reaction presupposes that there is no pretense or ego, no fashion or framing, no interpretive gaze or willful finger-pointing. Just the truth. In 1945, when the British photojournalist George Rodger arrived on assignment in Germany at the Bergen-Belsen extermination camp—the first photographer to get there— he felt ashamed to be looking through his viewfinder to assemble "thousands of Jewish corpses into nice photographic compositions," and thereafter refused to cover war and its aftermath. But a camera held by an innocent, the accidental photojournalist who has become a hallmark of our time, is another thing entirely. In Darnella Frazier's hands, the video becomes merely the transfer of *what hap-*

pened then to *our eyes now* as we open it from our inbox, watch it on cable television, or glimpse it from a post found on our own cell phones. All of which means that when it comes to the abuse of power, at least as it's rendered in public spaces, you can no longer hide. The camera—*some camera*—will always be there to remember you.

The video shot by Frazier provides an interesting study. By comparison, consider, first, how in 2015, Walter Scott, a fifty-year-old African American, was stopped by a North Charleston, South Carolina, cop for having a broken taillight. Scott, fearing arrest, fled on foot, and Officer Michael Slager ran after him. It was fairly early in the morning, and while Scott's car was parked in the lot of an auto parts store, he had run behind a metal fence near the back side of a pawn shop where there appeared to be no one in sight, Slager right behind him in pursuit.

Yet it turned out that there *was* someone present. Feidin Santana, a Dominican barber on his way to work, noticed the commotion, reached for his phone, and recorded the entire scene. The video Santana captured shows Slager shoot Scott eight times in the back, killing him. The officer then approaches Scott's body, checks for a pulse, and finally runs to retrieve his Taser and put it near the scene. This was done to fit the lie that Scott had been struggling to grab it from him and that Slager had been forced to kill him in self-defense. "Shots fired and the subject is down," Slager says into his radio. "He grabbed my Taser."

By contrast, Darnella Frazier's video of George Floyd's death has no apparent narrative. It tells no clear story. It's just a single scene showing a white police officer with his knee on the neck of a Black man lying prone on the pavement, his head pinned next to the right rear tire of the police cruiser. The officer has his hand in his pocket and his sunglasses perched on his head while he looks off nonchalantly. But here's the key: while it's a single scene, the video goes on for nine minutes and twenty-nine seconds.

No moral person can escape the gruesome awkwardness of watching it, the unpleasant feeling that even voyeuristic detachment cannot shield you from some level of responsibility for what you're seeing. In fact, viewing it, you have the sense that you, yourself, are guilty of a crime— which, in a way, if you believe in the spirit of the collective, we all are. There is even something of a crucifixion to it, a long, slow, painful end, carried out in public, with both official and unofficial viewers in attendance and a common cry from the dying—Christ for his "father," Floyd for his recently departed "mama."

Where the film of the Walter Scott shooting tells a story, there the killing happens in an instant. But with Floyd, the killing *is* the story, and, while the time elapsed is essential to its power, the focus on a single, unchanging scene also gives it the quality of an iconic still photograph or even a piece of sculpture. A man has his knee on another man's neck. That man is dying. The two could have been carved of Carrara marble and put on view in a museum or a public square, a mordantly askew rendering of the Pieta, with the Madonna and child replaced by the executioner and his prey.

It matters not who they are, really—George Floyd and Derek Chauvin—only that they're symbolic of a larger whole. And the symbolism is crucial to the reaction that the scene provokes, for one cannot read this arresting image, moving or still, without concluding that the death of George Floyd is neither surprising nor unusual. Its power is in its very ordinariness. It's a rendering of the whole sorry relationship between Black and white in America and, even more, the whole perverse relationship between the powerful and the powerless throughout the world. Indeed, no picture since the June 5, 1989, confrontation between a lone man with shopping bags and a parade of tanks—"Tank Man," as he came to be known, since his identity was never discovered—under the heat of the Tiananmen Square protests in China has had so much international resonance.

The comparison to Tank Man is appropriate, for that scene, too, works as both a frozen image and as video. Several still photographers captured the view, though AP cameraman Jeff Widener's shot, which he took from the sixth floor of a Beijing hotel, was the most tightly framed. Widener had been focusing his lens on the column of tanks as it moved down the street when Tank Man emerged into his viewfinder. At first, he found the man's presence annoying—he was spoiling the shot!—but then he realized that the column, no matter how imposing, wasn't the picture he should be after. No, it was Primeval Man *confronting* the column, humanity facing off against sixty tons of sinister steel. The result was a picture that requires no caption to generate its power. The iconography is that clear.

Captured in video, the image is enhanced by narrative. It's a historic moment. Young pro-democracy protesters, over a million of them, have gathered in Tiananmen Square to rail against corruption and call for a more open society. The Chinese government has moved its People's Liberation Army against them. A man in a white shirt and black pants, carrying a shopping bag in each hand, begins to cross a Beijing street just as government tanks are rolling toward the intersection. He isn't a protester, and in fact appears to be an incongruous part of the scene. What is he carrying, his groceries? But then he stops in front of the first tank in the column, blocking its path. He seems to be shouting something at it as he gestures violently with his right hand. The tank moves to one side to get around him, and the man moves with it. Finally he climbs on top of the tank with the intention, it appears, of confronting those inside. He squats at the hatch, perched like a hungry robin, then jumps down and stands to one side. The tank exhales gray smoke, like an animal awkwardly rising from its slumber, and begins to move again, and again the man leaps in front of the lead vehicle, before being led away by some men in blue shirts. Who are they—police? Sympathetic bystanders? We will never know.

Like George Floyd forty years later, Tank Man became a martyr, and why? Reporting would eventually show that he was far from the only civilian to confront the artillery in the dozens of Chinese cities where protesters were attacked and killed. There were better subjects for such tribute: thousands of people died in Tiananmen Square. Many more simply disappeared. No, what separated Tank Man from the others is that he had "the image," one that appeared to show how flesh and blood and the individual spirit could force an army, and with it state aggression, to stand down.

It all seems so silly now that we know how the history played out. Since no one knows what happened to Tank Man, it's presumed that he's dead, and that he was likely executed by authorities. The wished-for democratic reforms pushed by the university students in Tiananmen Square were never adopted. If anything, in the succeeding thirty-some years, the regime has tightened its hold on power. More important, no one in China knows Tank Man's story anymore. The confrontation has been erased by the state from all internet searches and has no place in the nation's history texts. It's as if it never happened. All of this means that the image, however powerful it may seem to be in isolation, is toothless. Man confronted the state, yes; but in the end, state power prevailed.

Comparing Tank Man to George Floyd, at least in the short term, seems to suggest the exact opposite story. There, in the picture, it appears evident that the state, as represented by the police officer, has won. He is in the dominant posture, and Floyd is inert and, eventually, unconscious. But unlike Tank Man, Floyd, in death, does not disappear. To the contrary: He is made immortal by the episode.

And Chauvin? Well, we now look at the picture of the two of them and can say to him, "You about to lose yo' job."

———

In the architecture of the George Floyd video, there are also parallels to John Filo's Pulitzer Prize–winning photo of fourteen-year-old runaway Mary Ann Vecchio kneeling over the body of Jeffrey Miller, one of four Kent State University students shot dead by the Ohio National Guard during a May 4, 1970, anti-war demonstration. In both the Floyd video and the Kent State picture, there is a person lying prone on the ground and another down on their left knee while looking back at us through the camera lens. But the roles of the three parties—prone, kneeler, and viewer—have been rearranged. In the 1970 picture, Vecchio is the one on her knee, her arms outstretched in a gesture that screams back at us, "Why?" Meanwhile, the viewer occupies the same space as the Guardsmen who had killed Miller. Chilling. *We* "did this," the picture seems to be suggesting. By contrast, in the Floyd video, the "Why" perspective, of course, is with the viewer—both the photographer, Frazier, and, in turn, the rest of us, *all of us*—while the killer, Chauvin, appears in the space that Vecchio occupies at Kent State.

All three pictures—Tank Man, Kent State, and George Floyd—are about the relationship between the powerful and the powerless, but there is a historical irony to the Kent State picture, when viewed in context. The Kent State killings are justifiably remembered as representative of state-sponsored violence against civilians, and they resonated with the public because so many American and Vietnamese youth were dying from state-sponsored violence in Vietnam. Indeed, Kent State was a story rife with important themes and no shortage of people ready to address them.

One of the first reporters on the scene that May Monday was Joe Eszterhas, who was working for the Cleveland *Plain Dealer* at the time but would soon join the staff of *Rolling Stone*. He would later become famous as the screenwriter responsible for the movie *Basic Instinct* and half a dozen other hits. Later in 1970, Eszterhas published a book based on his Kent State reporting. James A. Michener wrote about Kent State for *Reader's Digest*; I. F. Stone produced his own short book. Crosby, Stills, Nash & Young issued a hit song, "Ohio," that played on radios and on dorm room stereos everywhere. The song became the hymn of the anti-war movement. And then, of course, there was John Filo's photograph.

Filo was a twenty-one-year-old student at Kent State working in the university photo lab when word was passed of the shootings. Camera in hand, he ran to the scene of the confrontation. "I dropped my camera in the realization that it was live ammunition," he recalled years later. "I don't know what gave me the combination of innocence and stupidity . . . but I never took cover. I was the only one standing at the hillside. After I did that self-check and turned slowly to my left, what caught my eye on the street was the body of Jeffrey Miller and the volume of blood that was flowing from his body was as if someone tipped over a bucket."

Filo began to run, in fear for his own life, when he realized his obligation. "Where are you going?" he said to himself. "This is why you are here." As he brought the scene into his viewfinder, he noticed Vecchio and "the emotion welling up inside of her. She began to sob, and it culminated in her saying an exclamation." Later, he couldn't recall exactly what the teen said at the moment he snapped her picture, but remembered it was "something like, 'Oh, my God!'" The people around Filo objected to what appeared to them to be an attempt to profit off the scene. They called him a "pig" and a "vulture," but Filo's retort was one that resonates with the present moment.

"No one's going to believe this happened," he said. Then, gesturing to his camera, he said, "This is proof."

The image has been published and republished over the years. Vecchio's own father, she recently told the *Washington Post*, screen-printed it on T-shirts and sold them. Early on, as the picture was shared, Vecchio, who, like the Tank Man, was not identified in the moment, became the subject of considerable fascination. Who was she, and how did she come to be there at that moment, etching into the national consciousness the moral denunciation of a generation? Then details about her began to emerge. After the killings, she hitchhiked to Columbus, Ohio, and then to Indianapolis. Soon after, an anonymous tip that she was living there in a "hippie colony" led to a visit from an *Indianapolis Star* reporter. After getting his story, the reporter alerted authorities that Vecchio was a runaway, forcing a return home to her family in Opa-Locka, Florida.

It was a time, of course, before social media. But like Frazier fifty years later, the teen came under attack from those who blamed her for the killings. In Florida, Republican governor Claude Kirk wondered aloud whether Vecchio was part of some radical conspiracy and asked the US Justice Department to investigate if "professional agitators" were using Florida youth as "part of a 'chicks up front' strategy." Threats of violence were delivered to the Vecchio family mailbox: "It's too bad it wasn't you that was shot." "What you need is a good beating until you bleed red." "I hope you enjoyed sleeping with all those Negroes and dope fiends." As the picture itself gained fame, the FBI came looking for Filo's film and then, when he refused to give it to them, they hounded and intimidated him. People told him the picture had to be a "fake."

There are, however, two less remembered historical bookends to Kent State. On February 8, 1968, students at South Carolina State University, a historically Black college in Orangeburg, gathered to protest their treatment at a segregated bowling alley in town. In what is now known as the Orangeburg Massacre, South Carolina Highway Patrol officers, responding to the event, fired on the students, killing three and injuring dozens more. Nine officers, all of them white, were later acquitted. They claimed to be under small arms fire, but eyewitnesses reported hearing no shots coming from the students, and no guns were discovered among the protesters.

Then, on May 15, 1970—eleven days after Kent State—students at Jackson State College in Jackson, Mississippi, another historically Black institution, were fired upon by police. It started with the students pelting cars with rocks and continued as a false rumor spread through the crowd that Charles Evers (brother of the slain Mississippi activist Medgar Evers) had been shot and killed. When the police arrived, in force, they claimed there was a sniper in a women's dorm shooting at them. They then unloaded 150 rounds—the bullet holes are visible to this day—killing two and wounding twelve, and yet no evidence of a sniper was ever found.

Why is Kent State remembered and not Jackson State or South Carolina State? A considerable part of the outrage over the Kent State killings had to do with the fact that the dead were from the white middle class and that their story was amply told by a cadre of prominent white narrators, while the incidents at South Carolina State and Jackson State had only Black victims, which made them less interesting to the white press. You might also say that in May 1970, opposition to the war, and the youth revolution that attached to that opposition, was in the foreground even more than the racial turmoil that had been building since the 1950s. But perhaps the most important reason is Filo's picture.

The Black student killings had witnesses but no Vecchio, storytellers but no Eszterhas or Michener, no moment like the one Filo captured of Jeffrey Miller and Mary Ann Vecchio, no moment like the one Darnella Frazier captured on a Memorial Day morning fifty years later on the streets of Minneapolis. Or maybe there was such a moment, but no one was there to capture it. "What is the point of history?" nineteen-year-old Allison Krause wrote in 1970 on a final exam shortly before she became one of those gunned down at Kent State. "Dates and facts are not enough to show what happened in the past."

———

The American Civil War is one area where white storytellers have long controlled the narrative, with abiding consequences. Robert Penn Warren called it our "felt history," one that is carried forth in the "national imagination"—and he was writing in 1961, a time when the American nation-state seemed rock solid, undeniable, optimistic (even, in some quarters, on issues of race). It was just a few years after *Brown v. Board of Education* and a few years before the landmark 1964 Civil Rights Act and the 1965 Voting Rights Act—different from our own divided time, with schisms that are temperamentally and geographically similar to the ones that precipitated war in 1861.

In 1961, many people firmly believed in a version of Civil War history that reinforced the vaunted national creed and delivered to us, as Warren mockingly described it, the "ikon of a boy in blue striking off, with one hand, iron shackles from a grizzle-headed Uncle Tom weeping in gratitude, and with the other passing out McGuffey's First Reader to a rolypoly pickaninny laughing in hope." You might say that this was one example of the "national imagination" at work, the one that wrote history texts, built monuments, and informed the writing of title cards in museums; and it had a competitor in another fantastic vision, the one represented by the myth of the "Lost Cause" that was nurtured and protected by southerners out of the shame and trauma of defeat.

The Lost Cause maintained that Southerners fought the war not to preserve slavery but to defend state sovereignty. Slavery might have been the issue that prompted the two sides to engage in battle, but that was incidental to the South's real mission, which was to prevent the federal government from dominating the states and usurping the will of the people. This was the basis of the South's claim to be the true inheritor of the spirit of the American Revolution. It was only the industrial might of the North that vanquished Dixie, the "overwhelming numbers and resources" that Robert E. Lee referenced in his farewell address. But ideas? Those lived on in the minds of men, where the "oppressed" party in the Civil War was not the enslaved waiting to be freed; it was the slaveholders and their fellow countrymen enduring the aggression of Northern invaders.

It's critical to understand the word "myth" here, as it is too easily misinterpreted to mean only that the Lost Cause was a lie. As history, it was indeed a lie, and the record is there to prove it so. Look only at the address that Alexander Stephens, the Confederate vice president, delivered in Savannah, Georgia, on March 21, 1861, in which he said that the Confederacy's "cornerstone rests upon the great truth that the negro is not equal to the white man; that slavery, subordination to the superior race, is his natural and normal condition. This, our new government, is the first, in the history of the world, based on this great physical, philosophical, and moral truth." But the notion of "myth" in relation to the Lost Cause should be read more as a reference to legend, to the stories we write to explain things we cannot otherwise understand or, as in the case of the vanquished South, cannot bear to understand. Greek myth served the purpose of explaining the confounding elements of nature. The Myth of the Lost Cause served to explain the confounding elements of regional defeat, and thereby adjust painful memories into acceptable ones.

Like so many myths, the Lost Cause carried religious overtones. It was not just that the Confederacy was defeated; it was that an entire culture, identified by its agrarian character, was sacrificed. In this view, the antebellum South was a place of Edenic significance, where men were honorable and women were protected. It was America before "The Fall," an image that also conveniently defended against the South's reputation as a place of intellectual inferiority and backwardness. If the region was benighted, it was only because it had not defied God and eaten from the tree of knowledge. The North, by contrast, was industrial, acquisitive, greedy, and evil. With the sides so crisply drawn, the story of the war therefore became nothing more than that "genius and valor went down before brute force."

But was the South defeated? In the war's immediate

aftermath, it sure looked that way, with its rural land-scape charred and its cities turned to rubble. One-fifth of the adult white male population was dead, and many of those who survived the conflict were permanently maimed. In 1865, Mississippi spent 20 percent of the state's revenue on the issuing of artificial limbs for its wounded soldiers. Chattel slavery did end, destroying the region's economy, though one could argue that this was more accident than purpose, since Lincoln's primary goal was to save the union, a motive made clear as late as September 1862, when he released the first draft of the Emancipation Proclamation as more of a threat than an action. How, indeed, would history have changed if the South had met the demands provided there for a gradual, compensated end to slavery, according to no prescribed timetable (years? decades?), as a price for rejoining the constitutional order? It was only the stubbornness of the Confederacy in refusing such conditions that forced the actual proclamation of history, the one signed on New Year's Day of 1863.

But even beyond that, looking at what transpired afterward as the South navigated Reconstruction and its aftermath—the establishment of the Black codes, the voter suppression tactics, the rise of the Klan, the reassertion of control over Black labor through harsh contracts and con-vict leasing programs, and the violence, all of the violence—it's hard not to see that the South gained in spirit what it lost in law, and even gained in law what it had lost in law. "If you call this Freedom," wrote one Black veteran about Jim Crow, "what do you call Slavery?"

In the twentieth century, as the memory of the war became recast, the narrative of the Lost Cause gained a considerable following. It began with the memoirs of Stephens and of Jefferson Davis, where one might expect history to be refashioned. From there it moved to a few respected historians, on to veterans' groups, and then to the Sons of Confederate Veterans. Eventually it became the stories handed down in families and glorified at anniversaries. The South had lost the war, but it hadn't been vanquished. Indeed, it would rise again.

The first real history of the Confederacy was penned by the editor of the Richmond *Examiner*, who acknowledged that the South, in the terms established by its surrender, "submitted" to the restoration of the union and the "excision of slavery," but, as he went on to claim, the war did not decide the critical question of "negro equality; it did not decide negro suffrage; it did not decide States' Rights . . . it did not decide the right of a people to show dignity in misfortune, and to maintain self-respect in the face of adversity. And these things which the war did not decide, the Southern people will cling to, still claim, and still assert."

Whatever Robert Penn Warren meant by the Civil War being the "imagined" and "felt" history we all carry with us, we can make a distinction between these two words by saying with certainty that neither the northern vision of liberation nor the southern vision of a violated regional honor addressed the "felt" history of the Black American's Civil War. Indeed, for much of the nation's history, the Black experience has been left a mystery, its story told more by white people than Black people, by academic more than participant, by inference more than fact. The picture that emerged was often one-dimensional and dripping with condescension—Black Americans as a primitive people who were incapable of equality, either because they were congenitally inferior or because they were so developmentally arrested by the experience of slavery that they had been rendered inferior.

This was a lesson that was made clear when Lonnie Bunch, the founding director of the Smithsonian's National Museum of African American History and Culture, which opened on the National Mall in 2016, went about assembling a collection of Black American life. How do you use the traditional tools of museum work to tell the story of a people whose material culture has been systematically compromised? How do you recover or, in its absence, represent that which has been hidden, lost, or destroyed? Bunch and his team responded to the ostensible "collection gap" by searching widely for previously unknown artifacts. Through this search, which included formal museum spaces and the collections of everyday Black people, Bunch was able to gather critical contributions. Still, it's undeniable that the violence of slavery and institutional racism have left many holes for students of early Black American history to fill.

But then all that began to change in response to three profound developments. The Great Migration of African Americans from the South to the big cities of the North, which began roughly at the end of the First World War, brought a new visibility to Black culture, including music, religion, and politics. Second, there was a growing interest in anthropological studies of Black life and culture, explored through the work of Zora Neale Hurston and Melville Herskovits, especially Herskovits's *The Myth of the Negro Past*, which revealed a rich African American history, even while in slavery, through the oral histories of slaves conducted by WPA researchers in the 1930s. But the third reason for the shift of understanding of the Black experience may be the most significant, in that it intersects with all the others—and that is the arrival of new, more democratic communications technologies in the twentieth century.

For most of the nineteenth century, the camera was an expensive and cumbersome tool that required long exposure times, which meant that subjects were forced to sit for ten or more minutes without moving. Its principal application was for landscapes and portraiture, the latter evolving in form from the painted portrait and thus subjectively rendered and available only to the well-heeled. There was certainly no concept of photography as a method of discovery, no idea of its applications to journalism, and certainly no notion that the lives of Black people needed to enter the historical record—except, of course, when it was used to capture that stillest of subjects, a dead body left hanging from a tree.

There are two interesting exceptions to this. One was the abolitionist speaker and formerly enslaved woman Sojourner Truth, who, as a method of promoting her oratorical tours, sold *cartes de visite* (literally, "visiting cards") featuring a photograph of herself and the phrase "I Sell the Shadow to Support the Substance." Truth, who was born Isabella Baumfree, took her adopted name at age forty-six after a religious epiphany convinced her to become an itinerant preacher. But, unable to read throughout her life, she was an evangelist for oral culture who remained suspicious of written text for the way she insisted that it could be misconstrued by the reader. Her fame as a heroic standard-bearer on two fronts—abolition and women's rights—was achieved through her lectures, her dictations to others who would then faithfully (and sometimes unfaithfully) record her words, and pictures. On the subject of photography she appears to have been prescient, for she copyrighted images of herself and was keenly aware of the confusion that photography creates in its relationship to the real life it represents. That's the distinction she was drawing between "shadow" and "substance," though the term "shadow" also has overtones as a racial epithet.

The other was arguably America's first black celebrity, Frederick Douglass. As Celeste-Marie Bernier, John Stauffer, and Zoe Trodd, the authors of the fascinating history *Picturing Frederick Douglass*, discovered, Douglass was the most photographed American of the nineteenth century. Indeed, they can account for 168 separate pictures of him, while, for instance, only 126 of Abraham Lincoln. Worldwide, only the British royal family, the British prime minister, and the actress Ellen Terry surpassed him in his day.

The reasons for the abundance of Frederick Douglass imagery are several. For one, Douglass was a popular fascination, a curiosity whose very presence challenged assumptions about race and slavery. People wanted to hear him speak, but they also wanted to know what he looked like, and Douglass happily obliged.

Then there was Douglass himself. The author of not one but three books of autobiography, he was consumed with the process of self-invention, wanted very much to control his own image, and understood, with great foresight, the power of photography to set his story and the stories of others for posterity. In short, Douglass was an evangelist for the camera. In lectures, he spoke of a profound admiration for the Frenchman Louis Daguerre, inventor of the daguerreotype, comparing him to Samuel F. B. Morse and his telegraph. Together, he offered, these men had conceived of a way to collapse distance: Morse by bringing "the ends of the earth together" to form "a whispering gallery," and Daguerre by using little more than "simple but all-abounding sunlight" to transform "the planet into a picture gallery."

Douglass saw the democratizing potential of photography, a technology that allowed humble servant girls an opportunity previously afforded only to royalty, and, critically, he also saw the possibilities that picture-making afforded to the advancement of his own race. Drawings that had been done of him disturbed Douglass, for they tended to show him with "a much more kindly and amiable expression than is generally thought to characterize the face of a fugitive slave."

The artist—by which Douglass meant painters and sculptors—cannot, by definition, be impartial. For their version of the "truth" must first pass through their own filters and beliefs, making it "next to impossible for white men to take likenesses of black men." As evidence, he referenced a prevailing theory of Black physiognomy among the white ruling class that included comically exaggerated features intended to demean and ridicule. By contrast, the camera offered the opportunity for "true pictures" of reality. A new age, Douglass prophesied, was upon us. "Mind is everywhere asserting its potent, wise, and beneficent mastery over matter. The world is in motion. Industry, enterprise, discovery, and invention have in our day wrought wonders surpassing the wildest dreams of bygone generations. Oceans that divided have become, under the ministry of these great forces, but bridges to connect mankind in the bonds of common brotherhood."

Frederick Douglass was yet another Black leader whose mother was enslaved and whose father was, most likely, his mother's white slave master. Born in 1818 on a plantation in Talbot County, Maryland, he was given the stately name Frederick Augustus Washington Bailey. But after the death of his first brutal slave master, Douglass was passed to the master's son-in-law, and eventually to his son-in-law's brother, Hugh Auld, and his wife, Sophia, in Baltimore. There he lived the life of a "city slave," which meant a freer existence and, in his case, lessons from the well-intentioned Sophia in reading and writing. While Maryland was one of the few states where enslaved Black people were allowed such education, Hugh Auld objected. Douglass later described his master as believing that "if you teach that nigger (speaking of myself) how to read, there would be no keeping him. It would forever unfit him to be a slave. He would at once become unmanageable, and of no value to his master." In the end, Douglass would bring bits of bread with him when sent on errands and provide them to white "street urchins" in return for more lessons.

When Douglass was twenty, his master's prophecy

about the dangers of educating enslaved Blacks was ful-filled. Aided by the efforts of the Black abolitionist David Ruggles, Douglass stole onto a train out of Baltimore and eventually landed in New Bedford, Massachusetts, where he was taken in by a family of free Blacks. As a fugitive in need of protection, he changed his name—his first major act of self-invention—holding on to Frederick "to preserve a sense of my identity" and choosing the surname "Douglas" from "The Lady of the Lake," a poem by the Scotsman Sir Walter Scott, to which he added an extra *s*.

In Boston, Douglass came under the influence of the great white abolitionist William Lloyd Garrison and quickly rose to fame as an orator. His firsthand experiences made him different from other abolitionist speakers. He alone knew "something about slavery," he told his listeners, "as I have felt it." In speeches to church groups, he would explain that he was "not a fugitive from slavery but a fugitive slave," the distinction forcing the immediacy of the abolitionist movement upon those who heard him by acknowledging that at any moment, the doors could burst open and he could be returned to bondage.

But since his audiences often wanted less reflection on slavery from him and more accounts of the gruesome abuse that he suffered from it, this could be a humiliating enterprise. His listeners saw Douglass as more exhibit than speaker, more victim than philosopher, and while he would tell them in his much-admired baritone of the "bloody whip, the chain, the gag, the thumbscrew, cat-hauling, the cat-o'-nine-tails, the dungeon, the blood-hound" used to keep the slave a slave, he preferred to "not dwell at length upon these cruelties." His target was slavery, the institution, not the details of its manifestation, and, on this subject, he had little patience for those—both northerner and southerner— who "filled the air with whines of compromise."

Scholars have come to see Douglass's autobiographies as selective histories (all autobiographies are), and more interesting, perhaps, as artifacts of his life than as faithful renderings of it. But for anyone who seeks to understand this great American, a study of the pictures, and his writings about pictures, also offers no small reward. The photographs taken of him show the evolution of the man from young militant with clenched hands to elder statesman in regal repose. They are pictures rendered with a purpose, one driven by the poser himself, and the message he intended for viewers to receive from them went something like this: "Don't see me as a pitiable creature on display like a circus animal. I am a man equal to all other men." That these images live on—and not only as photographs but also as the inspirations for public murals and statues of him the world over—shows just how aware Douglass was to their lasting impact.

Douglass delivered four lectures about photography, and the insights there ring loudly into our own time. Writing in 1862, he observed how "no man thinks of publishing a book without sending his face into the world with it," and whether he was "handsome or homely, manly or otherwise, it makes no difference . . . once in the book, whether the picture is like him or not, he must forever strive to look like the picture." The notion that a photograph renders a kind of permanence upon its subject, so much so that the person themselves must thereafter strive to look like the picture and not the picture like the person, says a lot about technology and the image-driven culture that we inhabit today. But in 1862? Even then, Douglass apparently understood that a picture is not only a representation of the moment captured; it informs all succeeding moments as well, often taking on a life of its own.

Douglass also reflected on how a picture is understood, in part, by what one brings to it. "Our military heroes look better," he argues, "after winning an important battle than after losing one." The pictures themselves "do not change," but our attitudes toward the subject alter how we see them. He then connects that insight to race: "It is perhaps on the same principle of prospective beauty that ministers sometimes console the race to which I belong, assuring them that though black and ugly on the Earth, they will all be white and beautiful in heaven."

Broadening his discussion from photography to the visual arts in general, he pondered how an appreciation for pictures is what sets man apart from other animals: "The dog fails to recognize his own features in a glass." And then, prefiguring the ubiquity of pictures through reproduction, he reflects on how "the great cheapness and universality of pictures must exert a powerful, though silent, influence upon the ideas and sentiment of present and future generations." Pictures, and not text, have the quality of symbols and serve as "our natural and primary instructors, both as nations and individuals."

In a passage that anticipates ethnographic studies conducted decades later, Douglass said that the pictures we save provide unique insight into a people. Quoting approvingly the sentiment of the Scottish essayist Andrew Fletcher, who wrote "Give me the making of a people's songs, and I care not who makes its laws," Douglass added that "the picture and the ballad are alike, if not equally social forces—the one reaching and swaying the heart by the eye, and the other by the ear."

Amazingly, Douglass also seemed to foresee motion pictures. "Niagara is not fitly described when it is said to be a river of this or that volume falling over a ledge of rocks two hundred feet," he says. "This is truth, but truth disrobed of its sublimity and glory," truth that is "destitute of motion itself." He is speaking, of course, to the limitations of words and in appreciation for the ability of pictures, either paintings or sketches or photographs, to convey the *feeling* of motion—here, Niagara, where, by the way, he had gone on his honeymoon and sat for a picture in a studio, with a backdrop showing the waves and the rocks.

Douglass, who died in 1895, lived long enough, technically speaking, to have seen the camera used as a tool of social reform, though there are no accounts of his being aware of the work of Jacob Riis, for instance, whose 1890 *How the Other Half Lives* was a landmark of what would eventually, in more mature expressions, become known as "photojournalism." Riis's work, documenting the squalor of tenement life in the immigrant neighborhoods of the Lower East Side of New York, exemplified an unflinching realism that motivated progressives to seek relief.

But there was still a danger akin to the one that Douglass found when he felt himself on display as a "fugitive from slavery" that viewers who were used to travelogues and frameable images for their living rooms would react to scenes of social decay less as a call to action than as a daring peek into a world they found perhaps interesting but wished to keep exotic and remote. Indeed, Riis's pictures didn't only generate sympathy; they also produced horror from those who, armed with racial theories that saw white America as under assault not only from the freed slave and his descendants but from the Eastern European and the Mediterranean immigrant, found confirmation of genetic inferiority in the pictures. The term that Teddy Roosevelt used to describe the work of Riis and that of the photographer Lewis Hine, of the crusading journalists Lincoln Steffens and Ida Tarbell, was "muckraker," and he did not mean it as a compliment.

———

There are other George Floyd videos besides Darnella Frazier's cell phone capture, including those taken by the bodycams worn by the officers involved in the encounter. You can easily find these videos by searching YouTube under the heading "RAW: George Floyd Minneapolis body camera video," where they will then appear above a list of other suggested titles: Jason Alexander discussing the role of George Costanza, the character he played on *Seinfeld*; a clip from a 1972 episode of Johnny Carson's *Tonight Show* in which the chess wizard Bobby Fischer solves a special puzzle; a spoof on the game show *Family Feud* from *Saturday Night Live*; and the only suggestion that seems thematically appropriate: an interview with a paramedic who examined Floyd at the scene: "I thought he was dead," he says.

While they're less familiar, the bodycam videos are, in fact, even harder to watch than Frazier's video, which focuses on the time when Floyd has already been pinned to the pavement and is slowly expiring. If that video, as we say above, demonstrates the stillness of sculpture, the bodycam video is its opposite: all panic, bewilderment, paranoia, and rage, and seen not from the position of the human eye but, because the camera itself is attached lower down on the chest, from a vantage point that feels like you're offstage, peering through a hole in the curtain.

Faces are mostly out of view, meaning that torsos speak to torsos, adding weirdly to the drama and making the whole thing feel a bit like an experiment in film noir. The sound is choppy, interrupted by ambient noise and the rustle of clothing as the officer walks.

Officer J. Alexander Kueng's video starts with him entering Cup Foods and approaching an employee, who holds up the twenty-dollar bill that he says Floyd had just tried to use to buy cigarettes and that he says is counterfeit. The man points the officer toward Floyd's car outside. Kueng and his colleague go off to confront Floyd, and here you do see a face—Floyd's, as he sits in the car and is eventually dragged out of it, the officers standing over him. You watch Floyd's fevered reaction to being arrested, his immediate and frequent "I'm sorry" and "I'm so sorry, Mr. Officer. Dang, man." Ordered to step out of the car, Floyd says "Okay, Mr. Officer. Please don't shoot me. Please, man. I just lost my mom, man." His voice is shaky, he is near tears. He refers to having been shot at before. He is high. Panic in his voice, he repeatedly (twenty-seven times) says that he is "claustrophobic."

The expressions, so raw, resound as if lifted from an allegory: the formal address ("Mr. Officer") right out of Jim Crow; the request for leniency ("I'm so sorry") redolent of the misbehaving slave; and the signs that he is paralyzed by fear, that he is claustrophobic, not that he *will be* claustrophobic if he is apprehended but that he *is* claustrophobic, that this is for him a state of being, that he lives in terror of closed spaces, of being shut in, having no way out, caught in a predicament where he's wholly dependent upon his captors and his captors alone for relief. Through all of that, the mind takes in what it sees, but then adorns it with historical and cultural context, unaware of a disturbing irony.

While we cannot know it from a video in which his face is never seen, Officer Kueng is, actually, Black—his mother is white and his father Nigerian—and he was new to the force that day, working just his third shift. When he joined, he had spoken to his family about the police's reputation for abuse of Black people and argued that the way to change police behavior was to do it from the inside. Yet here, only days later, he's helping hold George Floyd to the pavement while Derek Chauvin applies pressure to the man's neck, and when that pressure results in Floyd's death, two of Kueng's siblings joined the calls for arrests of the officers involved, including their own brother.

This is more than record. It's surveillance media as narrative. In fact, it literally bursts with story, and watching it after we know what happened to Floyd is like having him talk back to us from the dead. What's your name? "George . . . George Perry Floyd." Date of birth? "October 14, 1973." Cars are driving by behind them. It's a busy intersection. The world will soon know what happened here. Tourists will make pilgrimages to the site. Plaques will mark the location. But for now, commuters make their way to work and delivery vans bringing goods to local retail outlets cut them off.

After Floyd's body has been removed by ambulance from the scene, Officer Kueng returns to the sidewalk where Floyd's companions are waiting for news. They ask the officer (at the 23:00-minute mark) for help retrieving Floyd's phone from the car. They say they want to take it to him. "No," Kueng says. "Leave it in the car. When he comes back, we need to be able to tell him where it is." When he comes back? "I am going to go talk to the owner," Kueng says. Inside Cup Foods again, he asks for the counterfeit twenty. There's confusion over who exactly passed the bill, "the big guy in the tank top" or the "one in hat and dreads." Floyd was the big one. "What did he purchase with it?" "Cigarettes." A couple of paramedics, having just arrived at the scene, come into the store like firemen arriving after the fire. They're looking for the ambulance. "They're up the street," Kueng tells them. "They moved to get away from the crowd."

Kueng asks the store manager if there's surveillance tape. There is, the manager says. You can get it from us anytime. The officer asks him to load it onto a flash drive and keep it until they can retrieve it. But the manager says it only lasts two weeks before it's erased. "Two weeks?" the officer asks. "Could you burn it right now?" The manager says they get the feed on their phones. "Oh, so you can pull it up right now? I'll be back with you, then." The officer makes his way out of the store (28:38), moving past what looks, oddly, like an old lunch counter with stools, the kind that are stationary but you can spin the seats. It looks unused, abandoned, as if it were part of another store in the same spot but another era. In fact, it recalls the famed Woolworth's lunch counter in Greensboro, North Carolina, where, on February 1, 1960, four Black college students, denied service in a whites-only section, staged a sit-in. Today that very lunch counter is on exhibit at the Smithsonian's National Museum of American History. As Kueng emerges from the store, in search of someone with an envelope in which he can deposit the counterfeit twenty, he faces another round of taunting. "You know you broke this man, bro," an off-camera male voice says. "You know you broke him. You can't say nothing right now."

THREE

The "Campaign"

On February 23, 2020, three months before George Floyd was asphyxiated by Minneapolis police officer Derek Chauvin, twenty-five-year-old Ahmaud Arbery went out for a jog near the coastal town of Brunswick, Georgia. It's unclear exactly where he started running, but security camera footage from a nearby home picked him up after he had crossed US 17 and entered the white, middle-class neighborhood of Satilla Shores, about two miles from the Fancy Bluff home Arbery shared with his mother. It was roughly one in the afternoon, and the area was bathed in broad daylight. Arbery's uncle, Paul Dix, told the *Brunswick News* that his nephew "loved to run" and recalled when Arbery, as a football player for Brunswick High School, had intercepted a pass and returned it eighty yards for a touchdown. "I've tried jogging with him a few times. Leaves me gasping after a quarter mile. He's a runner."

The film shows Arbery stopping at 220 Satilla Drive, where a house was under construction. He enters the site. A second camera at the construction site itself shows Arbery walking through the building. He is the only person there. He looks around. While Arbery is inside, a neighbor who was watching the scene from the across the street calls 911. He tells the dispatcher that there is man trespassing on the site—"Black guy, white T-shirt."

"And you said [he's] breaking into it right now?" the dispatcher asks.

"No," the man says. "It's all open. It's under construction." The man says that someone who looks like Arbery "has been caught on camera a bunch before at night. It's kind of an ongoing thing out here."

Then, suddenly, Arbery departs the building and continues on his way down Satilla Drive.

"There he goes right now," says the caller.

"Okay," the dispatcher says. "What is he doing?"

"He's running down the street."

"That's fine," the dispatcher says. "I'll get [the police] out there. I just need to know what he was doing wrong. Was he just on the premises and not supposed to be?"

It was true that a motion-activated security camera

had recently caught images of a few people inspecting the site—two white children, a white adult couple, and a Black man who appears on four separate occasions, though it's unclear whether that man was Arbery. No property had been taken and no damage was ever found. Nevertheless, the neighborhood had taken notice and was on the alert. Notices had been posted to the community's Facebook page. Two months earlier, Greg McMichael, sixty-four, a retired Glynn County law enforcement officer who resided nearby, had told the police that he would be willing to assist in apprehending any suspicious intruders. He asked them to tell the owner of the construction site, who lived two hours away, to "call [me] day or night when you get action on your camera." They texted the owner, notifying him of McMichael's offer, but the man did not follow up.

Nonetheless, on this day, as Arbery continued his jog, moving past their home, Gregory McMichael and his son, Travis, thirty-four, went into action. Convinced that Arbery was the Black man who'd been seen on the construction site before, they grabbed their guns—a .357 Magnum revolver and a shotgun—and, looking duty bound, pursued him in their 2011 Ford F-150 pickup. Another neighbor, Roddie Bryan, was on his porch when he saw the two men embark on their chase. "Y'all got him?" he called out before jumping into his own truck and joining them. When they reached Arbery, the McMichaels maneuvered to block his path, but Arbery reversed himself and started running in the other direction. Bryan, who, for reasons that are still mysterious, was filming the entire encounter from his car, then tried to block Arbery, too, but was also unsuccessful.

About four minutes later, the McMichaels had advanced ahead of Arbery and were now parked in the road, waiting in earnest. Travis was standing with his shotgun by the left side of the vehicle, while Gregory had climbed into the bed of the truck and was holding his revolver. The two men looked like a couple of game hunters on an expedition, which, following a perverted yet historically supported logic, they were—only their "game" was an innocent man.

The trio even had legal cover for their actions. Whether they knew it or not, what they were doing—civilians confronting a suspect they believed to have committed a crime—was protected by an 1863 Civil War–era Georgia statute intended to stop enslaved Blacks from escaping to join the advancing Union Army. Georgia, of course, would be a turning point for that conflict, with victory eluding the North until Sherman's historic march on Atlanta in 1864. But even after the war, the law, which broadly allowed for extrajudicial detentions and even executions, proved to be a convenient one for vigilante lynch mobs who cited it as justification for their actions. Georgia, with 531, ranks second only to Mississippi in the number of lynchings recorded since Reconstruction. In the 1890s alone, Glynn County was the site of three lynchings.

Gregory McMichael dialed 911. "I'm out here at Satilla

Shores," he said with urgency. "There's a Black male running down the street." Arbery continued toward them. Gregory McMichael later described him not simply as jogging but as "hauling ass," a phrase that suggests guilt, as if pace alone could be a sign of culpability. But if Arbery had accelerated his jog, it was more likely because he wanted to get out of the way of the danger in front of him: two white men with guns. As he got closer, he zigzagged to avoid the truck, eventually passing it on the right side before cutting back in front of it. Gregory McMichael yelled at him, "Damn it, stop!" Then shots rang out. The video recorded by Roddie Bryan is obscured for a second or two, but it then shows Travis McMichael and Arbery fighting over the shotgun. Arbery punches Travis; more shots are fired. Arbery stumbles forward, then collapses. Travis walks away. Gregory, holding his revolver, dismounts from the truck bed and approaches Arbery's body. He later said he was concerned that Arbery might be armed. He rolls him over to see if he can find a weapon. There is none. A pool of blood is gathering around him. He is dying.

———

Long before cell phone video and bodycams, before surveillance cameras and the advent of photojournalism, film was being utilized to frame the story of race in America. The first film to be screened at the White House was *The Birth of a Nation*, in 1915. The president was Woodrow Wilson and the filmmaker was D. W. Griffith, who, by developing the close-up, the fade out, backlighting, crosscutting, and a dozen or so other innovations, essentially settled the vocabulary of the modern movie. Before Griffith, filmmakers were still trying to find their way through that awkward phase when a new technology is defined by the thing that it is seen to supersede or replace. Thus, the first photographs were valued as cheaper, better, and certainly more objective captures of reality than paintings. The first films, in turn, were "living photographs"—not just a picture of a horse but, in Eadweard Muybridge's famous 1878 image sequence, a horse in motion, showing how, in its gallop, the animal actually lifts all four feet off the ground at once. Who knew? This was art as X-ray, revealer of subcutaneous truths.

Most early experimental films were like Muybridge's: events caught in a few seconds, in silence. They were more like modern-day GIFs than modern-day movies: a comic boxing match, a dance solo, or, in one bizarre experiment, the electrocution of a circus elephant called Topsy, named for the enslaved girl in the Harriet Beecher Stowe novel *Uncle Tom's Cabin*. Once the filmmaker's palette expanded a bit, comedy fit well in the new medium because, as mimes had been demonstrating since the beginning of time, one doesn't need sound to be funny. But to tell a story, to weave a narrative using only the projection of light through celluloid onto a blank screen, someone needed to first show the rest of us how that could be done. D. W. Griffith was that someone.

Born on a small farm in Kentucky in 1875, David Wark Griffith grew up inhaling the intoxicating aroma of his father's Civil War memories. While Kentucky was a slave state with southern sympathies, the plantation system of the Deep South had never taken hold there, and it was not among those states that seceded to form the Confederacy. Still, at the ripe age of forty-two, Jacob Griffith had volunteered for the First Kentucky Brigade, a makeshift regiment that saw action at the battles of Shiloh and Chickamauga, in the Atlanta Campaign of 1864, and in opposition to Sherman's March to the Sea. Because it didn't have official state sanction, its nickname was "the Orphan Brigade," though no doubt it carried a double meaning suggestive of its daring.

As a cavalry officer, "Roaring Jake" Griffith (a reference to his years of impassioned oratory on the political circuit) was wounded at least twice and maybe as many as five times, as his son claimed, leading to stories of gallantry that nourished the future filmmaker's imagination. Indeed, the younger Griffith would later claim that his father's sword was "the first memory I have of existence," an image he carried from watching the man proudly don his old gray uniform and engage in a saber fight with imagined enemies, delighting his children. Unlikely though it seems,

David Griffith even believed that his father's sudden death in 1885, when David was just ten, was merely the continuation of his war experience, the result of the inferior surgical thread used by a battlefield doctor that had finally "rotted and broke." (Others, however, were more likely to point to the ravages of drink as his cause of death.)

In his autobiography, published posthumously, Griffith the son describes an idyllic southern childhood adorned with stereotypical southern trimmings, including the dewy-eyed sentimentality of "innumerable darkies around our old Kentucky home" and how "as a rule, where these people are, so are music and laughter." In particular, he remembered the "old broad black mammy whom we called 'Aunt Easter'" who would make "hoe cakes that would have your mouth watering," and an "Uncle Henry" who "during the four years of the Civil War had been father's body servant and returned home with him." (It was not unusual for Southern officers to bring a slave with them to war.)

One day, "Uncle Henry" gave one of David's brothers a haircut to match a new style that the boy had seen becoming popular in Louisville. "Father appeared upon the scene towards the finish of the job and Uncle Henry queried: 'Like it suh?'" But Jacob Griffith didn't like it. He cursed the man for "ruining" his "best-looking son" and chased after him with his celebrated saber. The outcome of the tale changed with the telling, but the version in his autobiography had "Uncle Henry" returning with a glue pot and the hair clippings, whereupon he pretended to paste them back onto the boy's head. Griffith included the tale, he wrote, as a way of portraying "the peculiarly close relationship between the whites and Negroes of the old regime."

Griffith's love of theater is what drove him to a career in the movies, but his initial work fit the standard fare of the time: one-reel productions lasting a quarter of an hour that were shown to generally working-class audiences in tiny "nickelodeons," named for their five-cent price of admission. This was when the movie was a still a sensation merely because it "moved," while legitimate stage actors considered the medium unworthy of their talents, and religious groups held it in suspicion as an idle entertainment. But Griffith had big dreams for film, and indeed, when his signature epic, *The Birth of a Nation*, premiered in 1915, he realized them: a twelve-reel, three-hour creation that played on large screens in opera houses and stage theaters while specially composed musical accompaniment was provided by a live symphony orchestra. The sudden transformation from novelty technology to full-blown, mature art form was breathtaking. It was as if one had gone to sleep reading a dime novel and woken to find *War and Peace* on the nightstand.

The work showed that the camera could take in much more than mere information, more than motion. The close-up alone did something that no theater production could ever do. Through it, Griffith's camera "became a living, human eye, peering into the faces of grief and joy." There was something deliciously secretive about it, too, for you could do things through the movie camera that you could not do, or would never have the temerity to do, in real life—like stare at someone in an emotional moment or linger over the beauty in a face not from a distance but from a position of intimacy, or view realistically rendered corpses on a still smoking battlefield as if you were there at Antietam. This was "real life" portrayed on a screen, but with an emotional awareness one rarely achieved in real life.

All that alone would have secured a place in film history for *The Birth of a Nation*, but the story that the movie portrayed and its profound impact on audiences made it a landmark event in the history of American race relations as well. Working from *The Clansman*, a bestselling 1905 novel by the white supremacist author Thomas Dixon Jr., Griffith undertook the task of retelling the story of the Civil War and its aftermath in a way that borrowed heavily from his own rich imagination, giving flesh and blood and the power of the cinema to the myth of the Lost Cause. The plot involved the relationship between two white families—the Stonemans, from Pennsylvania, and the Camerons, from South Carolina—who had been friendly until the war drove them apart. The disastrous Reconstruction period follows, with Blacks now occupying the state legislatures and passing bills to allow for racial intermarriage—and with that, the free pursuit of innocent white women by Black savages was unleashed.

In the film, Blacks, who, with the exception of extras, are played by white actors in blackface, appear as sloppy, lazy, depraved, stupid, in power, and out for revenge. Black legislators, elected by a stuffing of the ballot box, are shown in the South Carolina state house, inebriated, feet up on their desks, eating fried chicken. Only the arrival of the Ku Klux Klan ("like a company of avenging spectral crusaders," wrote the *New York Times*'s reviewer, "sweeping along the moonlit roads") could end the horror of "Negro Rule," allowing for the healing of the split between white northerners and white southerners and a reunification around a shared revulsion for the horrid Negro who had forced them apart. The film's opening title card primed the audience for the story they would witness: "The bringing of the African to America," it read, "planted the first seed of disunion."

Thus, it was the shiftless Blacks, and not slavery or white supremacism, that caused the conflict—they, and the northern carpetbaggers and scallywags, including the Radical Republicans, who allowed them their freedom and saw them to positions of power, where they exhibited their natural inclination toward bestiality and barbarism. No, the only hope for America was through the resurgence of a paramilitary operation, a band of white knights bent on saving southern virtue from the African "voodooism" that slavery, and slavery alone, had kept in check. Indeed, in the climax to the film, when the men in white hoods arrive on horseback to save the South, the orchestra plays "The Ride of the Valkyries" from Richard Wagner's *Die Walküre*, and then segues to "Dixie" as a new title card emerges, announcing that northerner and southerner have reunited "in common defence of their Aryan birthright." (It should not be lost that the melodies of Wagner, who was a raging anti-Semite, would give comfort and inspiration to those plotting the rise of Nazism in Europe twenty or so years later.)

The ideas Griffith adopted using the new medium of film were all Thomas Dixon's. Through his Reconstruction Trilogy of novels he had already been successfully plotting a reinterpretation of the Civil War and explaining why the progress toward equality that was made from it was corrupt and wrong, and should be abandoned. But Dixon was never a writer in the pure sense. He cared more about his message than the medium he had adopted to deliver it, and he was a showman, determined to make a splash and recruit as many people as he could to his cause, no matter the means. To that end, he had already created a stage play version of *The Clansman* nine years earlier and traveled with the production, providing commentary between acts. He told audiences that his objective was to educate white people—especially northern white people—about just how much the members of their race had suffered under Reconstruction, and that now was the time to take the country back. Southern grace and paternalism had kept the Negro from endangering the white man, but once he was freed, his pre-Adamite nature was revealed. Hence, no less than Almighty God himself had "anointed the white men of the south through their suffering" to demonstrate that "the white man must and shall be supreme."

The play was an enormous success with audiences (less so with critics), but watching the development of the nascent movie industry, Dixon saw the opportunity in it for reaching even larger audiences. He shopped his story to producers and finally found, in Griffith, a willing partner, one whose personal history made him receptive to resentments over the war and toward the African American who had emerged free from it. In a speech during the opening-night showing of *The Birth of a Nation*, Dixon offered that he would have let no one but the son of a Confederate soldier direct the film. In the end, he got that and more. Griffith's impressive talents were the perfect vehicle for the propagation of florid lies packaged in southern agrarian nostalgia.

For Griffith, the movie was one long homage to a world conjured from the delusions of his youth. Years later, he argued that the film "owed more to my father and his gallant comrades than to myself," and that "underneath the robes and costumes of the actors playing the soldiers and night riders rode my father—on his head the crested cap of courage," a reference to Jacob Griffith's membership in the Klan. But Griffith, who had only a sixth-grade education, also believed in the film as history, one that couldn't be found in the "Yankee-written histories" that were provided to him at school. When, in 1930, an interviewer asked him if he felt that the movie represented the "truth," Griffith responded in a glassy-eyed reverie, recalling his father's fight and his mother "staying up night after night sewing robes for the Klan," which, he asserts, "served a purpose" at that time. "Yes, I think it's true," he finally says, pausing for effect and reaching for a cigarette. "But, as Pontius Pilate said, 'Truth? What is the truth?'"

Dixon was right on one point. The movies *were* different from books, the first example of a "mass" form of media, of a form of popular culture that would explode in the twenti- eth century to include radio and television and, eventually, the internet. Movies were radically different from anything before them in that they were aimed at a popular audience (including those who couldn't read and those who wouldn't read) and experienced in a ceremonial space in darkness, the way dreams are. Unlike reading, which is done in the privacy of one's head, watching a movie is an experience encountered collectively, with a large group of strangers. You might say that these last characteristics made film more like the theater—and, of course, that was the analogy that Griffith was working from—but the movies were dif- ferent from the theater, too, in that they were much more of a visual medium than could ever be imagined for the stage.

In the movies, the director could change the setting

from shot to shot, collapsing distance by cutting back and forth between scenes, and show things happening simultaneously without requiring the delay of a set change. He could also change perspective, from panoramic to close up. For audiences used to the legitimate theater, it was as if they were watching from a mobile seat that brought them onto the stage within inches of the actors' faces for close-ups at one moment and then back out for longer establishing shots at the next. Even the limitations on sound (the talkie wouldn't arrive until the latter part of the 1920s) contributed to the element of mystery. Rapt viewers, whose own imaginations would fill in the dialogue in their heads as they watched, were like collaborators on the story, involved in a wordless communion with the filmmaker.

The movies were "big"—both literally and figuratively. Theater was performed by actors on a stage, and they would always be the size they were in real life. One could see them as people and relate to them that way. But in the movies, the actors appeared like enormous celluloid gods, which made them that much more useful to the art of mythmaking. Indeed, the whole experience of watching a movie had the quality of magic. The images on screen were illusions, developed by a machine process that few understood. All of that made the suspension of disbelief, the artist's calling card, come so much more easily.

But movies were also "big" in that they were so very modern. They were "of the moment," part of an exciting "age of invention" that had descended onto the world around 1870 and that would last well into the twentieth century, bringing the megaphone, the phonograph, the automobile, the X-ray, radio telegraphy, air travel, and even the recoil-operated machine gun. Though its attribution is in all likelihood apocryphal, words associated with Woodrow Wilson, as he emerged from the White House screening of *The Birth of a Nation*, are perhaps typical of the time. "It is history," he is supposed to have said, "written by lightning," then added, ominously, "and my only regret is that it is all so terribly true."

——

The autopsy report on Ahmaud Arbery revealed that he had sustained fatal injuries from three gunshot wounds— one on the upper left chest, one on the lower middle chest, and a third on his right wrist. But justice, not surprisingly, remained elusive, and both Travis and Gregory McMichael were still free. In fact, for two months, the killing of Ahmaud Arbery received little attention. The COVID-19 pandemic was gaining steam, distracting seemingly everyone and driving people inside. Thanks to stringent restrictions on gatherings, there was no opportunity to build a public protest over the incident, either. At one point, friends and family planned to arrive at the prosecutor's office, and, observing social distancing, enter one by one to demand that the men who killed Ahmaud Arbery be arrested. But that, of course, could be easily dispensed with and would certainly never garner the attention that a public demonstration would.

Still, even if there had been no pandemic, it's hard not to recognize a familiar indifference applied to the vigilante killing of a young Black man considered dangerous because he was Black and moving through a largely white neighborhood. The number of well-known instances of the past few years—the 2012 shooting of Trayvon Martin by George Zimmerman, empowered by nothing more than the latter's role in the "neighborhood watch patrol," being only the best known—would suggest just how common such deadly encounters are.

Since Gregory McMichael had been both a police officer and an investigator for the court, Jackie L. Johnson, the local district attorney, recused herself from the case. Instead, the job at first fell to Ware County prosecutor George E. Barnhill, who, citing the 1863 citizen's arrest law as well as a right to self-defense, maintained there was insufficient cause to charge either Travis or Gregory McMichael. That position, of course, prompted a question. Forgetting for the moment the seamy history of a Georgia law adopted to encourage slave patrols and instead accepting it at face value, one could quite rightly ask precisely what crime Ahmaud Arbery had committed that demanded a citizen's arrest. Was it that he had trespassed on the construction site? If so, then why pursue him and not, say, the two young white children who were also seen on the surveillance video? Or the white couple? Since nothing had been damaged or stolen, was it a serious-enough crime to demand a citizen's arrest? Indeed, is there a construction site in any residential neighborhood in America that has not, at some time, inspired the curiosity of passersby? And why must guns be drawn to pursue anyone suspected not of armed robbery or some other violent crime but of trespassing? Yet on that justification alone, here, in rural Georgia, a Black man—unarmed, it was revealed—jogging on streets that were a short distance from his home was cornered by two self-appointed, gun-toting white men who demanded that he answer to them, and when he did not, they shot him dead. To Barnhill, this was, presumably, the law at work.

As it turned out, even Barnhill had an obstacle to prosecution, though one that he himself did not consider significant. It was Arbery's mother who pointed to a conflict of interest in the fact that Barnhill's son also worked at the Brunswick District Attorney's office where Gregory McMichael had worked, and that they'd worked together on a case involving a shoplifting charge against Arbery. Bowing to that pressure, Barnhill then recused himself, but as he did, he couldn't resist offering his own opinion on the case, and to that end he referenced a video—the one that Roddie Bryan had shot, which at that point was unknown and still unseen by the public—where he said it was clear that Travis McMichael was reacting in self-defense when he shot and killed Ahmaud Arbery. Dissecting the video with great care, looking for the angle of the gun barrel and the direction of the "blood plume," Barnhill even speculated that perhaps Arbery had shot *himself.* "While we know [that] McMichael had his finger on the trigger, we do not know who caused the firings. Arbery would only [have] had to pull the shotgun approximately 1/16th to 1/8th of one inch to fire the weapon himself, and in the height of an altercation this is entirely possible." Barnhill then followed up with a cryptic reference: "Arbery's mental health records & prior convictions help explain his apparent aggressive nature and his possible thought pattern to attack an armed man."

The strategy was clear, and it was not unlike the one adopted by Thomas Dixon and D. W. Griffith. Take a story that appears to be one thing—for Dixon and Griffith it was the macro story of the Civil War and its aftermath; for Barnhill, the micro story of a young Black man running from white men with guns—and explain it to be its opposite. Arbery wasn't jogging, he was running from a crime scene ("hauling ass"). It was therefore reasonable to suspect that he was armed and dangerous. He was dangerous both because he had a prior criminal record (a shoplifting charge and a firearms possession charge, though how would the McMichaels, acting as "citizens," have known that?) and because he was mentally ill (which, again, the McMichaels could not have known, and, in fact, is a charge that remains in serious dispute). This illness supplied him with an "aggressive" nature, or why else would he not see the foolhardiness in confronting two men with deadly arms? And in tussling with one of these law-abiding men, who were only looking to hold a suspected criminal until police could arrive, he may well have forced the gun to go off and died of his own act, tragic soul. The whole narrative recalls the trumped-up stories of rape and murder supplied to justify lynch victims, the ones that called upon racist tropes prepped to ring certain sentimental chords in the southern mind and that went unchallenged until Ida B. Wells began the movement to expose them as lies.

Still, it would be too easy to declare that Travis and Gregory McMichael are merely bad people and that they're served by a law enforcement community that includes more bad people like George Barnhill who function as after-the-fact enablers. This would be the "few bad eggs" argument we so often hear about murderous police officers like Derek Chauvin. Get rid of these outliers, goes the reasoning, and we will be good. Install a few more Black police officers in Black neighborhoods, provide sensitivity training in our schools, and form book groups to read about "how not to be a racist." It's much harder to see these men as the product of a worldview (and social, cultural, and economic arrangements) that we all have shared in, one established long before them and before us, before their forebears and before our forebears, and that still reverberates both consciously and subconsciously, history intertwined with history, shadow overlapping shadow, myth begetting myth.

"There is an aphorism attributed to Mark Twain (though no evidence exists that he ever said it)," writes Andrew Delbanco, "that while history does not repeat itself, it does rhyme. The fugitive slave story is a rhyming story. It is impossible to follow it without hearing echoes in our own time." For how difficult is it to recognize in Ahmaud Arbery not simply a man who was treated to an injustice in the moment but also the image of the fugitive slave, moving unchained through the master's grounds (jogging!) and brashly acting as if he belonged there ("Black guy, white T-shirt")—that is, until the posse arrives in a Ford pickup on a fevered mission ("in hot pursuit" is how Barnhill described them, as if he were writing for a bad television drama) to reestablish the natural order?

———

Throughout the country, wherever *The Birth of a Nation* was shown, it arrived with spectacle. Some of that was promotion. In New York, for instance, Dixon arranged for hooded cavalry to appear outside the Liberty Theater, and in other, smaller towns, groups of men in Klan garb rode on horseback through the streets in anticipation of the film's opening. But the film itself also had an incendiary influence on audiences, prompting outrage from Black viewers, and many whites, too, who found its rendering of American history a fiction that could be described only as a rousing form of propaganda, and from loyal southerners who harbored half a century of southern antagonism over the still unsettled war. There were reports from South Carolina that "men who once wore gray uniforms, white sheets, and red shirts wept, yelled, whooped, cheered, and on one occasion shot up the screen" in an effort to save young Flora Cameron from "Gus," a Black brute who pursues her through the woods, nostrils flaring, eyes red with rage, until, in fear, she leaps to her death. Indeed, the Klan, dormant for decades, chose this moment to reopen membership. In fact, when *The Birth of a Nation* arrived in Atlanta, an advertisement for recruitment appeared adjacent to an advertisement for the movie.

It is hard for us, today, to comprehend such violent reactions to any film, because we've become so used to the vocabulary and syntax of the medium. But in 1915, it was jarring, even frightening, to see one's fears played out not simply in the privacy of inner thoughts but in a form that successfully mimicked the external world. In this sense, the camera's ability to reproduce reality—not merely to comment on it, like painting or the word might, but to give human form to it—worked to inform and ultimately to confuse. Perhaps the most useful comparison in our own time would be to the role of deep fakes and artificial intelligence in challenging our notion of what's real and what's contrived to make us think it's real.

One of the interesting things about technology is that it rarely limits itself to the purpose its inventor, or inventors, conceived for it, and once it has been unleashed on the world to make its way through the unpredictable path of the marketplace, the impact it has is rarely based upon its technological achievement alone. No one, other than some critics and other filmmakers, looked at *The Birth of a Nation* and marveled at Griffith's effortless use of crosscutting any more than people (other than engineers, historians, and businessmen) looked at the first automobiles and marveled at the internal combustion engine or the genius of mass production. In each case, people cared little about what it was and more about what one could now do with it, what new experiences it could bring them. With the automobile, that meant the ability to travel long distances with ease. With the movies, it meant the ability to walk into a darkened communal space on Main Street and, like magic, be seduced by stories that required no particular intellectual gifts (not even literacy) to enjoy, just a pair of eyes and a willing disposition. Much as Leni Riefenstahl's *Triumph of the Will*, despite its criminal service to Nazi ideology, continues to hold a place in the hearts of critics ("Fascinating Fascism" is the title of a

Susan Sontag essay on the subject), *The Birth of a Nation* had an undeniable "something" that facilitated its service to a dark purpose.

For Dixon and Griffith, that purpose was showing audiences what it was "really" like for white southerners to live through the indignation of Reconstruction, no matter how fictional their vision may have been. The fact that truthtellers, be they white or Black, did not have a comparable answer to their motion picture, or not one that burrowed deep into the psyches of the viewing public the way that the movies could, disadvantaged not only racial progress but the whole rendering of American history. For white southerners, it was a way of striking back. "One could not find the sufferings of our family and our friends—the dreadful poverty and hardships during the war and for many years after—in the Yankee-written histories we read in school," wrote Griffith. "From all this was born a burning determination to tell some day our side of the story to the world." His movie did that spectacularly.

In Woodrow Wilson, the southern revisionists had a commanding ally. Wilson was a friend of Dixon's; the two had been classmates at Johns Hopkins. A Virginian by birth (though he went on to be president of Princeton University and governor of New Jersey before becoming the twenty-eighth president), Wilson was the son of a southern minister who had been a chaplain in the Confederate Army and who had owned slaves himself. During the war, he converted his church into an auxiliary hospital and built a stockade for prisoners on its grounds. In January 1861, just months before the secessionist attack on Fort Sumter that launched the Civil War, Joseph Wilson preached a sermon showing "how completely the Bible brings human slavery underneath the sanction of divine authority." He further argued that the Bible does not "ask for equality, but rather repudiates it, seeing that the best interests of all parties can be served only on the terms which nature and providence and scripture have fixed—the terms of mastery on the one side and servitude on the other."

Wilson was a progressive on economic issues ("a little less virile *me*," is how Teddy Roosevelt described him), but when it came to race, he was his father's son. Long before he was president, Wilson, in his 1902 *A History of the American People*, had written sympathetically of the white southerner, saying that Reconstruction was "a veritable overthrow of civilization in the South," and that the return of the Klan demonstrated an "instinct of self-preservation to rid themselves, by fair means or foul, of the intolerable burden of governments sustained by the votes of ignorant negroes and conducted in the interest of adventurers." The Klan, to Wilson, was "an 'Invisible Empire of the South' bound together in loose organization to protect the southern country." As president, he allowed for the segregation of the federal government, introducing separate work areas, lavatories, and lunchrooms. Indeed, anyone applying to the Civil Service was required to submit a photograph, which many interpreted as a method of weeding out Black candidates. Though he never issued an executive order mandating separation of the races, instead allowing his cabinet secretaries to initiate such policies on their own, Wilson privately expressed approval, arguing that it was for the safety of the "Negro" who would encounter the prejudice of the white worker, an absurdist and unprincipled trope proudly worn by segregationists well into the 1960s. It would take a "hundred years," Wilson told William Monroe Trotter, the Black Boston newspaperman and activist, to "eradicate" the feelings of prejudice. In the meantime, "we must deal with it as practical men."

Trotter was among the Black leaders who stood firmly in opposition to *The Birth of a Nation*, but he had plenty of company. Douglass was gone, and Booker T. Washington was just months from his own death. His form of Black nationalism had lost considerable favor among Blacks who now were likely to see Washington's pitch to accept Jim Crow and build their own society separate from whites as little more than cowardly accommodation, naivete, or, worse, sheer stupidity. The choice marked a shift in approach, one in which the ideas of W. E. B. Du Bois, who had first embraced Washington before distancing himself from him, were now taking precedence.

The root question was one of identity. Exactly who was

the Negro American? Dixon and Griffith had their definition. Washington had a different, though increasingly
unacceptable, one. Now it was Du Bois's turn. In fact, he
had been fighting this fight for some time, dating back to
his pioneering 1899 sociological study *The Philadelphia
Negro* and to the Paris exposition of 1900 when, as a professor at Atlanta University (later Clark Atlanta University),
he was chosen to mount an exhibit on the African American for the fair's "Negro Section," which he did by exploit-
ing the emerging new media of his time—photographs and
"infographics." Du Bois's presentation focused on Georgia, and it showed the dignity of ordinary African Americans there—"typical Negro faces" is how he described his
collection of pictures—countering the Black American's
well-worn reputation for sloth and ignorance. Du Bois's
catalogue of data was delivered not as rows of numbers
plotted on graphs but as colorful design experiments not
unlike modern-day data visualization projects. His aim
was to demonstrate the achievements of the American
Negro against great odds, and to do so in ways that were
accessible to ordinary fairgoers.

This approach alone distinguished Du Bois from Washington, but, in reality, the two men could not have been
more different. Where Washington was patient, Du Bois
was demanding. Where Washington was proud, Du Bois
was angry. Washington was of the rural South, Du Bois of
the urban North. And while Washington was focused on

achievement, Du Bois's vision, as he laid out in *The Souls of Black Folk* (1903), was to respect the triumphs of the African American while devoting commensurate attention to the ignominies he faced in a racist society, where a combination of "amused contempt and pity" left him with "no true self-consciousness," only the opportunity to "see himself through the revelation of the other world."

This was the source of Du Bois's most famous insight: the "double consciousness" of the American Negro. The African American cannot divorce himself from his American roots, Du Bois asserted, yet he cannot embrace them, either, for they are a negation of his very humanity. It was with this very revelation that Du Bois's break with Washington appeared most profound. "The history of the American Negro is the history of this strife," he wrote, "this longing to attain self-conscious manhood, to merge his double self into a better and truer self. In this merging he wishes neither of the older selves to be lost. He would not Africanize America, for America has too much to teach the world and Africa. He would not bleach his Negro soul in a flood of white Americanism, for he knows that Negro blood has a message for the world. He simply wishes to make it possible for a man to be both a Negro and an American, without being cursed and spit upon by his fellows, without losing the opportunity of self-development, without having the doors of opportunity closed roughly in his face."

Naturally, Du Bois was horrified by *The Birth of a Nation*, in which he found "the Negro represented either as an ignorant fool, a vicious rapist, a venal or unscrupulous politician, or a faithful but doddering idiot." But the well-spring of opposition that the film inspired among Blacks (and many white liberals) did more to advance the NAACP, the organization that he had helped found in 1909, than anything else to that date. In essence, it jump-started the movement for civil rights (a term without meaning at the time) that would culminate decades later in the landmark legislation of the 1960s. Along with many other groups, the NAACP campaigned to have the movie banned, an illiberal idea that only succeeded (where it did) because the Supreme Court had not yet gone through its transformative period of First Amendment doctrine, expanding the protection for free speech that would eventually encompass all manner of expression, including movies. But while censorship of the movies was common in that time, the criteria for such action tended more toward depictions of sexuality and violence than racism.

In fact, Du Bois's preferred response was not to see the movie censored but to hit back in kind—to create a different movie, challenging Griffith. Yet here he ran up against one of the central facts of race and media: the party that owns the means of the messaging controls the message. "If Negroes and all their friends were free to answer in the same channels, by the same methods in which the attack is made, the path would be easy," he said. "But poverty, fashion, and color prejudice preclude this." Briefly, Du Bois and the NAACP entered into negotiations for a film they called *Lincoln's Dream* that would highlight Black achievement. There was also an attempt for a movie based on *Rachel*, a play by the mixed-race author Angelina Weld Grimké addressing themes of racism and lynching. Meanwhile, Booker T. Washington made a pitch to have his autobiography, *Up from Slavery*, put on the screen. Yet in each instance, the lack of enthusiasm from white capital foiled the plan.

Respect for Du Bois may have commanded him more attention, but the loudest Black voice in opposition to *The Birth of a Nation* belonged to Trotter, a militant with a distinctively American pedigree. His mother was the great-granddaughter of Sally Hemings's sister, linking Trotter to the slave family of Thomas Jefferson's Monticello. His father fought in the Civil War for the Massachusetts 55th, a regiment of free Black soldiers organized in response to the Emancipation Proclamation's encouragement of Black soldiers to enter the Union Army. Harvard educated, Trotter considered careers as a minister, a banker, or a real estate broker before finding his calling as a journalist. Black newspapers had been prospering and, as Ida B. Wells demonstrated, they could be instrumental in establishing a voice, perhaps the *only* voice, in opposition to Jim Crow. Trotter saw his work as not only to object but also to warn, using the pages of the *Guardian*, the weekly he founded in Boston, as a kind of travel guide to emerging threats and reports of abuse that went unrecorded in the white press.

Like Du Bois, Trotter saw his work as a way of countering the caricature of the African American that had been established and repeatedly reinforced by all manner of media: novels, newspapers, magazines, and, ultimately, the movies. He worried that a spread of the racial values of the South could well result in a "fixed caste of color" nationwide. In that spirit, he took on Bostonians who, owing to the city's history as the center of the abolitionist movement, traditionally saw themselves as immune to what was universally described as "the Negro problem." Even in progressive New England, he demonstrated, the life of a "colored" man was held back, if not by law, then by custom. He recommended that people challenge distinctions observed by schools, churches, and hospitals lest "every colored American would be a civic outcast, forever alien in the public life." The *Guardian*, which occupied offices in the same space that once housed William Lloyd Garrison's abolitionist paper, the *Liberator*, carried the slogan "For every right, with all thy might."

Trotter was combative and angry. He despised Washington, whom he called "the Great Traitor," and once heckled him at a Boston lecture so fiercely that the disruption landed him in jail for thirty days on a charge of disturbing the peace. But he also rejected the NAACP for what he saw as its dependence on white money, preferring, as he said, "an organization of the colored people and for the colored people and led by the colored people." And so it was only in character that, unlike the NAACP and other organizations, he fought against *The Birth of a Nation* not by filing lawsuits or seeking municipal favor but by mobilizing popular dissent. A lawsuit, in his judgment, involved only a few legal minds and a judge. But a protest? That called upon the perseverance of masses of ordinary people, voting with their feet, and built the kind of undeniable human expression that anticipated the civil disobedience of Martin Luther King Jr. Decades before the now celebrated bus boycott in Montgomery, Alabama, Trotter was organizing mass gatherings to take down D. W. Griffith, Tom Dixon, and the gathering revanchist march of the southern cause.

Still, in the moment, Trotter, like Du Bois before him, failed. *The Birth of a Nation* played in Boston and throughout the country, and the criticisms leveled by Black and white leaders failed to blunt its success. Its influence continued to perfume the cinema for decades, most notably with the arrival, in 1939, of the lushly rendered, grotesquely sentimental David O. Selznick romance *Gone with the Wind*. The movie was based on the Pulitzer Prize–winning novel by Margaret Mitchell, who, as a youth, was so enamored of Thomas Dixon that she converted one of his novels into a stage play and performed it with the neighborhood children. Years later, after the publication of *Gone with the Wind*, Dixon wrote Mitchell a fan letter, apparently angling for the job of adapting the book for the screen, but Mitchell rebuffed him. Selznick, while impressed by the cinematic potential of the novel, planned to purge its most racist scenes and characterizations, but he ended up doing a light edit. He knew that to do anything more would strip the story of its obvious appeal, and while he professed a desire "that the Negroes come out decidedly on the right side of the ledger," he had an audience to please.

The result was a film that burrowed itself deeply into the American consciousness, where it remains, satisfying an appetite many viewers didn't know they even had and depositing characters into the popular culture that remain recognizable in all corners of the world to this day. This was not mere storytelling; this was nation-building.

For men and women both, it tapped into that unattractive human desire to be exceptional, superior, part of a vast civilization with a colorful and gallant history. One didn't just exist; one mattered. Lonely was the white girl of the day who did not dream of marrying Rhett Butler and being escorted into a flower-festooned ballroom on his arm while her friends looked on with envy. The movie delivered itself with such indelible impact that one does not need to have seen it to know it. Like Woodstock, or *Roots*, *Gone with the Wind* immediately conjures images without anything more being said.

By the time *Gone with the Wind* appeared, the myth of the South was so ingrained in law and custom and provided so much restored pride to southern audiences that it wasn't surprising to see one of the film's stars, Hattie McDaniel, who played the Black servant, Mammy, refused entry to the all-white theater for the world premiere in Atlanta. With Dixie enthusiasm running high, the actors paraded down Peachtree Street, bathed in klieg lights, and joined a costume ball hosted by the Junior League in honor of the film. There, elite Atlantans dressed in crinoline petticoats mingled with Clark Gable, Olivia de Havilland, and Vivien Leigh while, in front of a mockup of the plantation Tara, a "negro choir" entertained the white crowd with spirituals, the women outfitted with aprons and Aunt Jemima bandanas and a ten-year-old Martin Luther King Jr., dressed as a slave child, singing along.

The cruel ironies present in each instance did not go unnoticed. Gable threatened to boycott the premiere over the treatment of McDaniel but eventually backed down, and the Atlanta Baptist Ministers' Union raised objections to the presence of the choir, which was from, of all places, Martin Luther King Sr.'s Ebenezer Baptist Church. The ministers approved a resolution of censure on "Daddy King," as he was later known, for being complicit in this humiliation. But their complaints were a whimper compared to the hype the film generated. A wave of hysteria for southern culture was sweeping the nation, erasing principle in its path. Indeed, when McDaniel's name was announced as the winner of the Oscar for Best Supporting Actress, the first African American actress to be so honored, she rose from her seat at a segregated table. No one blinked.

Ten years passed before another Black actress, Ethel Waters, in *Pinky*, was nominated for an Oscar, and more than fifty years before a Black actress—Whoopi Goldberg, in *Ghost*—won another one. McDaniels's role in *Gone with the Wind* served to solidify the image of the happy and trusted Negro caretaker living in the white family's shadows and routinely named "Auntie" or "Mammy." It was the actress's fate to play such characters—maids, cooks, nannies—throughout the rest of her career. Waters's role in *Pinky* was as an illiterate Black maid. But the message was not only that Black people were inferior. It was that they were happiest when they embraced their subordinate status, like pigs in shit. They enjoyed cooking the white man's meals, raising the white couple's children, fixing the white woman's hair, and cinching the white woman's dress in time for her appearance at the ball. They had no names except Auntie and Uncle, no interior lives, and no rights.

The collapse of academia before the power of the narrative films like *The Birth of a Nation* and *Gone with the Wind* perpetuated was just as stunning. Respected scholars adopted the Lost Cause argument and published it uncritically, helping to burnish this fiction in the nation's consciousness as the accepted understanding of the Civil War. In what created a perfect storm, their efforts were indirectly aided by the work of the reigning historian of the early twentieth century, Charles A. Beard, who catapulted to fame with the view that the entire American story was best understood as a rivalry of economic groups and not as the playing out of philosophical or moral principles. In Beard's thinking, the Civil War, then, was a struggle between agriculture as it was practiced on the southern slave plantation and the industrialized capitalism that was moving to destroy it from the north. Slavery, as a moral issue, was insignificant compared to the larger issue of capitalist exploitation, and the targeted class, the one being eclipsed by the industrial engine, resided principally in the South. A whole generation of progressive scholars and policymakers emerged from Beard's influence, including those who worked to establish the intellectual foundation of the New Deal. And while it was not their aim, nor Beard's, to project sympathy for the Confederacy per se, their views provided much comfort to those who still clung to the rebel flag. This was a moment when popular culture and historiography became fused as a single expression. For how neatly did Beard's thesis fit Griffith's and Dixon's portrayal of northern carpetbaggers and scallywags who deviously attacked the South's economic foundation and installed the African American as the white man's equal?

If Beard's voice was not a redemptive one, it came close enough, aiding Confederate revanchists who saw a remedy for their suffering in a return of the Negro to chains and the white man's defense of his "Aryan birthright."

———

Until George Barnhill, the prosecutor, referenced a video in his opinion, no one other than the McMichaels and Roddie Bryan even knew there was one. Bryan later maintained that he had provided it to the police on February 23—there at the scene of the crime. But the police didn't release it. It only became available to the public more than two months later when it was posted online and traveled throughout social media, where it fueled outrage. The origin point for the release was WGIG, a local radio station, which received it from, of all people, an attorney, Alan Tucker, who had been conferring with the McMichaels about representing them. Tucker's reasoning was peculiar, to say the least. He said that by making the video public he "got the truth out there," which sounded noble, except that the "truth" he was looking to reveal would presumably be one that would defend his prospective clients. To that end, he said that he wanted the world to know that this "wasn't two men with a Confederate flag in the back of a truck going down the road and shooting a jogger in the back." Indeed, there was no flag.

Meanwhile, the lawyer for Roddie Bryan insisted that when his client jumped in his truck and joined the McMichaels on the chase, cell phone camera at the ready, he was doing what "any other patriotic American would have done under the same circumstances." He added that "whether Ahmaud Arbery was white, Black, or Martian, [Bryan] wouldn't have acted any differently on the day in question." But these statements became complicated to defend when prosecutors later found "pages" of racist text messages on Bryan's phone, including one about Martin Luther King Day, where he referred to it as "a Monkey Parade."

Considering how, in the end, the video incriminated the McMichaels as well as Bryan, the cameraman, it appears at face value to be a demonstration of overt stupidity. (Shortly after he issued the video, it was determined that Tucker would not, indeed, be representing the McMichaels.) Yet this act takes on a different meaning when we examine it as a lesson both in "how we see" and "how we aim to be seen." The "how we see" part includes not only the McMichaels and Bryan and their lawyers but also Barnhill and, presumably, everyone else in the Georgia law enforcement community who participated in the initial, protracted decision not to charge the group and instead let them go free. They looked at the video and saw it with eyes shaped by hundreds of years of racism, and if eyes can have "muscle memory," they reacted as they had long been taught to react. A Black man has invaded their neighborhood. When their reflexes tell them to chase him, he runs, so he must be guilty of something. When they pull their guns on him, he resists, so, of course, he had to die lest he threaten others in the area. The shooters, then, are not murderers; they are heroes.

By this notion, prosecutor Barnhill's reading of the event was influenced not only by what he could see in the video. He was also persuaded by what he was told about it, for the "narration" of the picture had one source: the testimony of the only (living) witnesses to the encounter, the McMichaels and Bryan—and because they had associations with law enforcement (to the prosecutor, they were "us"; Arbery was "them") they were deemed credible, even if they happened to be the ones who, both literally and figuratively, pulled the trigger.

In the "how we aim to be seen" aspect, the reason for the video and the reason for the release of the video is the same reason a hunter clings to a trophy, as a souvenir of achievement. This was video as glorification. They had done good and wanted the world to know. It was also video as justification, as a bulwark against any other telling of the story. For, without it, there was still the possibility that the narrative about the death of Ahmaud Arbery might be told in some other way, using an alternative explanation, and that's why the two lawyers' comments are so revealing. They're saying that lest you be inclined to view the situation differently, let us stipulate here and now that the

McMichaels carried no "Confederate flag" and that Roddie Bryan acted as "any other patriotic American would have done under the same circumstances." Anyone still looking to find progress in the American story must pause at the thought that one hundred fifty-five years after the guns were ordered silent at Appomattox Court House, a deadly encounter between three people on a random street in southeast Georgia can still revolve around the lingering suspicions and identifications that animated the nation's defining conflict.

"Photographs," wrote Susan Sontag, "are not so much an instrument of memory as an invention of it or a replacement [for it.] It is not reality that photographs make immediately accessible, but images." D. W. Griffith was seeking to use the emerging media of his day to replace the memory of the Civil War and Reconstruction with his own telling of those events—"inventing" history, in a sense—and he succeeded. But his effort relied on the investment of millions, on a cast of thousands, on his own pioneering cinematic genius, on Dixon's gift for promotion, and on the tenor of the moment.

We no longer live in D. W. Griffith's America. Our own time has a very different relationship with the media. One no longer needs to be a well-funded professional to replace one lasting image or understanding with another one. We have the two instruments necessary for doing that in our cell phones, and the ability, through social media, to "publish" what we record on them. The transformative nature of these two tools cannot be overstated. For once Roddie Bryan's video was released, as well as the surveillance video from the construction site, the audio of the 911 calls, and the bodycam video of the officers who arrived on the scene, and once all of it had been published on news sites and deposited into YouTube and shared through Twitter and Facebook and Reddit, where it had been downloaded and analyzed, slowed and magnified, and dissected for greater and greater detail—once all that had happened, a new crowdsourced counternarrative emerged. It was that counternarrative that demonstrated the lies that both the McMichaels and law enforcement had used to justify their actions, and it led to a public campaign that resulted, eventually, in murder charges and, later, convictions for Greg McMichael, Travis McMichael, and Roddie Bryan. It also led to a nearly unanimous repeal of the 1863 citizens' arrest law in the state of Georgia. The new tools of technology had been used to successfully challenge the criminal justice system. New Orleans Saints football player and activist Malcolm Jenkins captured the lesson at hand. "It's more likely that those in power will do the right thing," he said, "when they know we are all watching."

The police had told Arbery's family that he had been shot and killed while in the act of a crime, but clearly Arbery was innocently jogging when he was confronted by the McMichaels, guns drawn. The construction surveillance tape from minutes before shows him only as curious, and perhaps trespassing, but in no way could he be said to be burglarizing the site. His killers had assumed that Arbery was armed, but the video shows that he was not. The video also shows Arbery as alive and in distress after the shooting. There is a moment when he raises his head, moves his leg, and lets out a gasp, but neither the first police officer on the scene nor the McMichaels make any attempt to get him medical attention. Indeed, Travis McMichael seems more concerned about the trauma that he himself was experiencing for having just killed someone. The rapport between the police and the McMichaels is disturbing. It's as if they're conferring with colleagues (which, in a sense, they were) rather than grilling murder suspects. There is even a point when the police appear to be consoling the men.

How different would it have been if a white man, jogging in a Black neighborhood and stopping at a construction site to look around before emerging to continue on his way, had then been confronted by two Black men with arms, cornered, challenged, targeted, and finally killed? Would the Black killers, standing aside as the police arrived, showing indifference to the body bleeding out within feet of them, turning a deaf ear to the dying man's death rattle, have explained their way out of the situation to the satisfaction of the men in blue? No, of course they wouldn't have, because that's not how the narrative goes, the one planted deep in our soil and watered by history-telling and social custom, by the spoken word and the written word and by moviemaking, too, going back over a hundred years. Arbery might as well have been a half-breed like Gus and Satilla Shores the plantation of Tara. The McMichaels? The Klan. And the Glynn County prosecutor? The Master. For that is what myths are—stories handed down from generation to generation, informing our worldview and providing a method of settling the moral choices confronting us.

Still, this time, there was a counternarrative building. For once the news of Ahmaud Arbery's murder took hold on social media, all kinds of new information emerged. Support groups were established, an activist agenda drawn up, and instructions shared on how to fight back against injustice. "When they stop you," shouted one protester wearing an "I Run with Maud" T-shirt, "make sure you got your camera going. Make sure you got a video." A more expanded profile of Gregory McMichael showed that when he was serving as chief investigator for the district attorney, he had been derelict in his required training going back eight years, with lapses that included state-mandated instruction in de-escalation and the use of force. To explain these, McMichael referenced two heart attacks and colon surgery, medical bills that forced him and his wife to file for bankruptcy, problems with his teenage daughter, and clinical depression. As a result of the training gaps, his arrest powers and firearm had been revoked, along with his badge, but he continued to work as an investigator, a decision that now calls into question many of the cases he worked on. Even more disturbing was Gregory McMichael's statement, captured by police on bodycam video at the site of Arbery's killing. While McMichael was officially retired, and therefore a civilian at the time of the incident, he claimed that his .357 Magnum was "Glynn County PD issued."

It also turned out that Barnhill had once been involved in prosecuting a questionable case of "voter fraud" when he brought felony charges against Olivia Pearson, a Black city commissioner and voting-rights activist who regularly brought people to the polls. In one such instance in 2012, she had assisted a twenty-one-year-old Black woman in what was her first time voting by telling her how to operate the machine. Such assistance is allowed, but only if the person is disabled or illiterate, and the voter in this instance was neither. Still, no one claimed that Pearson had told the woman who to vote for or even touched the machine, and such small infractions are usually overlooked. Instead, four years later, just as the Black vote in the region was dramatically rising, Barnhill, in charging Pearson, brought Georgia's first "improper assistance in casting a ballot" case. When Pearson's trial ended in a hung jury, he tried her again, until a second jury, deliberating for just twenty minutes, delivered a verdict of acquittal. It was not surprising, then, when, in reacting to the Arbery story, social media users saw a trend of racist determinations.

A historical shift was being experienced. In the many crosscutting videos serving as a freshly revealing record of the event and in the exchanges on social media about them, in the research undertaken not by law enforcement but by ordinary people scouring the internet, technology— so long used as a weapon against Black people—was now being used *by* them, and by others working in their interest, where it served as a shield against such attacks. Imagine if an army of truth tellers had shown up at a lynching a hundred years earlier, jumped onto the platform, and in a multitude of voices disproved the allegations against the man and condemned the barbarism of the scene before them. Consider what it would have been like if that same army had carried the story forward to the mountaintops and, shouting in all directions, let all those in earshot know of the atrocity committed in the interest of preserving the hold of one race on a superior position over another. And then what if all those people listening had gone forth from their homes to travel to the next town to let them know, and those in that town to the town thereafter, and so on and so on until all the world knew? Consider, too, what it would have been like if technology, including the tools of the nascent art of moviemaking, had been available not only to embittered descendants of the Confederacy like Dixon and Griffith but to those who would call out their lies. Would our history, flowing through different waters, have made us a better people? More important, will the arrival of these tools make us a better people now?

FOUR

The "Influencers"

He was seventeen, but as Kyle Rittenhouse stood before a camera being interviewed on the night of August 25, 2020, he had the fat cheeks and boyish manner of someone four or five years younger. Wide-eyed, his manner betraying equal portions of apprehension and exhilaration, dressed in an army-green T-shirt, military boots, and a reverse-facing baseball cap and holding a Smith & Wesson AR-15 assault rifle, Rittenhouse looked the part of a guerilla fighter in some faraway revolution. In fact, he was in Kenosha, Wisconsin, about forty miles south of Milwaukee, standing by the service garage at a used automobile dealership named Car Source. Rittenhouse's mission was to protect the building from rioters like those who had torched the cars in the dealer's lot the night before. His role was an unofficial one, part of a contingent of volunteer "guards" who heeded the calls from right-wing groups on social media to come to Kenosha and face off against the increasingly violent protesters.

The activists had taken to the streets in response to yet another Black victim of police violence. This time it was twenty-nine-year-old Jacob Blake, who was shot seven times in the back as he tried to enter his car, leaving him paralyzed. Blake's children were in the car at the time and had witnessed the scene, and while the Kenosha police did not wear body cameras, a neighbor's cell phone had recorded it all. Released on social media, the video provided fuel to the already simmering national outrage over the George Floyd killing. In Kenosha, where this new incident had happened, that indignation took to the streets. The protests were initially peaceful, but by night they turned ugly, with demonstrators tossing bricks at police and lighting a fire that destroyed a corrections department building. Clutching his assault rifle, Rittenhouse, whose career dreams included becoming a policeman or a paramedic or both, spoke to the camera, offering that his primary role was to protect people. "If there's somebody hurt, I'm running into harm's way," he pronounced. "That's why I have my rifle, because I need to protect myself obviously, but I also have my med kit."

The previous night's fire had been a spectacular one—"I'm talking flames licking the sky," one neighbor colorfully said—and all that remained of Car Source's outdoor lot were the carcasses of Chevies and Dodges, Mazdas and Toyotas. Indeed, as Rittenhouse took his position, it was already the third night of protests, and the devastation wrought on the city of roughly one hundred thousand situated scenically along the shore of Lake Michigan had been substantial. Along with the car dealership and the corrections building, a furniture store had also been torched beyond recognition. Roughly thirty businesses sustained damage, and it was later estimated that civic buildings alone sustained $2 million worth of destruction.

Reacting to the scene, Kevin Mathewson, a former Kenosha alderman, reached out on Facebook. Calling upon "Armed Citizens to Protect our Lives and Property," he declared that it was time to protect the city from "evil thugs." His words were well chosen, particularly for a confrontation over the treatment of Black people who once *were* property, and at a time when "thug," as a dehumanizing term for a threatening Black man in a hoodie, had become the twenty-first-century equivalent of "brute." Earlier that summer, in response to the public protests over George Floyd, Mathewson had attempted to form the "Kenosha Guard," as he called it, but found little support. This time, however, as his plea spread from Facebook to Reddit to the conspiracy website Infowars and onto the air with right-wing talk radio, thousands responded. Pronouncing himself the commander of the group, Mathewson issued a warning to police: do not get in our way. "Do *NOT*," he wrote, "have your officers tell us to go home under threat of arrest." To his followers, he then laid out a mission redolent of the lynch mob: "You cannot rely on the government or the police to protect you," he asserted. You must take the law into your own (white) hands.

The Kenosha streets were now populated by groups with a confusion of loyalties. Mathewson and his Kenosha Guard were there to "police" the city but had no love for the actual police. In fact, they wanted to replace them. Meanwhile, some of the actual police were seen tossing water bottles to the militiamen, presumably as gestures of gratitude for their presence. "We appreciate you guys, we really do," affirmed an officer over his microphone. Downtown, the National Guard had arrived and installed a large fence around the courthouse to protect it. Their numbers would eventually swell to two thousand, including many troops requested from nearby states. By then, the FBI and other federal personnel, two hundred in all, had joined as well, creating a mélange of lawmen that carried the potential for different rivalries. Finally, there were the lone rangers, people with no affiliation whatsoever but who nonetheless arrived, weapons in hand, to take part in what was increasingly becoming an armed standoff, mostly civilian versus civilian, but also civilian versus police.

The protesters had formed into their own subsets, including members of the hastily formed Black Lives Activists of Kenosha (or BLAK), the New Black Panther Party, and the People's Revolution. But the militiamen read them all as one variation or another of "BLM-antifa," a catchall term for anyone on the Left, though when the Kenosha police later announced that they had arrested 175 protesters from forty-four different cities and seized twenty guns, it was unclear whether there was any consistent identification among them.

Among the many people on the street that night was a self-proclaimed "citizen journalist" named Kristan T. Harris, or, simply, "Kristan T," who livestreamed the confrontation on his web-based show, *The Rundown Live*. Harris, who was later mentioned in an extensive profile of Kyle Rittenhouse published by the *New Yorker*, which noted that Harris's work included "conspiracy content of the Pizzagate variety," had been streaming protests all summer and saw himself as a risk-taker, a sort of gonzo journalist in the style, perhaps, of Hunter S. Thompson. The *New Yorker* description seemed to get under his skin. "The @NewYorker can sit behind a desk and arm chair QB while people like me risk their life," he posted on Facebook when the article came out. He noted, with intended irony, that if you clicked on the hyperlink embedded in the word "Pizzagate" in the *New Yorker*'s online text, it actually took you not to Harris's musings but to a *New Yorker* article on that very subject. Now, he suggested, who exactly is the one peddling conspiracy theories?

In fact, Harris and his partner, Michael Paczesny, who began *The Rundown Live* in 2013, claim a broad though predictable collection of topics for their site and its associated internet radio enterprise, a list that includes "liberty, police state, corruption, philosophy, technology, futurism, conspiracy, globalism, elitism, technocracy, human rights, politics, secret societies, ancient history, alternative history, holistic health, United Nations, gun control, law enforcement corruption, space, science, esoteric, symbolism, new age, religion, military industrial complex, federal reserve, prison industry, lobby groups," and, very specifically, the "Bohemian Grove and Bilderberg Group," two longstanding exclusive clubs composed of world leaders and power brokers that are favorite targets of anti-globalists who see them as representations of the "shadow state." Harris and Paczesny, who work out of Milwaukee, claim that they cover "news and conspiracy that your local news won't" and have "some of the most liberty minded guests around."

Harris's stream of the night of August 25 was later uploaded to YouTube, a one-hour-fifty-two-minute feature film that appears with its very own tease: "Kristan T. Harris of KGRA-db independent news show, the Rundown Live, gets footage that will grip you from the beginning of the video until the end."

It opens with Harris greeting Rittenhouse and another armed guard at their posts by the car dealership. Before engaging with them, though, the cameraman aims his equipment at the snipers on the roof of the dealership—an establishing shot that suggests the kind of surveillance you see when the president is in town and the Secret Service is providing protection—and alludes approvingly to the fact that the men are volunteers. There are "militia on the 'ruff,'" he says, showing his quaint Wisconsin accent, "and that's pretty neat."

The exchange between Harris, Rittenhouse, and the other guard has the feeling of men greeting each other for the first time in a bar—a bit of posturing, a bit of small talk. As Harris brings his lens down to street level, the guard who is not Rittenhouse asks if the camera is getting his "good" angle. "Do you *have* a good angle?" Harris ribs him, laughing. Harris asks if they're local, and they say that they are. Harris pronounces that he is not too concerned for his own safety, that he operates on a "nonaggression principle," and that the protesters have medics who are "pretty helpful" if needed. "We got medics, too," Rittenhouse assures him.

The livestream, when seen on YouTube, has a different feel, of course, from when it was, well, a *live stream*. Back then, it was a window onto unfolding events, with the outcome unknown. Much later, on YouTube, it's a record of events that have already happened, video evidence to be played and rewound and played again. Because we know what happened—that two people would die, shot by the teenager Rittenhouse, and that he would eventually be acquitted on murder charges, prevailing in court on the principle of self-defense—we view it the way that a movie-goer views a movie they've already seen, with knowledge that even the protagonists in the film don't have. But on the night of August 25, 2020, in the video's first and primary purpose as a live stream, viewers were watching the story unfold in real time, guided not only by the camera but by what Harris chose to show with his camera—and not just those pictures, either, but by Harris's richly woven, and, yes, conspiracy-laden soundtrack. Far from a raw camera feed, the video is like a continuous two-hour-long selfie.

Harris wanders to a gas station called the Ultimate Convenience Center. Its windows are covered with plywood and a few dozen militiamen stand intimidatingly in front of it. They wander out to the street every now and then before retreating back to the building. There is a lot of testosterone-fueled posturing. Observing them, Harris says to his audience that "it looks like they're protecting their businesses, which is cool," though it appears that the only thing most of them have to do with the business is that they have arrived on the scene to "protect" it.

Harris tells them that the police are enforcing a curfew, "snatching and grabbing" those in violation of it, and that he therefore expects that the protesters at the courthouse will soon be fleeing the cops and making their way toward them. His message has the feeling of a call to arms. "You guys protecting your business? That's very cool," he says again, directing his words now to the crowd. He then ups the ante. "It's your American right," he shouts, then follows with something Eisenhower might have said before releasing the troops across the English Channel toward Normandy: "I'm proud of you guys." Harris seems to grasp that the men gathered here are drawn by the lust for the fight, and that the stakes are higher than Car Source or the Ultimate Convenience Center or even the streets of Kenosha. They see themselves as defending the whole American way of life from what they perceive to be an existential threat, one posed in the moment by the Black Lives Matter crowd, but, really, by a multitude of disruptive modern forces like the ones that Harris and Paczesny list on their site. They've watched the news from Minneapolis, Portland, Seattle, and dozens of other cities, and when they use the term "property," it is both as distraction—cover, that is, for more overtly racist motives—and code.

One of the men tells Harris that there's a school building burning downtown. "BLM, that's what they do," says another. "My issue is that the police are only protecting federal buildings," Harris says, citing one of his favorite targets, the federal government. A muscular man with a beard, dressed in a tight blue T-shirt and carrying a bottle of Coke that he sips from time to time, explains that there are not enough police to protect everything. "That's why we have militia," Harris responds. Harris says that he hopes that the men carrying arms will act responsibly. "Trust me, these dudes are responsible," the man says. "That's cool," says Harris, before a bit of reflection leads the two to agree that they have seen their fair share of "dipshits" and "boneheads" with guns, and they can be found on all sides.

By way of illustration, the man struggles to recall the story of a "fucking dipshit" carrying an assault rifle in Texas, before adjusting his description to a "libertarian fuck" and finally "some libertarian douchebag," emphasizing "bag" as if to say that this is not just any ordinary "douche." As though he's referring to a friend with inside knowledge, he says that he's "pretty sure the internet knows a lot about this." Harris takes mild offense and tells the man that he, himself, identifies as libertarian, or maybe, he says, as an anarchist. "Yeah," the man says, "but you're not a dick."

The "libertarian douchebag" that the man was trying to recall was in fact Garrett Foster, a twenty-eight-year-old protester who held libertarian views but marched with the BLM crowd, often carrying an AK-47. Exactly a month earlier, Foster had been shot and killed in Austin, Texas, when he confronted the driver of a vehicle that had turned into the midst of a BLM protest. Foster, a white US Air Force veteran, had been pushing the wheelchair of his fiancée, a Black quadruple amputee, when Daniel Perry, a white active-duty US Army officer who was working as an Uber driver on the weekends, stopped his car among the marchers. In the ensuing chaos, Foster, assault rifle in hand, approached Perry's car and asked him to roll down his window to talk. Perry did roll down his window, just far enough to point his pistol at Foster and pull the trigger. Perry claimed self-defense, citing Foster's posture and the positioning of the assault rifle. But to the Kenosha militiaman engaged in conversation with Harris, Foster only got what he deserved. "Guess what?" he said of the story. "Natural selection." Harris agreed. "That's just the law of guns," he said. "If everyone has a gun, the dumb people kill themselves."

The conversation continued. "I've noticed," the man says, exhaling an indignant breath, "I've seen a trend. A lot of these little antifa faggots? They're usually some little privileged white kid from the suburbs or from a big-ass house. You know, had a good life. They're easily influenced, they got influenced by college or the internet or whatever, and they have this false perception of reality, of how the world really is. And they're going to go out, act like a dick, and not expect someone to shoot them in the fucking face if they fuck with their business or their house or their car or whatever."

The man says that he trains for high-stress situations like the one they're about to face because you have to build the "muscle memory" that will allow you to react instinctively to a threat. Harris says that he's heard that you should run before going to the firing range because that will increase your pulse rate, simulating a "real-life scenario." The man agrees. "I mean, me, personally? I like to do burpees as I'm shooting—you know, get the heart rate up, get your hands jittering, right? And then, boom!"

Things are heating up. Just as Harris had warned, the protesters, pushed back by the police, are now being driven into direct confrontation with the militiamen. The police are using tear gas, and the air is filled with fog. Every few seconds a firecracker is set off, sounding like gunfire. Protesters claim that the snipers on top of the Car Source building are directing a "green laser" at them. (A laser is sometimes employed to improve shooting accuracy.) One of the guards yells up to the roof, "Hey . . . if you can keep people from pointing their guns at the crowd . . ." Harris interrupts him: "And no laser pointer, either." It feels like they're summer camp counselors setting the rules for a late-night competition between rival teams. The militiamen spread word that the protesters are using "chemical" bombs. Harris asks, "What kind of chemical bomb?" Rittenhouse, who has made his way back into Harris's shot, says that they're "mixing ammonia and gasoline" into an explosive device that, when detonated, "causes irritation to the throat and eyes." Harris says, "Like tear gas?"

"Worse than tear gas," Rittenhouse says.

"Appreciate what you guys are doing!" says Harris

again. Then, to his audience, he does one of his periodic station identifications. *"Rundown Live*, RundownLive.com. Please share the livestream, let your friends know to tune in. Follow us. If you guys want to support us, there's links to the Cash App and to PayPal."

———

The use of the term "influencer" to mean a stand-alone entity or, especially, a career choice is, of course, a fairly recent phenomenon. Before social media took hold, we might refer to people who *have* influence or whose words *carry* influence, but that was because what they said or what they did resonated with those in power. They didn't really set out to influence as an act distinct from opinion or reputation, and it was more likely to be their expertise, the soundness of their arguments, or respect for their achievements that drove their influence, not their style or skills at controlling audiences or even, as can be the case now, the peculiar nature of the technology used to deliver their messages.

That's not to say that people in the past weren't swayed by the sonorous tones of a populist politician or the oratorical skills of a dynamic rostrum speaker touching their heartstrings. The story of the twentieth century is filled with tales of leaders, most of them brutal tyrants, who achieved a near hypnotic hold on the masses. Technology aided their rise, too. Think, for instance, of how Adolf Hitler used the microphone and then the radio to sell millions of Germans on a distorted dream of an Aryan Fatherland, or, considerably more benignly, how FDR brought the presidency into the American living room, warming it to the sound of his "Fireside Chats." Or, for that matter, of the way that radio and its successor, television, influenced multitudes to buy soap, cars, and breakfast cereal, even when they didn't need them, and to lust for an ultimately unachievable way of life, one concocted in boardrooms, and all because of the hold that these forms of media had on the American imagination. Still, as a term, we might, at least in the past, be more inclined to associate "influencer" with "huckster"—that is, with people who sell us something disingenuously, aided by the aroma of snake oil and the bustle of the carnival.

Our recent notion of "influencer" arrived about a decade ago with Snapchat and Instagram, where social media practitioners would forge a personality, one usually composed from selfies and other, mostly staged photos and videos demonstrating some series of attributes—wealth, or beauty, or glamour, or confidence, or hipness, or a disinterested but practiced superficiality, or even a disingenuous relatability (the contradictions abound!)—and then watch as their performances commanded followers. This new digital fan base would stoke the interests of companies, who would place products and target ads to take advantage of the newfound market that these influencers had created. There was a lot of money to be made in such activity, even if the prototypical social media influencer was nothing more than a teenage girl whose both magnetic and solipsistic hold on her followers could be aggregated with those followers' followers and those followers' followers' followers until you could fill an arena with like-minded people all apt to look and act and think and, most important, shop the same way.

That seemed harmless enough. But since then, the term "influencer" has also taken on new meaning, one deeply revealing of the predicament of our new technological world. It goes like this: In an environment absent traditional media filters, it's as if we, the consumers, have entered a vast Egyptian souk with everyone shouting at us at once. Naturally, in such a competitive environment, the "influential" voice is at a premium. Indeed, it's a necessity. We either find the one person or several persons whom we can trust to guide us, or we become paralyzed by the chaos.

If we were to apply the idea to the story that began this chapter, we would acknowledge that we were watching a combustible confrontation on the streets of Kenosha, and doing so in real time. As we did, we would react the same way we would if we were watching a movie (which, of course, we are); that is, we try to make sense of it by orienting ourselves—in particular by separating the "heroes" from the "villains," or, perhaps even more accurately, the people we identify with from those with whom we do not. We cannot do that all on our own. There is simply too much going on, and while we see what's happening on the screen, we don't see what's happening off-screen, outside the frame, or even behind the lens. We don't know what happened before the camera was turned on, and we don't know what happened after the camera was turned off. We need more information, and then we need someone to help us interpret that information.

That's where Harris, our cameraman, comes in. He not only shows us what's happening, he tells us what to make of it. We tend to trust him because, while we can see what his camera sees, he is actually there, and he isn't a camera, he's a person. We live in an increasingly technologically constructed world, but when trying to understand what's happening in some far-off place, we tend to value the perspective of those who are breathing the air there.

Of course, as it turns out, Harris approaches the situation with a well-developed point of view, one that guides his camera and informs his narration. We see men with guns, but he reassures us that these "militiamen" are merely "protecting their property." Through his uncritical exchanges with the people he films, we learn that the BLM protesters are "white kids" from upper-class homes and that they burn school buildings and use weapons "worse than tear gas."

(Through this narration, we're taught that we shouldn't worry about the militiamen, but maybe we *should* worry about BLM.) We discover that there are insufficient police around to protect the community (another worry), but that's "why we have militia," to step in where the police cannot. We're encouraged to find relief in the fact that the militia has trained for times like these. They know how to work in the heat of the moment because they go to shooting ranges and get their heart rates up by doing things like burpees, all in anticipation of a moment when their adrenaline is high and they need to be ready at the trigger. Guns are necessary, but stupid people are not. After all, stupid people might as well be dead. In fact, if they died, it would improve the overall gene pool.

Only a few hundred people watched Harris's livestream in the moment, but the film was widely distributed. Each time it was shared, through Reddit or Twitter or Facebook, the story went with it. As a result, much as with the teenage influencer and her followers, a market for Kristan T's view of Kenosha—a worldview, really, that goes well beyond the events in that city on that night—was established and thrived. Mind you, it was not the *only* view.

There is no consensus around Kristan T any more than there is consensus around BLM or antifa or the Proud Boys or QAnon. Our new media and technologies defy consensus. Returning to the image of the souk, the sea of people in search of meaning becomes captivated by one influencer or another, some gravitating here, others gravitating there, until the market represents not one large community but hundreds of segmented mini-communities, each with its own unique identity, each seeing something different in the same scene.

Now, in that process, we confront something critical to understanding video in our times. Video can be a truth teller, yes, but, as D. W. Griffith quoting Pilate might say, "Truth? What is the truth?" For while the camera does give a faithful recording of what the lens captures, we tend to rely on other factors to make sense of what we see. One of them is the cameraman; another is the narrator, which, as here, could be the same person, but it also could be someone different (a complication that we will confront later). A third factor might be the source where we discovered it. If this was something we found in a Facebook group or our Twitter feed, endorsed by others whom we follow and respect, we might welcome it; if it was not, we might be more skeptical. And a fourth, very critical factor is us: Where do we see ourselves belonging in the scene we're watching? After all, we don't greet the morning with a blank slate. For all the many identities and groups represented in Kenosha, the situation is essentially binary. There are those who are with the protesters and those who seek to, if not obstruct them, then to contain them. Whose side are we on? What notions of right and wrong do we bring to what we're watching? Are they fixed, or can they be altered by what we see?

Back when the photograph was new, or at least when it became a common tool for journalism, it was regarded in much the same way that we might regard video today, as an incontrovertible record of reality. We couldn't all be in the places where news was being made, of course, but cameramen and camerawomen—many of them very daring—could be there, and what they shot with their cameras would serve as a substitute for our eyes. As technology then became more sophisticated, each generation refined that notion.

At first there was still photography, which, while often compelling, is artificial. It stops action—it is, to use a common phrase, a "frozen moment"—and becomes more of a symbolic representation of what happened than *what actually happened*. It may very well crystallize, for us, the meaning of an event, and even "become" that event for us, objectifying it, and that's important. We do this, for instance, with our personal memories. Like the shoppers in the souk looking for the ripest tomato, we're at a loss until we can order our memories according to certain conclusions. ("This was when Dad was his happiest: fishing.") So, too, with our national story. The picture of the marines raising the American flag at Iwo Jima during World War II tells a story of the triumph of the Pacific war. The war seems clean, accessible, understandable.

It pushes aside stories of the firebombing of Tokyo, the atrocities both suffered and committed by American troops, and the annihilation of Hiroshima and Nagasaki and counters the moral ambivalence that properly attends the stories of all wars.

Of course, sometimes the photograph can make an appropriately conclusive statement, or, at the very least, one that large numbers of us can agree to. Think back to the picture from the Kent State killings or of the shot of the man confronting the tank in Tiananmen Square—or, for that matter, even the freeze-frame of George Floyd. The message of each event is so evidently clear, and the picture is so evidently representative of that message.

Sometimes, too, a picture can be both appropriate *and* deceiving. The pictures of the Selma march are heroic, as the march itself was heroic, but they tend to be viewed as, perhaps, too conclusive. We're apt to think of them now the way that we think of the Iwo Jima photograph, as representing a story with a triumphant ending, concluding that, when challenged, America faced down racial injustice and did so by calling upon core themes of our history dating back to the founding. Yet such a conclusion, heartwarming to many Americans—indeed, the story is treated like scripture in our nation's classrooms—leaves out critical truths, the central one being that life does not freeze for us. It's always in motion, and stories like the Civil Rights Movement do not end with the Civil Rights

Act. In fact, the succeeding years may well reverse the successes of an earlier time, much as recent attempts at voter suppression reverse the achievements of the Voting Rights Act.

Once film and videotape emerged in a photojournalistic role, they provided something closer to a true record, but the cameras were cumbersome and required professional training, and what they captured had to be edited. Decisions needed to be made by intermediaries, which buffered us from the "truth." Video in our time, however, is different, in part because it's so portable and democratic—anyone with a cell phone can be an instant videographer—and because it's omnipresent. Not only are there people armed with cameras everywhere you go but so is the state, in the form of law enforcement bodycams and, significantly, other forms of surveillance, much of it put in place after 9/11 in the interest of national security. So, too, are corporate America and even the nation's infrastructure armed, both private and public, with cameras mounted in hallways, outside storefronts, and on the sides of buildings. For the first time in human history, there are cameras everywhere, gathering data on all of us, and, unlike in past generations when the camera was a tool to be utilized when needed, triggered by the human hand in an act of judgment ("This is worth capturing") and producing something tangible (in the case of a still picture) or having a beginning, a middle, and an end (video), these cameras are always on.

The revelation here is not so much that we have a running record of what's happening around us—okay, that's pretty stunning (and frightening, too)—but that even this record, remarkable though it may be, is no substitute for the human eye. Both the camera and the eye register imagery, but the eye interacts with the brain, which then serves as its own private editing room, minimizing one piece of information and inflating another according to some of the multiple influential factors outlined above. This explains why two people can look at the same image—not a Rorschach inkblot but a picture that comports with the physical world—and see something completely different. The brain merely matches what it sees with what it already knows and already believes, forcing, in effect, the past upon the present, old thinking onto new facts. Sadly, in America, there is a lot of old, failed thinking, particularly on matters of race.

———

Among Black American writers in the twentieth century, James Arthur Baldwin occupies a special place. He was a gifted novelist and one of the finest essayists the nation has ever produced. He was also a public person, in a way that none of the well-regarded Black writers before him were, someone who appeared on television and lectured widely and was featured on the cover of *Time* magazine. He was friends with Marlon Brando and a favorite guest on *The Dick Cavett Show*. He debated the prominent conservative intellectual William F. Buckley Jr. on Buckley's *Firing Line*, and he famously debated him at Cambridge University in England on the proposition that the "American Dream" was earned at the expense of the "American Negro." He was at the March on Washington in 1963, and in 1965 he marched from Selma to Montgomery. In fact, it's fair to say that unlike many serious writers who have emerged in the age of popular culture, Baldwin's work was well read but he was even better known.

You can watch many of his appearances by searching his name on YouTube, including what is now referred to as the "Pin Drop Speech," which was his closing argument in Cambridge, or the fiery exchange he had with philosopher and Yale University professor Paul Weiss on *The Dick Cavett Show*, or you can watch a fascinating roundtable discussion undertaken on the day of the March on Washington, when Baldwin sat with Brando, Charlton Heston, Sidney Poitier, Harry Belafonte, and Joseph Mankiewicz in a moderated discussion over the future of race relations in the country. Baldwin had been disappointed that he hadn't been asked to speak during the march itself, which he attributed to his more militant reputation. Nonetheless, he does not hold back here. The discussion, which was sponsored by the United States Information Agency, was intended to be shown around the world, in effect already spinning the story of the march to make it a selling point for American self-reflection and insight. One wonders if Baldwin knew that and, if so, whether he approved of it.

All of it is worth "the price of the ticket," to borrow the title from a collection of Baldwin's collected nonfiction. For even now, thirty-five years after his death, the man is riveting theater. When Baldwin occupies the screen, one is reminded of that cliché about the supremely gifted actor, because you simply cannot look away—a face as if carved from wood, with a wide gap between his front teeth, and large, bulging "frog-eyes" (his term) that appear to move in and out in a rhythm with each phrase, eyes that had once prompted his stepfather to pronounce him "the ugliest boy he had ever seen," an insult that Baldwin insisted held no sting, for he surmised that his eyes came from his mother, whom he considered "beyond any question the most beautiful woman in the world." There is all of that, and then that voice, a deep, resounding, coffee-colored baritone, enhanced by years of inhaling nicotine, one that he used to great effect, the way that a Sunday preacher—his stepfather's career and one that Baldwin once imagined for himself—might, with cadences promising both terror and salvation.

But Baldwin wasn't a preacher, he was an artist, by which we mean that his mind didn't work like a preacher's nor that of a politician, historian, lawyer, journalist, or activist. It didn't seek solutions to the "Negro Question" or "the color problem," as he preferred to call it. He didn't build "arguments," championed no "isms," and adopted no causes, and he made enemies and friends on multiple sides, both integrationists and separatists, Black and white. Militants and mainstream Black leaders objected to him, including, at times, both Malcolm and Martin, though Malcolm had genuine respect for Baldwin, and Baldwin for both men. Baldwin didn't even like the term "civil rights." He preferred "human rights," which confused some people and put others off. He also didn't believe in the "Civil Rights Movement," insisting that it was nothing more than a proper "white English" term for what was really just the "latest slave rebellion."

Appropriately, Baldwin was accused of demonstrating "intellectual inconsistencies," but he saw this as a characteristic of his profession. Politicians and lawyers and academics may need to carry a consistent message, but "a real writer," he offered, "is always shifting and changing and searching" and "he can never be absolutely certain that he has achieved his intention." He just keeps on writing. "All artists are divorced from and even necessarily opposed to any system whatever," he wrote. Their talent is to see what others do not and to bear witness to that vision. "Poets (by which I mean all artists) are finally the only people who know the truth about us. Soldiers don't. Statesmen don't. Priests don't. Union leaders don't. Only poets . . . We know about the Oedipus complex not because of Freud but because of a poet who lived in Greece thousands of years ago. And what he said then about what it was like to be alive is still true, in spite of the fact that now we can get to Greece in something like five hours and then it would have taken I don't know how long a time."

Baldwin described writing as if he were squeezing the juice of a fruit he had been handed at birth, for one can only write from experience, he said, and "everything depends on how relentlessly one forces" from it "the last drop." Indeed, if some have mistaken Baldwin for an activist, it is only because race dominated his lived experience. It was not his intention to be a "Negro writer," to "represent" the Black race. He wanted to be a writer without a qualifying adjective, but race "was the gate I had to unlock before I could hope to write about anything else." (Imprisonment is a persistent Baldwin theme.) This is the conundrum that, at times, forced him out of America, in search of someplace where he could discover who he was beneath the color of his skin, where "I didn't have to walk around with one half of my brain trying to please Mr. Charlie and the other half trying to kill him. Fuck Mr. Charlie! It's his problem. It's not my problem." And yet, finally, it was also what forced him back.

It was during one of his self-imposed exiles, while walking the boulevards of Paris, that Baldwin came upon a photograph staring back at him from "every newspaper kiosk." It showed fifteen-year-old Dorothy Counts "being reviled and spat upon" on the way to her first day at an integrated school in Charlotte, North Carolina. The picture is one of those "frozen moments," and, as such, stood symbolically for the bravery of those who were challenging injustice back home. "There was unutterable pride, tension, and anguish in that girl's face as she approached the halls of learning, with history, jeering, at her back," Baldwin later wrote.

It's a brilliant phrase, really, "history jeering at her back," as if an entire schoolbook subject could be transfigured into a sentient being, and a grotesque one at that, barking from the street corner. It is also telling. One thinks back to Frederick Douglass's own fascination with photography, and his audiences' fascination with him, a slave in the flesh, or of Du Bois's exhibition of photographs and infographics in Paris, or of the counterargument advanced by Jim Crow and then the film industry, "jeering" back with images of Black people as subhuman creatures in order to justify their inhuman treatment. The Black American has always needed to assert and then reassert their humanity, to say we are not strangers, we are like you. We can speak and write and go to school and love and lead and follow and laugh and bleed and die.

Baldwin was sensitive to such imagery, and he had a lifelong fascination with the movies, revealed in his frequent role as a film reviewer. He knew the history of the medium, too, including *The Birth of a Nation*, which he described, in a phrase, as "an elaborate justification of mass murder." Here, though, in Paris, it was a still image that riveted him. In fact, it so jarred Baldwin that it was then, in the moment when he first saw it, that he decided he would leave France. "I could, simply, no longer sit around in Paris discussing the Algerian and the Black American problem. Everybody else was paying their dues, and it was time I went home and paid mine."

Of course, like Sophocles with Oedipus, it can be said of Baldwin and his work that what he said then is still true now, and less because he wrote of universal truths (though he did) than because the central injustice that he identified remains unaddressed, his warnings, sadly, unheeded. Indeed, it is disturbing to read, or even just to listen to, Baldwin and recognize his reference to the "white policeman" and "the anguish of the Black people around him" to be as familiar to us now as it was then to him, and, equally, his follow-on that one day "to everyone's astonishment, someone drops a match in the powder keg and everything blows up," precipitating "editorials, speeches, and civil-rights commissions . . . demanding to know what happened. What happened is that Negroes want to be treated like men."

The formation of Black Lives Matter as a movement dates to 2013 and the killing of Trayvon Martin. But it owes its surge in popularity to Twitter, especially the so-called Black Twitter defined by hashtags like #iftheygunnedmedown and #wearetrayvonmartin, and of course #blacklivesmatter itself. In fact, if Twitter broadly represents the transformation of the public sphere as originally defined by the German philosopher Jürgen Habermas—a democratic discursive space, where ideas are traded freely—to the tools of social media, then Black Twitter represents the arrival of a "digital counterpublic"—that is, a virtual place where countermajoritarian messages can be traded free of mediation, and while the evidence was initially anecdotal, scholars of digital media (yes, the study of Twitter has reached the academy) having analyzed tens of millions of tweets, "digitally archived and made computationally tractable at massive scales," have confirmed that one of the most frequently cited BLM counterpublic voices is Baldwin's. He is "the movement's literary touchstone, conscience, and pinup" as well as its "most-tweeted literary authority."

There he is, tweeted out by Ya Momma @thewrong words, three days after George Floyd was killed, when racial unrest was just beginning to build and again by @tipsfromyoursis on November 20, after a summer and fall of turmoil, each citing Baldwin's "I object to the term 'looters' because I wonder who is looting whom, baby." Those are some of literally scores of tweets and retweets appearing on Twitter and from there branching into all forms of social media, inspiring new insights, bringing like-minded people together, and fortifying justice movements worldwide.

James Baldwin, who came of age as a cultural figure in the 1950s, is a twenty-first-century influencer.

Two quotes in particular—"Not everything that is faced can be changed; but nothing can be changed until it is faced" and "To be black and conscious in America is to be in a constant state of rage"—have been perhaps the most shared, but it will surprise no one who knows something about the man that scholars have uncovered James Baldwin quotes on Twitter representing multiple sides of the author's personality. One researcher used reverse engineering to delineate "six subtly different Baldwins" crafted from quotations that have "excised, revised, botched, remediated, and wielded Baldwin's words anew."

In fact, Baldwin reduces nicely to Twitter, which may seem surprising for a writer of novels and long essays, but he had a knack for language that was well suited to oratory (which may be another reason why he's so captivating as a speaker), and Twitter, while a silent medium itself, likes the pithy phrase that can "silence" a room. Then, too, a key part of Baldwin's use of language is the way that he creates the confrontation of opposites—"Not everything that is faced can be changed; but nothing can be changed until it is faced"—and the reversal of accepted truths: "I object to the term 'looters' because I wonder who is looting whom, baby." He can also be found combining both approaches, as in "The purpose of art is to lay bare the questions that have been hidden by the answers." In the Twitter age, these are the kind of concise expressions, twisting accepted wisdom, that can carry a movement, for they transfer comfortably from the screen to the street and back again.

One could argue that the Baldwin we meet on social media trivializes the man, or simply that any representation of Baldwin, broken into fragments, is not Baldwin at all. But Twitter can be deceptive, and in the case of Baldwin, the quotes are often just the tease that brings you to a fuller excerpt or a broader comment, and from there to a deeper conversation, one triggered by Baldwin's words. Soon, connections start to be made, from Baldwin to Trayvon Martin, to Eric Garner, to Michael Brown, to George Floyd, to, say, Assata Shakur and Richard Wright and then back to Baldwin in a never-ending loop.

Someone, for instance, provides context by inserting the origin of the "looters" quote—an interview that Baldwin gave *Esquire* magazine in July 1968 (three months after the assassination of Martin Luther King and the riots that followed)—and the conversation expands. Someone else cites the next line in the interview, where Baldwin says that "The looter doesn't really want the TV set. He's saying screw you." Soon the entire article is being shared, diced, minced. Someone with the user handle @ThisIs AfricaTIA takes a screenshot of it, focusing on the passage where Baldwin says, "Anyone who has ever struggled with poverty knows how extremely expensive it is to be poor." Another, with the handle @larwoolf but who goes by the name "La femme merveilleuse invisible" ("The Wonderful Invisible Woman"), posts a 1963 picture of Baldwin outside the "Colored Entrance Only" to a Durham, North Carolina, ice cream shop.

It turns out that in *Esquire*, Baldwin offers not only a reversal of the moral standing of "looting" but a very prescient critique of how television accounts of the looting lead the viewer to think about what they're seeing in a certain way. "The mass media—television and all the major news agencies—endlessly use that word 'looter.' On television you always see Black hands reaching in, you know. And so the American public concludes that these savages are trying to steal everything from us. And no one has seriously tried to get where the trouble is. After all, you're accusing a captive population who has been robbed of everything of looting. I think it's obscene."

Critically, Twitter is also the way that a new generation "teaches" Baldwin, for mediating is what "media"— be it social or any other form—does. Just as a still picture carries a different meaning from a picture in motion, so, too, words read on a printed page become different when heard spoken, different still when they are excerpted and mounted on placards or chanted in protest, and different again when they are sent electronically over a pixelated portal that links people across the world. Twitter distorts and even maims words, taking them out of context and flipping them upside down. But what emerges can be instructive in a new way, words peppered with emojis and GIF files, surrounded by an audience of others tweeting back with their own, like a crowdsourced rap without audio.

The operative goal is not to simply state something but to change it, make it your own. Consider, for instance, that Baldwin's comment that "not everything that is faced can be changed" comes from a January 1962 *New York Times* essay on the future of the American novel. There, Baldwin is in fact complaining that he and other young writers are being unfairly compared to Ernest Hemingway and F. Scott Fitzgerald, if only because the past, being past, was a more comfortable subject to contemplate than the unjust present that Baldwin and others were revealing in their own literature.

Baldwin's "to be black and conscious in America is to be in a constant state of rage" has different issues with its origins that are equally compelling. It comes from the writer's participation in a January 1961 WBAI radio roundtable on "The Negro in American Culture," when the moderator, Nat Hentoff, asked him if he found it hard to reconcile his artistic responsibilities with his responsibilities to speak out for his race. Baldwin then says something slightly different than what he's commonly credited as saying today: *"To be a Negro in this country,* and to be *relatively* conscious, is to be in a rage *almost all the time.*" It was the Black Panthers Huey Newton and Eldridge Cleaver (otherwise a critic of Baldwin who published demeaning statements about Baldwin's being gay) who picked it up and made it a rallying cry. When they did, they not only shifted the language to be more direct and incendiary but they took it out of context as well. For Baldwin is again addressing his profession as a writer, and he follows those words by saying that ultimately, as a Black writer, you have to "control" the rage, and determine "that what is really important is not that the people you write about are Negroes, but that they are people, and that the suffering of any person is really universal." In other words, he was arguing for rebellion, but it was a *controlled* rebellion.

The point, however, is not that Twitter users got it wrong, even where they objectively did. It is that through Twitter, ideas get massaged and pulled like taffy, and while sometimes they break, other times they simply get new applications or modifications that befit the times. What Baldwin said about the novel can certainly be applied to a sphere greater than its literary origins. The fact that he actually recommended modulating your rage "so that it won't destroy you" may be an important distinction, but once released into the conversation, phrases, like tweets, take on a life of their own. When you consider that Baldwin's original language was first altered by Newton and Cleaver and then passed down through the ages until—in a decades-long process reminiscent of the game of Telephone—it was finally resurrected to apply to our own times, the issue may be less one of its contents than its unqualified attribution to Baldwin. Of course, since he reveled in his own inconsistencies, Baldwin might even have approved of the process.

For all his changeability, there is one consistent element to Baldwin's vision, and it's the assertion that race is a social construct. "Color," he wrote in 1962, "is not a human or a personal reality; it is a political reality." That was not a new notion then, as scholars like Franz Boas had been making such a claim for more than half a century. It wasn't even a new notion for Baldwin. In 1947, at the age of twenty-three, in a review of a new biography of Frederick Douglass, he had written that "relations between Negroes and whites, like any other province of human experience, demand honesty and insight; they must be based on the assumption that there is one race and that we are all part of it." Still, he understood how radical a proposition this was, and one imagines that he would not be surprised to learn that sixty years later, we're still far from that place.

To read Baldwin, or to listen to him, is to see racial identity as one more limiting sphere to be conquered by human expression. In an unpublished draft of his essay "The Price of the Ticket," he describes the twentieth century as a time of "cataclysm" that "begins with the smashing of the clock—Proust, Joyce, Stein, for example, and even, in fact, Henry James—and the violent rearrangement of space—Picasso, for example—and reaches its terrifying climacteric with the smashing of the atom." Baldwin doesn't directly connect the thought to race, but one imagines that he intended to, or maybe, in a moment of uncharacteristic reticence, simply left it to his readers to do so. For the idea of smashing things—breaking things up so that they have to be reconceived and rebuilt—is central to his thinking about race and is one of the reasons why, on the divide between the nonviolence of Martin and the radical urgency of Malcolm, Baldwin tended to feel more comfortable with Malcolm.

Baldwin was impatient with America because he saw it as trapped in its own history, and he wasn't satisfied with half measures, nor interested in incremental change. "We talk about integration in America as though it was some great new conundrum," he said in that Cambridge retort to Buckley. "The problem in America is that we've been integrated for a very long time. Put me next to any African and you will see what I mean. My grandmother was not a rapist. What we are not facing is the result of what we've done."

Baldwin wanted white America to make this admission, to say that the nation hadn't merely struggled with a few mistakes but that it owed its very existence to an ideology of white supremacy. And no papering over of this, no liberal social program aimed at raising the poor from the depths of despair, no "affirmative action" got at this central, throbbing issue. In light of that, it was the responsibility of the writer, he said, to persist, to "disrupt the comforting beat" of language and "tell as much of the truth as one can bear, and then a little more."

A favorite image of Baldwin's was that of a rotting corpse in a closet, the result, he would postulate, of a friend having murdered his mother, and both he and the friend know it but have sort of wordlessly agreed not to talk about it. "Now this means very shortly since, after all, I know the corpse is in the closet, and he knows I know it, and we're sitting around having a few drinks and trying to be buddy-buddy together, that very shortly, we can't talk about anything because we can't talk about that. No matter what I say I may inadvertently stumble on this corpse."

Reading that passage today is chilling, and not just because the picture of injustice is so clear, the impasse between white America and Black America he describes so seemingly immovable, but also because now, a fifth of the way through the twenty-first century, it feels as though the tectonic plates of history have shifted. The explosion of our racial myths was perhaps a prospect too cataclysmic for the time of Picasso and Einstein, but the calendar has turned to a new age, one in which we cannot avoid the "corpse." Our new forms of media simply will not let us. And Baldwin remains present to guide us through it all.

———

Kristan T. Harris was not the only videographer at the scene in Kenosha on August 25, 2020. Richie McGinniss of the *Daily Caller*, a right-wing news site founded by Fox News host Tucker Carlson and his Trinity College roommate, Neil Patel, was there, too. So was Brendan Gutenschwager, who publishes through Storyful, a site that describes itself as the "first social media news wire," aggregating information from Twitter, Instagram, YouTube, and many other sites to "deliver clarity in a world of confusion." (Storyful is owned by Rupert Murdoch's News Corporation, generally known as News Corp and parent of Fox). There were also hundreds, if not thousands, of people recording the scenes on their cell phones.

A few months after the events, Harris posted a longer, two-and-a-half-hour assemblage from that night that used his own video as well as that of forty-four additional sources. He synchronized the footage so the entire scene unfolded in real time, allowing viewers to watch while following the time of day down to the tenth of a second. (It's a remarkable achievement in video editing.) And it is there, at the spot marked by Harris as 23:47:37 p.m., that the film picks up a confrontation between the teenager Kyle Rittenhouse and Joe Rosenbaum, a thirty-six-year-old man who suffered from bipolar disease and had only that afternoon been released from a psychiatric hospital where he had been placed for monitoring after a suicide attempt. At 23:48:37 the camera shows Rittenhouse, his

AR-15 at the ready, running by a second Car Source garage with Rosenbaum in pursuit. Rosenbaum throws a plastic bag at Rittenhouse, but he misses his target. At 23:48:44, a BLM protester fires a warning shot in the air. The video is unclear on what happens next, but eyewitnesses reported that as they entered the car lot, Rittenhouse turned around to face Rosenbaum, who then reached out in the direction of Rittenhouse's rifle. In the video, we hear four shots ring out, and Rosenbaum is down.

Rittenhouse waits a few seconds while one of the videographers—McGinniss—kneels to attend to the man. McGinniss tells Rittenhouse to call 911. Instead, he turns and runs from the scene, speaking into his cell phone. You can't tell from the video, but it's later reported that he said, audibly, "I just killed somebody!" That exclamation—whether delivered in exaltation or in shock—prompts the crowd to recognize him as a shooter on the loose.

We hear "Cranium that boy! He just shot a man" at 23:49. "Why'd he shoot him?" someone asks incredulously. "Why?" In fear, some people run from Rittenhouse; others move toward him with the intention of stopping him in his tracks. Rittenhouse, running down the street, trips and falls.

Anthony Huber, a twenty-six-year-old who had been a regular at Kenosha BLM protests, throws his skateboard at Rittenhouse's head. From the ground, in a prone position, Rittenhouse fires his rifle at Huber. In fact, the teenager would shoot three people that night: Rosenbaum, who died of his wounds; Huber, who also died; and Gaige Grosskreutz, a BLM protester who carried a pistol and a medical kit. Grosskreutz drew his gun on Rittenhouse—believing, he later said, that the teen was an active shooter—and as he did, Rittenhouse, who later claimed that he feared for his own life, fired at him, inflicting a severe wound on Grosskreutz's arm. Grosskreutz later said that the bullet from Rittenhouse's gun had "vaporized" his bicep.

On the video, we can now hear what must be Grosskreutz shrieking in pain. Rittenhouse gets up and slowly jogs toward the police vehicles at the end of the street, his hands up. His gait is unhurried, but now people have moved completely away from him. There is more gunfire going on behind him, but it's unclear who's delivering it. From a distance, people point at Rittenhouse. "This dude here," one person shouts to no one in particular. "He just shot them!" The moment is tense. You can hear the cameraman, Gutenschwager, breathing heavily with anxiety. The police, in their armored vehicles, move toward Rittenhouse. They are alert to the news of the shootings, but despite the crowd's warnings, they don't appear to recognize that Rittenhouse is the shooter. Over a loudspeaker, they tell him to get out of the road. Then they drive right past him on their way to attend to the dying Huber, bleeding out on the pavement.

There was plenty of documentary evidence in the videos, and much of it was soon being shared on social media, where a fuller picture of Rittenhouse, and the events of that night, emerged. Twitter, which had been used to organize both the protesters and the militia, frothed at the excitement. Someone tweeted out pictures of Rittenhouse with the line, "This is the shooter in Kenosha tonight. Find him," and within minutes, he had indeed been identified, his Facebook page posted. Rittenhouse was a Trump supporter and gun enthusiast. He came not from Kenosha but from the town of Antioch in neighboring Illinois, about half an hour's drive away. He lived with his mother, Wendy, whose Facebook page was also shared. He liked the police, perhaps even wanted to become a policeman. He had heeded the call to come to Kenosha to protect "property."

Later, we learn that Rittenhouse had left the scene and met up with his sister's eighteen-year-old boyfriend, Dominick Black, who had been one of those patrolling on the roof of Car Source. Since Rittenhouse was too young to buy a gun, it was Black (only months older) who had purchased Rittenhouse's assault rifle for him at an Ace Hardware in Kenosha. The two men returned to Antioch, and by early morning, Rittenhouse had turned himself in to Antioch police. (He would eventually be charged with five felonies, including first degree intentional homicide.) Later, official video of this moment would be uploaded to YouTube. We see Rittenhouse and his mom, sitting in a stark interrogation room with two police detectives. Wendy Rittenhouse expresses concern for her son's reputation. "You're already labeled as a white supremacist gun person. You need to look at your safety and stuff like that," she says to him. "Will you stop talking, Mom?" Rittenhouse replies. Later, he asks if the police will delete all his social media accounts.

Over the next few days, weeks, and months, the story, like all conversations on social media, expands into shapes heretofore unimagined. In effect, we descend again into the souk, with a steady run of new information and commentary pulling us in every direction, much of it repeating a familiar rhythm, the one that reacted to the stories of lynching victims by further demonizing them and Floyd's death by demonizing him, too. Rittenhouse had just shot and killed two men—that much was incontrovertible—but in the eyes of the far right, he was a hero, a patriot, someone who had acted in self-defense, and his targets were people who deserved to die. The most tantalizing news for victim shamers was that Rosenbaum was a registered sex offender, having been sentenced to fifteen years in prison for molesting young boys. But Huber, too, is exposed on a charge of domestic violence. And Grosskreutz had been convicted of more minor charges, including being "armed while intoxicated."

As with other killings, the message is clear: These lives don't matter. On a GoFundMe page established to receive donations for Rosenbaum's funeral costs, someone posting as "Richard Adams" comments, "This guy is a child molester piece of sewage," and then follows up with a warning. "Protest with ill will and you'll end up like this sack o shit. He got what he deserved along with the other two clowns . . . Play stupid games win stupid prizes." Someone using the handle @anntensity tweets "I want Kyle Rittenhouse as my bodyguard." The conservative commentator @AnnCoulter responds, "I want him as my president." A year later, $26,409 had been raised for Rosenbaum's survivors. Over $2 million had been raised for Kyle Rittenhouse's defense.

There is plenty of pushback. A tweet from Michael Hamilton COYS (@NLAHamilton) compares the Kenosha police reaction to the 2014 shooting of a young Black boy in Cleveland: "Tamir Rice was playing with a toy gun and was killed by a cop. Kyle Rittenhouse walked around Kenosha, WI for 4 hours with an illegal AR-15, killed two people, injured one and then was allowed to walk right by cops. Rice was 12. Rittenhouse is 17. #Blacklivesmatter." @JalenElrod tweeted "Kyle Rittenhouse is a white supremacist and a domestic terrorist. #JusticeForJacobBlake #BlackLivesMatter. ✊🏿 ✊🏾 ✊🏽 "

Someone using the handle @LilRedRooster who goes by the name "Crowing for Days" wrote, "Kyle Rittenhouse exposes the rotten, decaying innards of America so well. Capitalism and racism both roll so well into one another when you have an angry white kid able to kill other humans over property value. America has always valued white property more than black lives." On the subject of capitalism, at least, the tweet is prophetic, for within days, there was a cottage industry in "Free Kyle" merchandise, including T-shirts showing a silhouette of Rittenhouse with his AR-15 and a message bragging about the "Kenosha Trifecta." For a while, the Rittenhouse family even got in on the act, selling their own tees, hoodies, and hats, until the hosting website took their page down.

Soon, social media researchers turned up another video, this one apparently of Rittenhouse punching a girl in a parking lot. There is more video of Rosenbaum, too; he's shown shortly before his confrontation with Rittenhouse engaged in an angry tirade at Ultimate Convenience Center, where he looks at some of the armed men patrolling the store and shouts, "Shoot me, N***a!" It was filmed by Julio Rosas, a reporter for Townhall, another conservative website. Rosas is one of a handful of videographers sent to capture what has sometimes been referred to as "riot porn," video of protesters committing violence that, when posted, undermines their peaceful message.

Rittenhouse attracted the attention of two prominent defense attorneys in civil litigators John Pierce of Los Angeles and L. Lin Wood of Atlanta, who stepped forward to offer their services. Both Pierce and his firm, which describes itself as a "law firm for the digital age," one "dedicated to the lost art of combat by trial," have been associated with right-wing causes. In fact, Pierce would later become the favorite lawyer for those charged in the January 6 assault on the Capitol building, representing seventeen defendants in federal court despite never having tried a criminal case before. (He had signaled his support on the day of the attack, tweeting, "When tyranny reaches a certain point, the time for peaceful protest comes to an end.") Wood, meanwhile, was a personal-injury lawyer who made a name for himself when he stepped forward to represent Richard Jewell, the security guard falsely accused of the 1996 Atlanta Olympics bombing, in a defamation lawsuit against CNN, NBC, and *Time*. More recently, Wood has been tied to the election fraud conspiracies of Donald Trump.

Shortly before the unrest in Kenosha, Pierce established a foundation, #FightBack, with the aim to "defeat the evil forces of the left." The language was dramatic, but it fit Pierce's worldview, one that sees modern-day America as engaged in a domestic battle akin to the American Revolution. To underscore that, he peppers his language with references to Lexington and Concord and the Minutemen, uses the hashtags #thomasjefferson and #declarationofindependence, and sells T-shirts with the rebel slogan "Don't tread on me #FightBack." Like the militiamen (a loaded word, too, for its resonance with the language of the Second Amendment), Pierce and Wood looked at the story of Kenosha and saw an existential battle for the future of America.

Engaged by the Rittenhouses to shepherd Kyle's defense, Pierce declared his client to be caught "in the crosshairs of institutional forces that are much more powerful than him," and that the only reason the Kenosha prosecutors charged him was "to appease the divisive, destructive forces currently roiling this country." The prosecutors relied on video throughout their investigation—the word "video" appears fifteen times in the complaint—yet, Pierce argued, they had rushed to judgment without performing an "in-depth review of the available video footage." To counter their claims and build a public following for his client, Pierce then offered his own edited video of the events of that night, "The Truth in Eleven Minutes."

The film is well-produced. Using dramatic music, graphics, B-roll, and punchy narration, it takes the chaos of that night and tidies it up into a simple morality tale: Kyle Rittenhouse, servant to his community, was one of many "Good Samaritans" who had shown up in Kenosha to "prevent the total destruction of their community" when he came under threat from an angry mob—the same mob that had been terrorizing American cities all summer. The people he shot in self-defense were criminals who aimed to kill him. These and other protesters were the ones who acted outside the law, and yet Rittenhouse, "a lifeguard who risked his safety to protect his community and give first aid to wounded protesters, was the only one charged with a crime." What happened to Rittenhouse was an outrage, but it shouldn't surprise us. The left's "endgame is to strip away the constitutional right of all citizens to defend our communities and personal property, our lives and the lives of our loved ones." And that was why we mustn't sit idly by, for now is the time when the "home of the brave" must rise up "to defend the land of the free."

You can watch the film on YouTube, after first clicking past the warning that the contents have been identified as "inappropriate for some users." And, a year after it was first posted in September 2020, roughly a million people had done just that, appending comments that cheered on Rittenhouse and condemned the Black Lives Matter crowd. The footage is real. For the most part, the raw information that the narrator recites is true. It's how the film presents that information that adjusts our understanding of the event—what it chooses to highlight and what it chooses to omit, what music it applies to accompany the visuals, and what graphic elements it employs to drive us toward a particular conclusion, to "influence" us to see things a certain way.

There is, for instance, only one tiny reference to Jacob Blake, which, after all, is the most immediate reason why the protesters are there. There is no mention of George Floyd or Breonna Taylor, of Trayvon Martin or Michael Brown, of Eric Garner or Sandra Bland or Philando Castile or Oscar Grant or Tamir Rice or Walter Scott or Jordan Davis or Freddie Gray or the long, sad history of state and vigilante violence against people of color, which, of course, is the broader reason why the protesters are there, just as they had been marching on streets all over the world during the summer of 2020.

In fact, to watch this film is to see the unrest in Kenosha presented as if it had happened spontaneously, that a midsized midwestern city had been going about its life in peaceful tranquility and then, suddenly, "to everyone's astonishment," someone dropped "a match in the powder keg" and all hell broke loose. The protesters are portrayed as wantonly violent, and the three men Rittenhouse shot as criminals. As each enters the story, the picture freezes on their image and a chyron appears, like a wanted poster, identifying them by their crimes ("JOSEPH ROSENBAUM, AGE: 36, Registered sex offender, Convicted of sexual misconduct with a minor and crimes against children"; "ANTHONY HUBER, AGE: 26, Convicted of domestic abuse, Use of a dangerous weapon, Battery, Strangulation and Suffocation, 2nd Degree Reckless Endangerment").

Of course, equally verifiable video could be constructed to offer a counter story. Support for the Black Lives Matter movement in the summer of 2020 was commanding. If there was a public value at stake in Kenosha, it was the reckoning the nation was undertaking on the issue of race, not some exalted expression of the value of real estate. Over the three days, the protests were largely peaceful, and the tone changed only when the militiamen appeared on the scene as a provocation. In deciding to come to Kenosha, Rittenhouse had been inspired by the chatter of right-wing extremists. After he shot Rosenbaum, he began running away, and what more noble purpose could there be than to try to stop him, a killer on the run? Those who tried to apprehend Rittenhouse were the ones acting to protect the community; it was Rittenhouse who was endangering it. The criminal pasts of those who died is irrelevant, as irrelevant as it would be to explore the criminal histories of the militiamen. Why do we value property over lives? Why did Rittenhouse, a killer, walk right past police unchallenged? How would the police have treated a Black man walking down the street, assault rifle in hand, while bystanders outed him as a killer?

We could even posit a third view, one that reacts in large part to "The Truth in Eleven Minutes." It goes like this: Everything that happened in Kenosha was, in fact, code. The protesters weren't simply demonstrating in response to the shooting of Jacob Blake, and not even the larger principle that "Black lives matter." They were objecting to a system of white supremacy that is so deeply embedded in our society that at times it feels as though only violence can dislodge it. Wood and Pierce and the militiamen knew that, and they were (perhaps properly, given their allegiances) threatened by it. When they say that they're protecting "property," then, they are in fact looking to guard not so much a physical structure as the social structure, one that benefited their ancestors just as it continues to benefit them.

This clash is nothing new. It represents just the "latest slave insurrection." You can hear in the language of the film, for instance, echoes of the same insults that have been leveled at Black people throughout American history. The marchers are charged with disorderliness, criminality, untrustworthiness, and disrespect—the very same kinds of charges that undermined Reconstruction and led to Jim Crow. This is the purpose of laying out the criminal pasts of the two dead marchers. They are white, yes, but they have aligned themselves with a threatening Black cabal, and therefore are subjected to the same judgment, the same fate.

It's telling that Wood and Pierce use the Rittenhouse story to reignite the spirit of the American Revolution. While the war itself was a challenge to tyranny and an assertion of the equality of all men, the central contradiction in the cause was that slavery was, of course, legal in the colonies, and it survived in the new republic when the Framers inserted the three-fifths and fugitive slave clauses into the Constitution. (Though even that document spoke in code, never using the words "slave" or "slavery," preferring instead "person held to service or labor.")

The Rittenhouse family eventually fired Pierce after they became uncomfortable with the way he was promoting Kyle as the poster boy for the militia movement. But it's worth following Pierce's story at least through his role in defending those accused of the January 6 storming of the Capitol and Wood's support for the same cause when, after tweeting that Vice President Mike Pence "is a TRAITOR, a Communist Sympathizer & a Child Molester" who should be "jailed for treason" and "face execution by firing squad," he followed, on the morning of the attack, with the phrase "The time has come for Patriots." Belligerents in civil conflicts often clash over who is the truer descendant of the founding spirit, and it is the claim of the militiamen that America has strayed from its liberty-loving (and slavery-embracing) roots.

The point here is not to say that all video renderings of the story of Kenosha (or any other event) are equal, or that video evidence is inherently untrustworthy. To say that would be to also negate video validating claims of police brutality on people of color. It is, instead, to acknowledge that seeing is a both a cognitive and an optical activity and that, again, as Baldwin told us, "the visible reality hides a deeper one" and that in the end, "all our action and achievement rest on things unseen."

Every technology has its moment when, like a new love, it can do no wrong.

Early on, a future with the internet, and then social media, seemed golden. The old oppressive hierarchies would come tumbling down, and in their place citizens would "report news, expose wrongdoing, express opinions, mobilize protest, monitor elections, scrutinize government, deepen participation, and expand the horizons of freedom." And much of that has indeed happened, especially around issues of racial justice. In 2015, Black Twitter users forced the release of the name of Michael Brown's killer, Officer Darren Wilson. That same year, national media did not cover the story of Sandra Bland, the Black woman whose refusal to cooperate with a Texas state trooper who had pulled her over for failing to signal a lane change and who was later found hanging in her jail cell, but Black Twitter did, adopting the hashtag #sayhername (long before Breonna Taylor) to emphasize that police violence targets Black women as well as men. More recently, the story of Ahmaud Arbery would likely have faded if social media hadn't kept it alive, and, largely because of social media outrage, the story of Taylor, the twenty-six-year-old emergency-room technician who was killed by Louisville police, became a cause célèbre that featured appeals from Oprah Winfrey, Cardi B, Alicia Keys, Jay-Z, and just about the entire NBA.

But while our new technologies are very good at assembling small pockets of resistance, broad-based consensus is frustrated by the bewildering new mood of competition that our techno-democracy has forced upon us. Operating in a digital environment where all our voices are roughly equal, the racist and the antiracist occupy the same amount of space. The situation is further complicated by the persistent belief that "leaderlessness" is a virtue of the internet and of social media, and that modern-day justice movements need to eschew command structures and hierarchies because they are inherently corrupting. That may seem appealing as an idea, but in practice it has meant that small groups of extremists, whose absolutism could not have survived in a majoritarian world, thrive, and that any attempt to use the new media to make a better, more equitable society must contend with those who, motivated by fear and bigotry, would tap into the same technology's vulnerabilities to violently steer us away.

FIVE

Another Chance

Anyone who still believes that the present rash of violence against Black people—or, we should say, the sudden technology-driven awareness of the persistence of violence against Black people—isn't historically rooted must finally explain Charlottesville. It was on August 12, 2017, two years after Trayvon Martin and three years before George Floyd, that a "Unite the Right" rally was held there for the express purpose of protesting the removal of a statue honoring Confederate general Robert E. Lee and the renaming of the square once known as Lee Park. The gathering was an unusual display of comity between two generations of white supremacists, including old-style Klansmen like the former Imperial Wizard David Duke, and newer alt-right activists like Richard Spencer, who originated the term, and Jason Kessler, a Charlottesville local who was once a member of the Occupy movement, did fieldwork for Democrats, and even voted for Barack Obama for president in 2008 but who then underwent a slow conversion fueled by racist resentments. He now runs a blog called *Protect the West!* that's filled with anti-immigrant, anti-Semitic, and anti-Black expressions. "You talk about black people, you talk about gay people, you don't give a damn about white people," Kessler said before the City Council as it considered the renaming proposal earlier that summer. "White people have the right to organize and advocate for our rights as well."

The proposal before the Council, which was drafted in response to a petition originating with a fifteen-year-old local high school girl, also involved the removal of a statue of the Confederate general Stonewall Jackson and the renaming of Charlottesville's Jackson Park. But while Jackson joins Lee and President Jefferson Davis on the Confederate holy trinity carved in the seventeen-thousand-square-foot bas-relief on Stone Mountain outside Atlanta, neither of the other men carries quite the stature of the white-bearded Virginian. That's not only because Lee outranked Jackson and outshone the much duller Davis. It's because in Lee's farewell address to the troops, officially General Order No. 9, when he announced that "[a]fter four years of arduous service marked by unsurpassed courage and fortitude, the Army of Northern Virginia has been compelled to yield to overwhelming numbers and resources," he laid the foundation for the myth of the Lost Cause.

It was that argument—that the South wasn't in fact defeated but had instead been the victim of an unfair fight whose outcome was driven by statistics and not by a superior cause; that the North had nothing but money and manpower and industry, and lots of it, while the South had dignity and grandeur and noble, even divine, purpose—and the fact that the general himself was the one who spoke these words, indeed spoke them in his surrendering statement, that stoked the fires and generated the clamor that Dixie would one day rise again. This is what the historian James M. McPherson has called the "virgin-birth theory of secession," with Lee at the forefront of a battle struck not to defend slavery but to protect the South's constitutional liberties from the acquisitive, aggressive North.

The Charlottesville monument to Lee was commissioned in 1917, two years after *The Birth of a Nation*, and dedicated in 1924, the same year that historians believe the Ku Klux Klan reached its peak membership nationwide, a number that ran somewhere in the millions. The addition of 1920s-era Klan sympathizers would no doubt have inflated that total severalfold, but it's important to note that the Klan in the 1920s was a different organization from the one that terrorized the nation during the days of Reconstruction, a little cleaned up and more mainstream, more popular in the North than in the South. Its message still targeted Blacks, yes, but also Catholics, Jews, and immigrants. Together, they became the focus of a familiar Klan theme, the protection of the national gene pool from "inferior" peoples.

This was a time when there was a fascination for the "science" of eugenics and a fear that the shifting patterns of immigration that were then bringing people from the Mediterranean countries and Eastern Europe would spoil the racial and ethnic character of the nation. In 1924, Congress passed the Johnson-Reed Act, which limited immigration according to certain quotas. The law aimed to match the makeup of foreign-born residents as demonstrated in the 1890 census, a date chosen to be representative of the last time America hadn't had to contend with "hordes of the most undesirable people in Europe" arriving at its shores. But it also directed that in 1927 the basis for those quotas should shift from the makeup of foreign-born residents to the "national origins" of the entire American population as reflected in the 1920 census, but only after that census had been purged of all descendants of "immigrant slaves"—virtually every Black American. To do anything less, offered the xenophobic Immigration Restriction League, would be to "open the country to an African invasion." The time had come to get free of the "jumbled-up mass of undigested race material" that was threatening the American future.

As justification for this discrimination, immigration-reform advocates cited the intelligence studies of Carl C. Brigham, a Princeton psychologist also credited with inventing the original Scholastic Aptitude Test (SAT), introduced in 1926. "At one extreme we have the distribution of the Nordic race group," he wrote. "At the other extreme we have the American negro," with Jews and Mediterranean peoples falling in between, though "closer to the negro."

The Klan's expanded appeal (achieved with the help of public relations, another new "science") was market-driven. Membership had waned when whites no longer felt an urgent need to protect themselves from the Negro. After all, they had essentially won that fight. By putting white people back in power and returning the Black population to subjugation, Jim Crow had wiped out any progress Blacks had made during Reconstruction. Seen this way, then, the arrival of Confederate monuments (and there were many being built across the country at the same time) was nothing less than a victory lap for white supremacist principles and a reversal of the outcome of the Civil War: Slavery was illegal, sure, but segregation now kept Black people under the white man's thumb, and, looking forward, arrangements were being made to preserve the nation for the Anglo-Saxon race.

The oration at Lee Park on the day when the Charlottes-ville statue was unveiled reflected that spirit of triumph, a classic demonstration of the way that the remnant images of the war continued to be employed long after the fighting was over, to serve the purposes of "regional defense, self-flattery and polemics." There, the president of Washington and Lee University—the successor to Washington College, where Lee served as president from 1865 to 1870, and which was renamed for him shortly after his death—pronounced that "the undefeated spirit of Robert E. Lee" was the "real victor of Appomattox," not "Ulysses S. Grant and his swarming armies" (note the degrading adjective, as if comparing the Union soldiers to insects). Thus, any twenty-first-century attempt to, quite literally, remove Lee from his pedestal could only be a repudiation of this "victory" and a return of the general, along with those who continued to venerate the racist cause that he championed, to the loser bin of history. "You will not replace us," shouted the tiki-torch-carrying marchers as they moved throughout Charlottesville in 2017 (not "Lee," not "Jackson," but "us") before completing their thought. "The Jews will not replace us."

It's helpful to pause a minute at that last phrase and understand it more deeply. For while "replacement" theory—the European-born idea that non-European immigrants are "reversing" settler-colonialism by moving to the continent where they're gradually replacing the native population and erasing its culture—is rampant in right-wing circles internationally, its emergence in America includes specific racist, anti-Semitic, and anti–Big Tech messages.

As Eric Ward, of the Southern Poverty Law Center, has written, the success of the Civil Rights Movement in beating back Jim Crow in the 1950s and 1960s embarrassed the white supremacist ideology in part because the triumph of a Black-led movement, built by strong leadership and effective organizing, challenged the well-worn caricature of the docile, passive, ignorant Negro. Surely the "inferior race" could not have done this alone. "For that matter, how could feminists and LGBTQ people have upended traditional gender relations, leftists mounted a challenge to global capitalism, Muslims won billions of converts to Islam? How do you explain the boundary-crossing allure of hip-hop? The election of a Black president?" wrote Ward, assuming, for dramatic purposes, the mind of a white supremacist. "Some secret cabal, some mythological power, must be manipulating the social order behind the scenes. This diabolical evil must control television, banking, entertainment, education, and even Washington, DC . . . What is this arch-nemesis of the white race, whose machinations have prevented the natural and inevitable imposition of white supremacy? It is, of course, the Jews."

The marchers in Charlottesville didn't go directly to the Lee statue. On the night before their proposed event, an impromptu gathering of around 250 of them shouted "Blood and Soil" and "White Lives Matter" as they paraded through the University of Virginia campus on their way to the Thomas Jefferson rotunda and the 1910 statue of the third president there. Charlottesville is, after all, Jefferson's town. It is he who founded the university and designed its first buildings, including the distinctive rotunda. Jefferson was also the architect of his own Monticello, the Palladian plantation home that sits high on a mountaintop a few miles away. More important for both the argument the marchers hoped to make and the one that would greet them from counterprotesters as retort, it is Jefferson who serves as the imperfect prophet of the American civil religion. He is justly credited with the celebrated principle of equality that he drafted into the Declaration of Independence, even as he, hypocritically, benefited from the work of four hundred slaves at Monticello, among them the mulatto Sally Hemings, with whom it's now believed with considerable certainty that he fathered more than one child. (In 2021, on the university's Founder's Day, six months after the "Unite the Right" rally, the Jefferson statue was vandalized when the words "racist" and "rapist" were sprayed across the base in red paint.)

Despite the importance to racial justice of the Declaration's phrase "all men are created equal"—in and of itself an astonishing statement for an age emerging from centuries of feudal darkness—there is plenty to Jefferson that would endear him to the white supremacists. For one, while there is no doubt that Jefferson understood the word "equal" to be incompatible with slavery, he viewed the end of bondage as an aspirational goal, believing that the practice would die naturally as reason increasingly came to govern man's affairs. Along with that, the term "equality," to the eighteenth-century mind, or at least to Jefferson's, meant only equality before the law, the "self-evident" nature of that equality referring to its being an element of our humanity, that rights were not bestowed upon us by other men but arrived instead with the first breath of life. But "equal" most certainly did not mean that the races were the same, that they were intellectually or socially equivalent. On that, Jefferson was clear: The Black man was inferior to the white man.

In his *Notes on the State of Virginia* (1781), Jefferson waxed on about the supremacy of the white race, insisting that Blacks "secrete less by the kidnies, and more by the glands of the skin, which gives them a very strong and disagreeable odour." White complexions were preferrable to the "eternal monotony" and "immoveable veil of black which covers all the emotions of the other race." He found Blacks to be "at least as brave and more adventuresome," but that this was "perhaps from want of forethought, which prevents their seeing a danger till it be present." Love was, for them, "more an eager desire, than a tender delicate mixture of sentiment and sensation." He found

Blacks to be inferior in reason, and in imagination to be "dull, tasteless, and anomalous." While the Black life may contain "misery enough," there was "no poetry," a claim buoyed by his dismissive criticism of Phillis Wheatley. Observation of those instances when Black blood had mixed with white showed "improvement" in "body and mind," demonstrating that "their inferiority is not the effect merely of their condition of life." No, these were all natural-born inadequacies of the race itself.

Like many, Jefferson was pessimistic about the chances for Black and white to live together in peace. Therefore, his preference was for an emancipation that would be followed by Black expatriation, probably to somewhere in the West Indies or Africa. On this, he found much agreement in his time. Indeed, the idea of colonization as a solution to America's race problem was popular throughout the nineteenth century as well. Lincoln showed interest in the idea. So did Harriet Beecher Stowe. Some part of the instinct for sending the freed slaves away, off the continent, was the fear that a race war would eventually ensue if they remained. Another part was a recognition that the wounds of slavery were so deep that they could never heal in the presence of those who inflicted them. (Both notions, in a sense, proved to be true.) "Nothing is more certainly written in the book of fate than that these people are to be free," wrote Jefferson in *Notes*, "nor is it less certain that the two races, equally free, cannot live in the same government. Nature, habit, opinion have drawn indelible lines of distinction between them." It says something about the American need for whitewashed heroes that the first part of that expression is etched into the Northeast Portico of the 1943 Jefferson Memorial in Washington, DC, but not the second part. We prefer our Jefferson to be the one we craft, not the one who was.

For the white supremacists marching across the University of Virginia campus on their way to the Jefferson statue, there was all that background, and more, to reinforce their steps. Like many of them, Jefferson was a southerner who remained suspicious of northerners for his entire life. Like them, he thought of himself as the revolutionary that he literally was. But unlike his fellow Founders, he never really strayed from the impulse, believing that "a little rebellion now and then" was cleansing for the national soul, like "a storm in the atmosphere." Indeed, violence was like "natural manure" to the "tree of liberty." If pressed, the marchers could even recite Jefferson's maxim that the "spirit of resistance to government" was so crucial that it would be better to "be exercised when wrong . . . than not to be exercised at all."

A Francophile, Jefferson was by all measures an elitist, except when it came to principle, where he embraced not simply the common man but an idealistic vision of the independent yeoman farmer, which he rendered in contrast to the greedy industrialist and the elite wielder of entrenched power. "State a moral case to a ploughman & a professor," he wrote. "The former will decide it as well, & often better than the latter, because he has not been led astray by artificial rules." Jefferson was anti-banker, anti-church, and anti-government, in large part because of the way that these institutions restrained the liberty of the individual. And he was all for casting off the "dead hand of the past" for the earth belonging to "the living," even proposing to James Madison that all debt, laws, and constitutions should expire after a generation, which he defined as nineteen years. Madison, wisely, disagreed.

By the time the marchers reached the Jefferson statue, it had been circled by a group of about twenty university students who locked arms behind a banner that read "UVA Students Against White Supremacy." They were protecting "their" Jefferson. The marchers with the tiki torches, who vastly outnumbered them, saw themselves as guardians of the same man but different principles. Still, one has to wonder how many of them knew that the monument before them was created by Moses Ezekiel, the first Jewish cadet to enroll at the Virginia Military Institute, or that the base of the structure includes a tribute to Jefferson's support for religious freedom by showing a spirit holding a tablet that lists multiple deities: "God, Jehovah, Brahma, Atma, Ra, Allah, Zeus." (Even so, Ezekiel remained a devoted Confederate veteran whose studio in Rome was decorated with a Confederate flag and who took seriously the words of his friend General Lee, who urged him to become an artist "and prove to the world that if we did not succeed in our struggle, we were worthy of success.")

The tiki torches, so reminiscent of Klan rallies and lynchings, provided a disturbing tone to the gathering. In the amber glow cast by their flames, the marchers looked threatening, like a pack of hungry jackals awaiting their prey. The two sides taunted each other with slogans until someone sprayed mace into the conversation and a flame was tossed, leading the police to move in and disburse the crowd. The next day, however, a much larger contingent of white supremacists, some waving Nazi flags, set off for the Lee statue. Along the way, counterprotesters engaged them, and fights broke out.

James Alex Fields, twenty, had traveled 543 miles from his home in Maumee, Ohio, to join the marchers. Born and raised in Kentucky, he had led a troubled life. His father died in a car crash a few months before he was born. His mother, a paraplegic, raised him by herself. When he was fifteen, she called police to the home when, told to stop playing video games, he hit her. On another occasion, he threatened his mother with a knife. He had been treated for bipolar disorder, schizophrenia, anxiety, depression, and ADHD. A middle school classmate told the *New York Times* that she recalled him as a loner who occasionally would yell obscenities and racial slurs. High school classmates remembered him touting Nazi ideology and express ing an infatuation with Adolf Hitler. Others recalled a class trip to Europe in 2015 that included a visit to the Dachau concentration camp, where more than forty-one thousand Jews were murdered. "This is where the magic happened," Fields said. After high school, he enrolled in the army but was discharged after just five months. Since then, he had been a security guard.

Before he departed for Virginia, Fields dropped his cat off at his mother's house and texted her that he was going to attend an "alt-right" rally. She later claimed a habit of not engaging with her son about his political views and that she only thought that the rally "had something to do with Trump." In response to his text, she told him to be careful. "We're not the one [*sic*] who need to be careful," he responded, adding a meme displaying an image of Adolf Hitler.

Once in Charlottesville, Fields was seen dressed in a white polo shirt and khaki pants, the new unofficial uniform of white supremacy. He was holding a shield with the insignia of Vanguard America, a quasi-secret fascist and white supremacist organization whose slogan is "Blood and Soil." The phrase borrows from the cries of *"Blut und Boden"* that were heard from Nazi supporters in Germany in the 1930s. It refers to a sentimental, almost mystical connection between "racial purity" and the "homeland." But later, Vanguard America insisted that Fields was not a member of their group and had only picked up a shield when offered one at the rally. (With entirely different motives, Tiki brand torches issued a statement that the company "is not associated in any way with the events that took place in Charlottesville.")

At roughly 1:40 p.m., Fields drove his gray 2010 Dodge Challenger to downtown Charlottesville. He entered 4th Street NE, a narrow, downward-sloping, one-way passage, and moved toward an area where counterprotesters, who had gathered in the pedestrian mall below, had begun marching. When he reached the bottom of the street, a silver Toyota Camry was in front of him, and in front of the Camry was a Honda Odyssey minivan. The vehicles were stationary as they waited for the counterprotesters to move past them. In fact, the driver of the minivan had parked and gotten out of her car to take pictures of what she saw as a historic moment, and a happy one. The marchers were filled with enthusiasm, shouting "Whose streets? Our streets!" and they carried signs that said "Love" and "Solidarity," as well as "Black Lives Matter." A special kind of bonding seemed to be happening. The driver of the Camry noticed it, too, later saying that while the crowd itself was diverse, she had "never seen so many white people standing up for Black people."

At first, Fields idled along with the other cars, but then he suddenly backed up almost a block—not to change directions and get away from the traffic logjam, as one watching may have thought, but to gain momentum for what he was about to do next: drive his car forward at a high speed, plowing directly into the crowd, a four-thousand-pound glass-and-steel bowling ball striking anyone in its path. People began screaming, some in pain, others in shock. Then, just as quickly as he had driven forward, Fields backed up again, striking pedestrians as he moved in the other direction before speeding off in retreat. It was all over in a matter of seconds, but the damage was heartbreaking. Heather Heyer, a thirty-two-year-old paralegal, was killed, and thirty-five others were injured, many of them permanently. In the mayhem, Jeanne Peterson, whose own injuries required six surgeries, saw Heyer's body flying over her. "That's what someone's eyes look like when they're dead," she recalled thinking.

At trial, jurors were shown posts from Fields's social media accounts. His Facebook page had an assemblage of photographs, including one of him with his Dodge and another of his cat. But there was also a picture of Hitler as a baby; a rendering of Pepe the Frog, a cartoon meme that started traveling around the internet in 2008 and, for reasons that remain mysterious (especially to its creator), was adopted by the alt-right; Donald Trump sitting on a throne; a character from the animated series *Archer* named Algernop Krieger, whose father was a Nazi scientist and is thought to have cloned Hitler to create him; and an angular graphic symbol known as the Othala Rune that dates to pre-Roman Europe, but which was adopted by the Nazis as a symbol of racial purity. Fields's Instagram posts were even more disturbing, for it was there, on May 16, three months before the attack, that Fields had shared an image of a car running into a crowd of people. "You have the Right to Protest," the post read, "But I'm Late for Work."

———

It would be easy to dismiss the "blood and soil" crowd in Charlottesville as little more than the latest expression of a pernicious strain in American life, the same one that has protected slavery and sought to drive immigrants away. It is certainly all of that. But we must also acknowledge that we live in an era that is engulfed in what James Baldwin, writing about a different era, once called "cataclysmic" change, much of it driven by the technological wonderland that we find ourselves living in, and that the anxiety we all seem to feel in the early twenty-first century has in some quarters taken on a frightening intensity, inspiring new communities of white supremacists generating turgid manifestos intended to break all forward progress. It's humbling, for instance, to ask ourselves if, say, a generation ago, before the internet had really taken hold and before social media had been invented, before Facebook's algorithms were turning mildly conservative users into frothing QAnon faithful, a twenty-year-old security guard suffering from bipolar disorder and schizophrenia, even one already captive to a sinister ideology like Nazism, would have been inspired on his own to do what James Fields did.

But this is where we are. In a relatively short time, we have created a new world to replace (there's that word again) the old world, which itself was once a new world replacing another old world, and on and on. All change, of course, is accompanied by some measure of apprehension, and part of our anxiety is no doubt the by-product of constructive opportunity, the growing pains that have, historically, accompanied progress. The difference is that along the continuum of technological advancement, the changes started coming faster and their reach became more comprehensive. This, of course, describes Moore's Law, which has to do with computer processing doubling in power every two years. But if this is the case, what we're seeing is Moore's Law writ large. The world we inhabit now is not only exponentially different from the world of twenty years ago; it is vastly different from what it was five years ago, or even two years ago. And if we take the far-right marchers at their word, absent the clear racist message they intend, the new world we're creating for ourselves is indeed "bloodless" and "soil-less." It is virtual.

All communications technologies, starting with writing, have broached this notion of virtual experience. When the telephone was invented, for instance, it brought the human voice—and through the voice, the person—across distance. It didn't physically deliver the person to us. Instead, it approximated their being there. It wasn't completely satisfying, in that a voice disassociated from a face and a body lacks the ineffable quality of "presence," but it was new and exciting, and it provided profound new economies to the human experience that we incorporated into our lives. So did the phonograph, the radio, the microphone, and the television. All were substitutes for elements of the real world, breaking the barriers of space and time, and we grew to understand them, to incorporate them into our lives, even as they changed us.

But the virtual world being created in our time is different. Technology is now so intimately wrapped up with existence that it has ceased to be something we use and become, instead, a region we inhabit. The relatively short history of the internet illustrates this. Early on, we struggled to adopt metaphors to describe it. The "World Wide Web," coined by Tim Berners-Lee, is the original one, of course, which lives on primarily in the "www" of internet addresses. The image of a web, the kind that a spider might weave, captured the decentralized nature of modern computing and its "stickiness," how once inside it we find it hard to get out.

"The Information Superhighway" had a good run, but it seems peculiarly antiquated now. In its day, it provided utility for those who, arguing for internet access in disadvantaged communities, worried about a repeat experience of the interstate highway system when it was designed in the 1950s. Real highways, like the one that divided George Floyd's Houston, devastated America's inner cities and set back racial progress. But a highway is something that you get on and get off—you don't stay there (though anyone from Southern California might disagree)—and as early as 1998, the economist and future AI entrepreneur Michael Moynihan correctly predicted that this would become a transitory image, sort of the way that "horseless carriage" was first used to describe the automobile or "wireless" to describe the first radios, emphasizing their difference from both the telegraph and the telephone. To Moynihan, logging onto the internet felt more like entering a "glorified library than a car." But, of course, "library" wouldn't work, either. It was too fixed, immobile, and, as we now know, way, way too limited.

Moynihan liked "cyberspace," which at least had the quality of being somewhere outside the physical world, and he likened the future of cyberspace to be a bit like the early days of the American West, a metaphor that worked for him because it suggested a new generation of swashbuckling cyber "buccaneers" settling uncharted territories, and because, like the old West, the internet was ripe for American business to explore and eventually exploit. "The basic building block of wealth on this frontier," he continued, "will be what I call cyberestate . . . real estate out in the void." Well, that's one that didn't exactly catch on. But in trying, Moynihan was onto one of the more confounding aspects of our new digital existence: What exactly constitutes the "property" of the internet—an invisible medium, both infinite and absent at the same time—and who can be trusted to control it?

Moynihan was writing more than twenty years ago when he was one of the early internet evangelists, but a lot has happened since then. Today most of us lead double lives, and one of those lives, maybe even the primary one, is in cyberspace. Our family pictures are stored up there. So are our medical reports and test results. Records of our financial accounts are kept there. Google Calendar keeps track of where we've been and where we plan to go. Twitter monitors our moment-to-moment expressions and those of others whom we "follow." Sleep apps create records of our REM cycles. Meal pack apps order our food. Uber Eats and DoorDash deliver it. TikTok and Twitter and Snapchat and Instagram and Facebook are where we spend our social lives. We find dates and sexual partners on Bumble, Hinge, Grindr, and Tinder. Thanks to the COVID-19 pandemic, our work lives are conducted on Zoom or Skype, where we have completely capitulated to the cyber-surveillance state. The exposure of inappropriate comments or behavior at a meeting used to require a brave whistleblower; now it's all on video record. But the main way that we live our lives in cyberspace is that we carry it around with us. No one is ever out of touch anymore, because, armed with a cell phone, we can always be found. Where are we? We're in cyberspace.

Gradually, we're dismantling our real-world communities (what we now quaintly call "brick-and-mortar," an unnecessary term only a few years ago when everything was brick-and-mortar) and moving them to cyberspace as well. Shopping malls are either being demolished or refashioned into housing or some other new purpose. Music stores survived the transition from records to tapes to CDs but collapsed once every recorded performance known to man became available through Apple Music or Pandora or Spotify. Businesses are abandoning the nation's commercial skyscrapers and telling their employees to work from home. COVID, of course, hurried all of this all along, too. But the trend was already there, and when the pandemic has fully passed, the transition will be so settled that there will be no way to reverse it. Why would we want to? Real estate is expensive. "Cyberestate" is free. (Well, sort of. We just pay for it in a different way.)

All of this talk may well seem quaint in a few years when we enter the metaverse—the next stage of the internet, where, as Mark Zuckerberg describes it, "you're in the experience, not just looking at it," and you accumulate new assets to furnish your virtual existence, apart from your real-world existence, and move seamlessly between the two. One of the distinctive aspects of cyberspace is that it is inherently unstable or, to use a more friendly term, "fluid."

Journalists know this. Stories they write aren't fixed. They're updated so that they reflect new information and correct old errors, a phenomenon that will frustrate future historians who need to mine events to understand how they were viewed in the time that they happened. But cyberspace is unstable in other ways, too. Lies go uncorrected. In fact, they get replicated ad infinitum. The pandemic has displayed these phenomena amply. New medical information today may change yesterday's best advice on warding off disease, but yesterday's advice has already left the station and will be well-traveled throughout cyberspace, getting twisted and pulled, before today's update can amend it. Meanwhile, fanciful notions or outright falsehoods find traction, in part because the truth is complicated and a lie can be both simple and satisfying, particularly when it taps into gut-level fears and resentments.

Still, the invisibility of cyberspace may be the main reason for the feeling of instability that it projects. No matter how much we live our lives there, we don't really know where "there" is. We wake up, turn on our devices, and go through "windows" where we're lost for hours. We move effortlessly from device to device as if we're floating off into the void. And even when the day is done and all devices have been turned off, we may have disconnected, but cyberspace has not disconnected from us. There's something inherently unstable about that feeling, and it leaves us craving authenticity. It's interesting to note, for instance, that no matter how heated an argument may become on social media, we measure it differently when it gets transferred to the streets. The summer of 2020 became a historic period of racial reckoning only after the outrage over the police killing of George Floyd led to protest marches worldwide. No matter how key social media was to the organization of the two sides that clashed in Charlottesville, it was, finally, to a physical object that they brought their confrontation.

Unlike cyberspace, a monument is something you can see and touch. You can march to it, kneel before it, hold ceremonies in front of it, stand on it, punch it, throw things at it, chip away at it, and write degrading messages on it. Most important, it is fixed in the ground, anchored to the soil. A thing to encounter and behold. To the community that erected it, and the descendant community that lives with it, it is representative of a shared value, a connection to the past. If it's a representation of a person, the monument, in effect, says "We admire who they were and what they did"; if marking an event, it says "We remember what happened here and learn from it." But most important, monuments and memorials are symbols of permanence. They tell us that however much we may change, there's something to us that is eternal and enduring. But what is that something? And what will it be once we complete the move to cyberspace?

Now, if we follow Michael Moynihan's analogy to the

American West, we arrive at a curious revelation about America and race. After much bitter argument, the original Framers of the American Constitution settled on a system that provided some protection for the practice of slavery even as they built in provisions that were intended to lead to its eventual collapse; in effect, "two constitutions," wrote the late historian Don E. Fehrenbacher, "one for their own time and the other for the ages, with slavery viewed bifocally—that is, plainly visible at their feet, but disappearing when they lifted their eyes." Seen and Unseen.

But slavery did not disappear. In fact, with the arrival of the cotton gin in 1794, it prospered. At the same time, the nation grew. In 1803, during the presidency of Thomas Jefferson, the United States acquired vast amounts of western land through the Louisiana Purchase. The region had previously belonged to the French, of course, who, not coincidentally, had been the target of a revolution in Haiti, a slave rebellion, one that frightened Napoleon, who now wanted nothing to do with the Americas.

When the land from the Louisiana Purchase was combined with the land acquired through the Mexican-American War of 1846–48, the United States actually tripled in size over the first half of the nineteenth century. Development of these lands was the next step, and technology, in the form of the locomotive (or "iron horse," which was the train's own original metaphor), intervened to help.

Unlike Europe, where the first tracks followed the outline of existing roads, many of them dating to antiquity, in America the laying of track was by itself the founding act in the conquering of the wilderness. The spirit that drove American development was "Manifest Destiny," the belief that nature was something to be tamed and indigenous people something to be removed to make way for white settlers and the march of American civilization to the farthest shores. This attitude, sometimes expressed as a divine right, predominated throughout the rest of the nineteenth century until the closing of the frontier in 1890.

The importance of the railroad as a symbol of technology cannot be overstated, and the equestrian metaphor for it captured something special. The steam locomotive "breathed" smoke, made loud belching noises, and galloped through the countryside like a thoroughbred. It was a romantic sight. Children would run to watch the trains as they came roaring through. Both Emily Dickinson and Walt Whitman wrote poems to the locomotive. Whitman admired the "black cylindric body," the "gyrating side-bars" and smokestack, the "swelling pant and roar," the "great protruding head-light," the "train of cars behind, obedient, merrily following" an "emblem of motion and power-pulse of the continent." Dickinson liked to see it "lap the Miles/ And lick the Valleys up/And stop to feed itself at Tanks" until it rested, "docile and omnipotent/At its own stable door."

The locomotive was the logo for the machine age that was descending on the world, and there was just as much excitement then, maybe even more, as there is now for the future. They had not yet experienced the dehumanizing aspects of a machine-driven life. Ironically, the locomotive also provided the image of the "underground railroad," the clandestine movement to funnel runaway slaves from house to house until they reached freedom in the North. Examined together, they provide quite the picture: the romantic steam engine motoring through the white world, taking out indigenous peoples in its path, while the inferior races crawl through dirt tunnels in search of safety. For even as the nation grew, the old questions, the ones that the Founders punted to future generations, persisted: Would slavery be tolerated in the new republic? Would slavery be allowed in the new territory being added to the republic? The northern states argued no, the South argued yes.

With the 1820 Missouri Compromise, Missouri was admitted as a slave state and Maine as a free state, and a line was drawn through the new territories, with slavery allowed below it but not allowed above it. But this hardly settled the argument. In 1854, Congress passed the Kansas-Nebraska Act, which repealed the Missouri Compromise by leaving the decision on slavery up to the voters of each new state. The Supreme Court's 1857 Dred Scott decision followed, a case that involved a slave who had traveled with his master, an army surgeon, from Missouri to the free state of Illinois, and then into the Wisconsin territory before eventually going back again to Missouri. Scott argued that because he had gone to a free state, where slavery was prohibited, and a territory where it was also prohibited, he had become free and therefore his continued enslavement was a violation of his right to liberty as granted by the Constitution. The suggestion was that territory was not only land to be inhabited; it was also an opportunity for new freedoms to be enjoyed.

But the Court found against him, declaring that members of the "negro African race" were not American citizens, because when the Constitution was adopted, they were "regarded as beings of an inferior order and altogether unfit to associate with the white race." Therefore, neither enslaved Blacks nor anyone descended from them possessed any rights "which the white man was bound to respect." No manner of public opinion on the subject, wrote Chief Justice Roger B. Taney, could be said to alter the law as the Constitution had long ago determined it. Taney thought he had settled a problem that Congress had failed to solve. In fact, he had just fanned the flames.

The Court's decision was awful, surely the worst it has rendered in the nation's history. In essence, when it came to the clash of liberty and property, the justices had valued property. Worse, they had valued property in man. Frederick Douglass worried that it could mean that every "emancipated colored man" would have "burned into his very soul the brand of inferiority." In essence, Taney had declared that Congress had no power to limit slavery in the territories, invalidating the principle established with the Missouri Compromise. With his defense of slaves as property, the Chief Justice had also cast doubt on the validity of the Kansas-Nebraska Act. Indeed, Abraham Lincoln predicted that the next decision from the Taney Court would assert that no state at all could prevent slavery within its boundaries. War, of course, followed, and after war, Jim Crow. But throughout the nineteenth century, as the West opened up, it was land, new frontiers, that had repeatedly renewed the argument over race, and each time, an opportunity was lost.

What then, will it be for our own time? The internet is to our time as the locomotive was then. New technologies can be and are used in ways that reflect old patterns of racism in America, but each new technological jump reveals a new frontier of space for us to start over again, an opportunity to go where our forebears could not or would not go. "Cyberspace is not only a place to obtain information," Moynihan predicted, with prescience. "Like previous frontiers, it's a blank canvas on which entrepreneurs seeking profits and others seeking less clear-cut goals from religious salvation to political revolution will paint their destinies and their future."

In short, it is another chance.

———

Despite all the videos shot at Charlottesville, for many people it was a still photograph that came to stand for what happened there. Ryan Kelly was working for the *Daily Progress*, Charlottesville's only newspaper, when he found himself on 4th Street at precisely the time that James Alex Fields's sedan came barreling into the crowd. Kelly's photograph, which won him a Pulitzer, was among the last he took for the paper. Feeling burned out, tired of the meager pay, he had already decided to leave journalism to work as a social media coordinator for a local brewery. August 12, the day of the rally, was his last day on the job.

The picture will never be as famous as the one of Jeffrey Miller at Kent State or the man and the tank near Tiananmen Square. Those belong to a different time, when the still photograph had its own form of "stickiness." But for an age that seems to have left still imagery behind, Kelly's picture was a surprisingly riveting sight. Ironically, just as the video of George Floyd suggests the stillness of a life quietly expiring before us, so this still image of Charlottesville has the clatter and tumult of an action video. And it, too, is ultimately about needless death. A test of a picture is what it tells you before you read the caption, and this one wordlessly rewards careful analysis.

In the foreground is a man of undetermined race with his back to the camera. He provides us a focal point; we are watching with him. What we see, at first, is what appears to be a collage: odd, almost surreal juxtapositions of imagery, so much incongruity that the viewer looks at it and begins to turn the picture this way and that just to ensure that they are holding it right side up.

There are dozens of people. Some are on the ground, others are flipped upside down, careening downward. One man is suspended almost perpendicular to the pavement, his T-shirt falling from his waist to reveal an elaborate tattoo on his lower back. There is so much chaos that the scene has the feeling of the aftermath of a bombing, though one carried out immaculately, without the usual fog of war. At center is a Black man in a white tee. His is the only face that we see in its entirety, and he's in trouble. Indeed, he's floating in air, having just been struck by Fields's car. Surely, gravity is about to send him to the asphalt as well. All around there are limbs—an arm protruding here, a leg there—and pieces of clothing, shoes and hats. There are also many signs. Two red official stop signs mock the moment. Nothing is stopping here. In the distance is a Black Lives Matter placard, but the word "matter" is obscured, so that it simply reads "Black Lives," a poignant comment, perhaps, maybe even an appropriate title for the image as a whole.

At center is a sign reading "Solidarity" with a raised fist. To the right is another that simply says "Love." And in the foreground, parked to the right of the line of traffic, is a Toyota Tundra pickup truck, pointing away from the camera. Its dominant presence makes the picture feel oddly like a billboard, as if someone is selling us something in the middle of a tragedy. A pair of legs is protruding from beneath the carriage of the truck, looking vulnerable, and a small sticker is visible on the rear bumper. You have to squint your eyes to read it: "No Man Stands So Tall as When He Stoops to Help a Child."

Nothing in the picture tells us that the white supremacists were there or that President Donald Trump, responding to the story, praised Robert E. Lee and declared that there were "very fine people on both sides," or that on the scale of virtue he equated Lee and Stonewall Jackson, both of whom entered into armed rebellion against the United States, with the nation's founders. Looking at the picture alone, we know only that a crowd that appears to be both racially and economically diverse was gathered in recognition of their shared belief in love, solidarity, and the importance of Black lives. We also know that some form of violence was used against them, and that it appears that it was cold, hard steel in motion. But really, how much more do we need to know to understand Charlottesville? Maybe only the fact that somewhere in that scene, buried by the sea of bodies, is a young white woman who, marching for Black lives that day, paid with her own.

Charlottesville was a turning point. The city has now joined Selma, Birmingham, Montgomery, and Little Rock in the lexicon of America's racial history. The Robert E. Lee statue has come down; so, too, the statue of Stonewall Jackson and another of the explorers Lewis and Clark that depicted Sacagawea beneath them in an obedient crouch. The statue of Thomas Jefferson on the campus of the University of Virginia remains, of course, but the administration has committed itself to a "digital contextualization" initiative so that future visitors can point their cell phones at the third president and enter cyber-space to gain a fuller picture, adding Jefferson's slave-holding contradictions and racist writings to the story of a man who, in one of the great paradoxes of history, also authored the two competing principles of American life: liberty and equality. The section of 4th Street in Charlot-tesville where James Fields rammed his car into protest-ers is now called "Heather Heyer Way," which is a fitting act of mourning and recognition. It belongs to the "we remember what happened here and learn from it" genre of memorial. Meanwhile, the "we admire who they were and what they did" genre is mercifully undergoing some reconsideration.

Once the streets of Charlottesville quieted down, things in cyberspace began heating up. Almost immedi-ately after the event, Twitter became enflamed in pursuit of the identities of those who participated in the rally. A North Carolina progressive activist named Logan Smith used the handle @YesYoureRacist to post close-ups from the event and to ask people to provide names and pro-files of the "Nazis marching in Charlottesville." He said he would "make them famous." He did. Within days, Cole White, a cook at Top Dog, a hot dog shop that's a favorite of students in Berkeley, California, was outed.

The eatery, which flaunts its libertarian allegiances on its website and dining room walls ("Freedom Works Better Than Government"), took a defensive posture as it announced that White, after being recognized, had resigned. "There have been reports that he was terminated. Those reports are false. There have been reports that Top Dog knowingly employs racists and promotes racist theology. That too is false. Individual freedom and voluntary exchange are core to the philosophy of Top Dog."

University of Nevada at Reno (UNR) student Peter Cvjetanovic was also identified, and responded with a defense of white nationalism, insisting that white "cultures are being threatened" and that "everyone is melding together." He was soon reconciled to his newfound fame. "I understand that things will never return to a sense of normalcy. The picture is out there. It is my choice. I will be living with it. I won't be running away. I hope I can attend UNR safely and that anyone out there who is upset at me would be willing to talk with me. Maybe they could see that I'm not the hateful bigot I'm shown to be." His sentiment captured one of the perplexing characteristics of social media. On the one hand, it's so immediate that it can capture an entire societal argument pulsating in real time and crowdsource criminal prosecution and injustice. Yet on the other, its permanence is profound, too. Thanks to tweets and retweets and screenshots, the past is never past. Peter Cvjetanovic has, perhaps appropriately, been branded a racist for all time.

Meanwhile, in reaction to Charlottesville, the process of more broadly identifying the nation's longstanding attachment to white supremacy began to take on momentum. If cyberspace could be used to shame those who showed up for the Unite the Right rally, to "make them famous," in Logan Smith's words, maybe it could also be used to make those who were already famous infamous, to not only force Charlottesville's Robert E. Lee and Stonewall Jackson statues off their pedestals but to force reconsideration of every representation of Lee, Jackson, and hundreds, if not thousands, of others, those who despite their having been part of an insurrection against the government of the United States continued to be held up for reverence. This included not only the many monuments and statues to Confederate leaders and others whose history we're only beginning to rewrite to comport with the details of their treason or other unsavory and racist acts but also all the many streets and squares named for Confederates—so many it remains daunting to even contemplate changing them all. In Alexandria, Virginia, only a short drive from the Capitol building in Washington, DC, there are forty such streets, including ones named for Lee, Jackson, and Jubal Early, the CSA general whose postwar lectures and writings helped establish the Lost Cause mythology.

Unrepentant, viciously bitter, in exile from the US in the years after the war, Early wrote "I have got to that condition, that I think I could scalp a Yankee woman and child without winking my eyes." So, of course, a street was named for him, which probably happened sometime after 1951, when a provision was built into the city's code that all new north-south thoroughfares must honor the Confederacy. Again, like the erecting of monuments, the naming of streets served a political purpose. Alexandria's rule was adopted three years after Dixiecrats ran Strom Thurmond for president on a segregationist platform, winning four states, and three years before *Brown v. Board of Education*. The measure was only repealed in 2014.

There is a street in Alexandria named for Confederate general Pierre G. T. Beauregard (for whom Donald Trump's first attorney general, Jefferson Beauregard Sessions, is also named; his "Jefferson" referred to Jefferson Davis) and one Forrest Street, which is named either for French Forrest, a CSA naval commander, or, more likely, Nathan Bedford Forrest, the Confederate general who was responsible for the 1864 massacre at Fort Pillow, Tennessee, where over a hundred surrendered Black Union soldiers—"a damned nigger regiment" is how Forrest described them—were murdered; "shot down like dogs," remembered a soldier under Forrest's command. The soldiers were former slaves, a detail that probably only increased Forrest's ardor, and word of the bloodbath passed quickly through the Union ranks. Afterward, some Black Union soldiers wore homemade buttons emblazoned with the battle cry "Avenge Fort

Pillow." Now with cyberspace arrives an opportunity to rewrite this sordid history in a way that acknowledges the shame of what really happened.

Forrest is worth pausing on, as he is revered among white supremacists, even sometimes preferred as the simple, plain folk answer to the stoic, well-born West Pointer Lee. Both a slaveowner and slave trader from Memphis, Forrest was unschooled in the art of war, rough-hewn, a rebel in the outlaw tradition. His legend preceded him as the "Wizard of the Saddle," so called because of the many times (twenty-nine, so the legend goes) he survived having horses shot out from under him. He was full of bravado and was temperamental, impulsive, and an exceptional cavalryman with considerable battlefield instinct. But there was something of the mad warrior to him as well, and he was an unabashed racist. In the postwar years he became the first Grand Wizard of the Ku Klux Klan. He died in 1877 but reemerged as a cult figure with the rise of the Lost Cause.

In 1905, when Forrest's hometown of Memphis unveiled a Forrest statue in Forrest Park, which was also named for him, thirty thousand people—about a third of the city—attended the ceremony. The remains of Forrest and his wife had been buried underneath the stone structure. As the myth around Forrest grew, so did his appeal, particularly to men. He seemed to embody an unbridled and ferocious masculinity. In 1990, when Ken Burns's

PBS documentary series on the Civil War appeared, providing many Americans with their first extensive history lesson on the period, the writer Shelby Foote, who was the series' star interviewee, praised Forrest, inflating his reputation. To Foote, Forrest was "one of the most attractive men who ever walked through the pages of history," insisting that he was, along with Lincoln, one of two "authentic geniuses" of the war, that his role in the massacre at Fort Pillow had been overblown, and that he ended his relationship with the Klan before it started committing atrocities. Most historians today will vigorously dispute all those claims.

The statue of Forrest in Memphis, now a majority Black city, stood for more than 112 years, with city leaders unable to move it or another statue of Jefferson Davis without running up against fierce opposition and legal obstacles intended to save Confederate symbols. The most recent was the Tennessee Heritage Protection Act of 2013, which forbids municipalities from removing or renaming any memorial on state property without a two-thirds vote of approval from the Tennessee Historical Commission, which is essentially controlled by the governor. In 2013, the city changed the name of Forrest Park to Health Sciences Park. (That they could do on their own.) Shortly thereafter, they worked the state's official procedures to remove the Davis and Forrest statues and were rebuffed. Then came Charlottesville. The city again petitioned the state, and again the state refused. So, the city council came up with a plan: They would sell Health Sciences Park, as well as the park where the Davis statue stood, to a nonprofit group, Memphis Greenspace, that would then remove the statues without having to answer to state law.

That set the stage for a legal drama over the remains of Forrest and his wife that resulted in the exhuming of the caskets and their transport, along with the original memorial, to a new $5 million museum of the Confederacy in Columbia, Tennessee, two hundred miles away. There, presumably, the worship can continue. And if not there, then at the 2,500-acre Nathan Bedford Forrest State Park in Benton County, Tennessee, where, on the park's website, the only acknowledgment of Forrest's brutal past is to say that he is "a controversial figure."

But the question that lingers is, now what? Streets are one thing. For instance, proposals in Alexandria include renaming two streets to honor George Floyd and Breonna Taylor. But the difference between a street and a monument is the difference between recognition and reverence. As the nation comes to terms with the rewriting of its history, there are an increasing number of empty pedestals and plinths begging for a new purpose. The easy fix would be to replace a monument to a disreputable person with a monument to a reputable person, perhaps to a person neglected by history. Yet the idea of "monumentality" feels like it belongs to another age, perhaps the one that embraced the now long discredited "great man" theory of history, and not to the intensely democratic moment that our technology is forcing upon us now. One could even argue that the notion of monumentality is itself wrapped up with supremacy—not just white supremacy but supremacy in a wider sense. Monuments are, by definition, larger than life. They put mortals on pedestals to tower above us like Goliaths. Democracies that too often resort to such veneration risk undermining their own principles. The tendency for twenty-first-century social justice movements to embrace leaderlessness only seems to reinforce this humbler perspective.

By contrast, consider Trump's July 4, 2020, visit to Mount Rushmore, where the governor of South Dakota, Kristi Noem, presented him with something she said she knew he would "appreciate": a bookshelf-size bronze replica of Gutzon Borglum's sixty-foot-high mountain carving with the face of Trump himself added to the array of Washington, Jefferson, Lincoln, and Teddy Roosevelt. The real Mount Rushmore, the one that Trump and Noem stood before, was birthed in the 1920s from an idea hatched by the state's official historian, who had something more modest in mind—a paean to the American West that was to include not only images of Lewis and Clark and Buffalo Bill Cody but also Native Americans like Sacagawea and Lakota chief Red Cloud.

Borglum's interest, however, was more in line with Manifest Destiny, and his ambition was unbridled. He compared his project favorably to the unrealized dreams of Alexander the Great, who wanted to "convert the Olympian mountains to sculpture," and "Michelangelo, who wished to carve colossal figures into the Carrara Mountains." America alone, he offered, would succeed in putting its imprint on nature. In fact, the Black Hills mountains, where Mount Rushmore is located, had once been part of the Great Sioux Reservation, recognized by treaty with the US government; that is, until gold was discovered there, leading to the Black Hills Gold Rush and the trampling of the pact with the Lakota.

Borglum had his own history with white supremacism. While he sculpted a marble bust of Lincoln in 1908 that is displayed to this day in the US Capitol building and a full-figure bronze of a seated Lincoln in 1911 for the county courthouse in Newark, New Jersey, he soon came under the influence of the Klan—likely, his biographers write, through D. W. Griffith's *The Birth of a Nation* and Madison Grant's influential white supremacist book *The Passing of the Great Race.* Until creative differences and disputes over money ended his relationship with the United Daughters of the Confederacy, he had been the original sculptor for the Confederate carving at Stone Mountain, and, while he was never an official member, he

was intimate with Klan leadership of the time. He condemned slavery, but he wrote that "it has been the character of the cargo that has eaten into the very moral fiber
of our race character, rather than the moral depravity of
Anglo-Saxon traders." And he was a believer in eugenics,
determining that if you breed two races, the lower race
prevails. "If you cross a thorough-bred with a jackass you
get a mule," he wrote. "A Negro and a Jew will produce [a]
Negro," but any member of a "European race and Jew, offspring Jew." Immigrants were "slippered assassins" who
were turning America into an alien "scrap heap."

Seen through this lens, Donald Trump's ceremony at
Mount Rushmore becomes an especially cunning coun-
terpunch to the progressive aftermath of Charlottesville,
one rich with code. "Today, we will set history and history's record straight," he said. "Before these figures were
immortalized in stone, they were American giants in
full flesh and blood, gallant men whose intrepid deeds
unleashed the greatest leap of human advancement the
world has ever known." There will be no reassessment,
for American history has already been chipped into the
granite, right here before your very eyes. You can't take
it down. You can't erase it. You can't "rewrite" it. It's part
of nature now. It's property. Real estate. Soil. The men
whose images are chiseled before you were no mere mortals but American "giants" in "full flesh and blood" (Blood

and Soil), "gallant" (Lost Cause mythology word) men (only white males) who are responsible for the "greatest leap of human advancement" (Manifest Destiny).

We've had more success, it seems, when memorials or monuments are not in human form but instead are shapes that the viewer can use to project their own meaning. That's certainly more in the spirit of democracy, too—the one reflecting the many rather than the many reflecting the one. The Washington Monument is an obelisk, beautiful in its simplicity and understatement. No words etched on it anywhere. No representations of Washington himself. It's still a monument to a man, but it feels less like aggrandizement. Maya Lin's Vietnam Veterans Memorial in Washington, DC—inspired by funereal architecture and first modeled by then twenty-one-year-old Lin from mashed potatoes in the Yale dining hall—is composed of two triangular-shaped vertical panels of polished granite sunk ten feet into the earth and inscribed with the names of the fifty-eight thousand Americans who died in the war. When standing before it, you discover your reflection looking back at you, bringing you into communion with the dead. The tone is appropriately somber, which initially raised vigorous objections, but when it opened in 1982 the overall effect was unifying.

The Statue of Liberty is a monument to an idea, but when it was first conceived, that idea had nothing to do with immigrants. It was the brainchild of a Frenchman,

Édouard René de Laboulaye, writer of both fairy tales and histories, including a three-volume history of America. Laboulaye was also a professor of law and, significantly, an anti-slavery activist. He was fascinated by America, "almost," one historian wrote, "to the point of fetishism." Inspired by the North's victory in the American Civil War, he wished to celebrate American democracy as demonstrated in the abolishment of slavery, and in so doing inspire his own country, then under the thumb of Napoleon III and the corrupt Second Empire, to a republican future.

The image he seized upon was one of a broken shackle and chains, which, in the original sketches, Lady Liberty held in her hands. There have long been rumors, stoked considerably by the arrival of the internet and social media, that the original Lady Liberty was Black, which would have made sense if it was indeed a direct reference to the Civil War, but these are based on scant evidence. Even if true, the political climate in America, and France, in the 1870s was such that any monument to the end of Black slavery, whether it showed a white Lady Liberty or a Black one, would have been received awkwardly, if not completely rejected. Napoleon III had supported the Confederacy. Reconstruction came to an end in 1877 when President Rutherford B. Hayes withdrew federal troops from the South. The war was something that many Americans wished to forget, and others—

those now reasserting white power in the South—saw as misunderstood. If anything, the image of a white woman on a pedestal seemed more in sync with another kind of fetish, the white southerner's fascination with protecting the fragile sex and, implicitly, the threat posed to her by the Black race.

In the end, both Laboulaye and his sculptor, Frédéric Auguste Bartholdi, opted to morph the idea into one celebrating freedom in a broad sense, timed not to the end of the Civil War but to the centennial of the American nation. The chains were removed from Liberty's hands and put at her feet. In place of them, she holds a tablet inscribed with the date July 4, 1776. Thus, a plan to dignify the moment when freedom from slavery was finally realized by the Black race in America vanished, appropriated to connect instead to the white American colonies' political freedom from British power.

The Emma Lazarus poem ("Give me your tired, your poor . . .") was added in 1903, branding Lady Liberty as an immigration icon, but the close association of immigration with the statue only started to gain attention in the 1930s when, well beyond the passage of the Johnson-Reed Act, white Americans could celebrate "their" immigrant roots, the kind that had been purified from the intrusion of darker peoples, restoring America into an Anglo-European Eden. In 1965, when Congress passed a new immigration act that overturned Johnson-Reed and ended the quota system, President Lyndon B. Johnson signed it into law in a ceremony at the base of the Statue of Liberty.

The new measure began a steady stream of immigrants from underdeveloped parts of the world that has provided us with the diversity we have today. But the vast majority of Black Americans were not, of course, immigrants; never had been. Their ancestors had come here on slave ships. As Tyler Stovall wrote in *White Freedom*, no one ever proposed putting up a statue in Charleston, South Carolina, or any of the other ports of the Middle Passage. To Black people, the Statue of Liberty was little more than another symbol of exclusion.

Yet somehow, as a monument, as an emblem of freedom, the Statue of Liberty still works. First, because, as a harbor sculpture, she is so appropriately majestic, especially when seen, for instance, from the Staten Island Ferry or from the window of a jet plane as it weaves its way up the Hudson before making a sharp right turn out to LaGuardia Airport. Lady Liberty also works because she's so malleable. On the internet and in social media, Lady Liberty, like the words of James Baldwin, gets appropriated with abandon, one of the few symbols that can be both kitschy and profound at the same time. No matter the edifice's original reasons for being; she has become a liberty totem, a place that can be used to form a statement of either respect or disrespect and still matter.

For Black Americans, Lady Liberty has served as a convenient vehicle to troll American claims of freedom, as when she appeared, during the rise of the Black Power movement of the 1960s, on a poster holding a list of demands ("free yourself, free the Panther 21, free the streets, free food, free housing, free medicine, free Bobby Seale, free education . . .") or in 1972 when Shirley Chisholm mounted the first-ever serious African American campaign for the office of president by choosing the Statue of Liberty and "Liberty and Equality" as, respectively, her logo and slogan. Lady Liberty has been Black, gay, Asian. She is pictured crying, laughing, dancing. Black women dressed as Liberty regularly joined protests against police violence in the summer of 2020. And when a white woman dressed as Liberty defaced the Black Lives Matter mural outside Trump Tower, Twitter users responded: "Lady Liberty drenched in red while desecrating 'Black Lives.' Ironically accurate."

Still, what do we do when the "we remember what happened here and learn from it" statement gets rejected by a community that effectively doesn't want to remember, or, perhaps even worse, would prefer to co-opt the event to serve a completely different, and false, narrative?

The story of Emmett Till is so well-known that it barely needs repeating. Till, of course, was a boy of fourteen from Chicago who, while visiting his cousins in Mississippi in 1955, took a dare from other boys to enter a grocery store and whistle at the white woman behind the counter. When word reached the woman's husband, Roy Bryant, who owned the store, he and his friends retrieved Till from his cousins' home, tortured him, and then murdered him, tossing his body into the Tallahatchie River.

The writer John Edgar Wideman was the same age as Till when he first came upon the picture of the dead boy, his face mangled beyond recognition, in an article in the Black magazine *Jet*. At first the image appeared to him only "as a blurred grayish something resembling an aerial snapshot of a landscape cratered by bombs or ravaged by natural disaster." When he realized it was in fact the face of a dead Black boy, he jerked his eyes away. The late boxer Muhammad Ali was fifteen, hanging out "on the corner with a gang of boys" in his hometown of Louisville, Kentucky, when he saw the picture in *Jet*. Ali was startled by the contrast between an accompanying photograph of the boy "laughing and happy" and the image from the casket with "his head swollen and bashed in, his eyes bulging out of their sockets, and his mouth twisted and broken." Ali was determined to get back at white people. He and a friend stole their way down to the Louisville railyards. "[A] poster of a thin white man in striped pants and a top hat . . . pointed at us above the words 'Uncle Sam Wants You.'" Ali and his friend threw stones at it, then broke into the shoeshine boy's shed, stole some iron shoe rests, and used them to sabotage a stretch of track. Writing of Till and the moment in his 1975 memoir, Ali added, "His mother had done a bold thing." It was indeed Mamie Till Bradley's decision to have her son's casket open, and to do so at a public funeral. "I wanted the world to see what they did to my baby," she said.

The funeral was attended by fifty thousand people, and the picture of Till gained national and international attention, provoking outrage not unlike that which attended the killing of George Floyd sixty-five years later. But until relatively recently, the only on-site recognition was an often-vandalized sign marking the spot where Emmett Till's body was recovered. The courthouse where Bryant and his friend J. W. Milam were tried for murder was restored in 2015, though considering that the two were acquitted and then promptly sold their story to *Look* magazine, where they actually admitted their guilt, one looks out on the empty seats and the jury box with despair. Elsewhere, several small, independent museums have been established.

The building that housed Bryant's Grocery long ago went into decay. Ironically, its business in the 1950s relied on Black sharecroppers, who, upon the acquittal of Till's murderers, refused to shop there. It closed a month later, and a new owner soon moved in. That business, too, closed in the 1980s, and shortly thereafter the building was bought by the descendants of Ray Tribble, who had been a juror in the trial of Till's murderers—and had voted for acquittal. Despite the former grocery's significance to civil rights historians, the Tribbles have refused many offers to buy it.

Instead, working with $200,000 provided to them by the Mississippi Civil Rights Historical Sites commission, they restored the adjacent Ben Roy's Service Station, which they also own, arguing in their grant application that "it is very likely that the events that transpired at Bryant's Grocery . . . were discussed underneath the front canopy" at Ben Roy's, and besides, those who wished today to look in on the site would need somewhere to stop. The work was completed in 2014, and, amazingly, the signage includes no reference to Emmett Till or his murder. In what you might describe as one more variation on the southern myth of the Lost Cause, Ben Roy's describes the 1950s as a time "of interracial fraternity . . . where the social strictures of Jim Crow were tempered by the communitarian bonds of life in small-town America."

———

One of the most commanding emotions of our new age, our life in cyberspace, is the fear of mind control. It manifests itself in arguments at school boards over Critical Race Theory, in conspiracy theories about the COVID vaccine planting computer chips in our bloodstreams, in shouts of "fake news" and charges of bias. It informs suspicions of science in general and of the science of climate change in particular. It is implicit in replacement theory. It has many analogues, among them the one popularized in science fiction for centuries, of man and machine melding to create a new, often frightening, species. Its most recent manifestation flows from our relationship with the virtual world. The more we trust our identity to the great void, the question will not only be "Where will we be?" but "Who will we be?" Will we be defined by our biology or by some other criterion? Will we be something new, maybe a robo-man or a techno-human? Will old earthly distinctions like race still matter, or will we adopt new ones? The fact that Google and Facebook and just about every part of the internet greets us each day not as strangers but as entities that know something about us—indeed, know us very intimately from the patterns of our search histories and other keystroke hints that we drop along the way— makes this seem not only possible but imminent.

There are serious concerns wrapped up in this, and they are worth discussing at length in a different context. But it's important to note that, as Americans, we have all been here before, indeed many times, as a nation that reinvents itself with regularity. When America began and the reigning technology was nothing more than the printing press, the goal was, in a manner of speaking, to create a new "species": a free and independent people, unencumbered by the demands of monarchy, religion, and dogma. The world sat up and took notice—so much so that when in 1782, shortly before the end of the American Revolution, a high-born Frenchman named Michel-Guillaume-Saint-Jean de Crèvecoeur published a series of essays he titled *Letters from an American Farmer*, it became an instant hit throughout Europe.

Crèvecoeur had moved to America in 1755, served as a cartographer in the French and Indian War, married an American woman, and settled in Orange County, New York. His book, which he wrote in English under his new American name, J. Hector St. John, addressed the subject that captivated his European readers: "What, then, is the American," asked Crèvecoeur, "this new man?" This "strange mixture of blood, which you will find in no other country"? Crèvecoeur's answer may well have been the first expression of what later became known as American Exceptionalism. Here in America, he posited, "individuals of all nations" are "melted into a new race of men." In the process, "all his ancient prejudices and manners" are left behind in favor of a new mode of life that stressed self-determination and equal opportunity. Crèvecoeur denigrated life in Europe as persistently clouded by the "mist of ages." By contrast, in America, he asserted, we have had "no war to desolate our fields, our religion does not oppress," and "we are strangers to those feudal institutions which have enslaved so many." Indeed, "nature opens her broad lap to receive the perpetual accession of new-comers." Such unbridled idealism.

But the Frenchman's identification of the emerging nation's essential hypocrisy went less noticed. Americans were different, he argued, but their achievements were realized at the expense of those they excluded. Visiting Charles Town (Charleston), South Carolina, he contrasted the scenes of joy there with the plight of the "poor slaves, from whose painful labours all their wealth proceeds." He described the "cracks of the whip" and the "showers of sweat and of tears which from the bodies of Africans daily drop and moisten the ground they till." The "chosen race eat, drink, and live happy . . . without labour, without fatigue, hardly subjected to the trouble of wishing," he wrote, while whole families are torn apart, dragged to the "rich metropolis" where they are "arranged like horses at a fair . . . branded like cattle and then driven to toil." They work for "persons they know not, and who have no other power over them than that of violence."

Crèvecoeur's chapter on Charleston offers more than reflection. Toward the end, he describes a walk through a wooded patch of countryside. He is on his way to dinner at a plantation when he suddenly comes upon a cage "suspended to the limbs of a tree" and inside it a Black man left to die of starvation and the flesh-eating habits of vultures. "I shudder," Crèvecoeur writes, "when I recollect that the birds had already picked out his eyes; his cheek-bones were bare; his arms had been attacked in several places; and his body seemed covered with a multitude of wounds." Despite his condition, the man spoke to him, and Crèvecoeur provided him some water before joining his hosts at dinner. There he learned that the slave's fate was the result of his having killed his master, and that his torture was necessitated by the "laws of self-preservation," a chilling admission that still resonates.

Crèvecoeur's instrument was the pen, but the pen was the camera of his day, and what he was doing was simple and, from our vantage point nearly 250 years later, all too familiar. Behold this great new species of man, he was saying, but do not ignore the injustices that attend his arrival—indeed, that make his arrival possible. In this sense Crèvecoeur was doing what generations of truth tellers after him, utilizing the technologies of their day, would do: point at the stain on the national landscape and say, "Look, see." Witness what violence is at the core of the American story. Recognize this injustice before you. It's the same impulse that drove Frederick Douglass half a century later to stand before audiences of the curious and lend the voice of a slave to the campaign for abolition, fielding questions about the grisly horrors of life in shackles, and to adopt 168 separate poses for photographs, determined to show that he was not an ape but a man, not an animal but a human, damaged but not broken, all the while knowing that his extraordinary gift for oratory might sway some while leading others to scoff that such brilliance could only be the result of his having had a white father (yes, the slave master who raped his mother).

It's what drove Ida B. Wells to reveal the lies at the core of the hundreds of lynchings of Black men after the failure of Reconstruction, both those charged with rape and those whose crime was little more than an "impertinent" gesture of defiance, and to publish pictures of lynchings displaying those hideous acts in all their gruesome detail. The cartes-de-visite that Sojourner Truth passed out at her appearances ("I Sell the Shadow to Support the Substance") and the thirty infographics on Black life that W. E. B. Du Bois brought with him to the 1900 Paris Exposition all served the same purpose. So did the urgent campaigns mounted by Du Bois and Monroe Trotter in resistance to *The Birth of a Nation* (and what greater example of "mind control" is there than a film that purports to reverse history and turn villains into heroes, heroes into villains?), James Baldwin when he patiently and persistently exposed the lie at the core of American identity and American history, and Mamie Till Bradley when she insisted on an open casket for her dead son. It is what animated the social media frenzy around the killing of Ahmaud Arbery, forcing the arrests of the McMichaels; the BLM protesters in Kenosha objecting to the shooting of Jacob Blake; and what inspired Darnella Frazier when she stood curbside at the killing of George Floyd, camera held high. Without the accounts that they wrote, shot, filmed, and tweeted, who would tell the truth about America?

Acknowledgments

We are grateful to many who provided assistance, small and large, in the research and writing of this book, and to the even more who provided much-needed inspiration and encouragement. We would especially like to thank Sylvia Steinert, Melissa Valle, R. L'Heureux Lewis-McCoy, Jack Brewster, Ben Brewster, Chris Brewster, Brandon Cardwell, Ralphie and Bagel Brewster. Dan Okrent offered important advice on the immigration history outlined in chapter five. Melanie Walsh's scholarship on James Baldwin and Twitter was particularly eye-opening and informs our section on Baldwin in chapter four. We look forward to reading more of her work. Jane Townsend offered occasional copyediting advice, which was much appreciated. The cover design benefited from the reactions of many of the above and also Kayce Jennings, Justin Moore, Evisa

Gallman, Oscar Almonte Espinal, Dia Lee, Alexis Tucker, Zenobiah Abdul Malik, George Carey, Alexa Kantgias, Mike Masella, John Masella, Tristam Osgood, Peter Bachmann, Dan Wellers, and Kevin Howat. Our agent, George Greenfield, was a tireless advocate, and our editor, Sean deLone, was an expert guide. We are grateful to both for making this book possible.

Endnotes and Sources

INTRODUCTION

2–3 *"A patient . . . is not invited to the consultation of the doctors on his case"*: Steve Luxenberg, *Separate: The Story of Plessy v. Ferguson, and America's Journey from Slavery to Segregation* (New York: W. W. Norton & Company, 2019), 391. The quote originally appeared in Lyman Abbott's newspaper, the *Christian Union.*

3 *"Metaracists . . . acquiesce in the larger cultural order which continues the work of racism"*: Joel Kovel, *White Racism: A Psychohistory* (New York: Pantheon Books, 1970), 212.

3 *"illusions of change . . . mostly white neighborhoods"*: Betsy Hodges, "As Mayor of Minneapolis, I Saw How White Liberals Block Change," *New York Times*, July 9, 2020, https://www.nytimes.com/2020/07/09/opinion/minneapolis-hodges-racism.html.

5 *"Invisibility . . . power and longevity"*: Isabel Wilkerson, *Caste* (New York: Random House, 2020), 23.

5–6 *"The thing about King . . . anything that's existed before in black struggle"*: DeRay Mckesson, quoted in Bijan Stephen, "Get Up, Stand Up: Social Media Helps Black Lives Matter Fight the Power," *Wired*, November 2015, https://www.wired.com/2015/10/how-black-lives-matter-uses-social-media-to-fight-the-power/.

6 *"use clubs on us in the dark corners . . . television"*: David J. Garrow, *Protest at Selma: Martin Luther King, Jr., and the Voting Rights Act of 1965* (New Haven, CT: Yale University Press, 1978), 152.

10 *"Seeing, which comes before words . . . is an act of choice"*: John Berger, *Ways of Seeing* (New York: Penguin, 1977), 8.

CHAPTER 1: THE SPECTACLE OF DEATH

13 *"had no requiem . . . sad and horrible fate"*: I. Garland Penn, *The Afro-American Press and Its Editors* (New York: Arno, 1969; originally published 1891), 186.

14 *"another face on a T-shirt . . . list that won't stop growing"*: Robin Bravender, "George Floyd's Brother: 'Make Sure That He Is More Than Another Face on a T-Shirt,' " *Virginia Mercury*, June 11, 2020, https://www.virginiamercury.com/2020/06/11/george-floyds-brother-make-sure-that-he-is-more-than-another-face-on-a-t-shirt/.

18 *"Momma! . . . Momma! I'm through"*: Lonnae O'Neal, "George Floyd's Mother Was Not There, but He Used Her as a Sacred Invocation," *National Geographic*, May 30, 2020, https://www.nationalgeographic.com/history/article/george-floyds-mother-not-there-he-used-her-as-sacred-invocation.

19 *the city's old neighborhoods went into a rapid decline*: Lori Rodriguez, "Some Fear Historic Black Neighborhoods Are Losing Identity," *Houston Chronicle*, July 15, 2001, https://www.chron.com/news/article/Some-fear-historic-black-neighborhoods-are-losing-2014193.php.

21 *Slowly, Houston is catching up with its history*: Cindy George, "Community Celebrates $33.6M Makeover of Houston's

Emancipation Park" *Houston Chronicle*, June 17, 2017, https://www.chron.com/houston/article/33-6-million-Emancipation-Park-redo-unveiled-11227617.php.

21 *Floyd began hanging out with . . . DJ Screw:* Insanul Ahmed, Tia Hill, and Russel Abad, "George Floyd Was Connected to Houston's Screwed Up Click With DJ Screw," Genius.com, May 30, 2020, https://genius.com/videos/Breaking-down-george-floyds-connection-to-houstons-screwed-up-click?utm_source=recirculated_content.

23 *the "lie," as DuBois called it . . . "cheating them and killing them":* Philip S. Foner, ed., *W. E. B. Du Bois Speaks: Speeches and Addresses: 1920–1963* (New York: Pathfinder, 1970).

25 *"unless we conquer our present vices . . . heritage from slavery":* W. E. B. (William Edward Burghardt) Du Bois, *The Conservation of Races* (Public Domain, 2012), 20.

26 *"no longer concerned . . . control of the dispossessed":* Michelle Alexander, *The New Jim Crow* (New York: New Press, 2020), 188.

27 *What is today known as the "Memphis Massacre":* Stephen V. Ash, *A Massacre in Memphis: The Race Riot That Shook the Nation One Year After the Civil War* (New York: Hill and Wang, 2013).

30 *his genitals removed "with tailor's shears":* Memphis *Commercial*, May 25, 1892, as quoted in Paula J. Giddings, *Ida: A Sword Among Lions: Ida B. Wells and the Campaign Against Lynching* (New York: Amistad, 2008), 212.

30 *"Somebody must show . . . fallen upon me to do so":* Jacqueline Jones Royster, *Southern Horrors and Other Writings: The Anti-Lynching Campaign of Ida B. Wells, 1892–1900* (New York: Bedford/St. Martin's, 2016), Kindle locations 1119–20.

32 *In the perverse logic . . . extralegal means to eradicate the problem:* Amy Louise Wood, *Lynching and Spectacle: Witnessing Racial Violence in America, 1890–1940* (Durham: University of North Carolina Press, 2011), 63. "Our statute books held in all their pages of fact and precedent, no law worthy to mete out justice in such a case."

32 *"a concession of the right . . . rapists and desperadoes"*: Ida B. Wells, "Lynching and the Excuse for It," *Independent* 53 (May 16, 1901): 1133–36, Northern Illinois University Digital Library, 2021, https://digital.lib.niu.edu/islandora/object /niu-gildedage%3A24185.

33 *"after coal oil . . . set fire to him"*: Royster, *Southern Horrors and Other Writings*, Kindle locations 2420–22.

34 *the persistence of images that one could not bear to see but could forever "hear"*: James Weldon Johnson, *The Autobiography of an Ex-Colored Man* (Seattle: Amazon Classics, 2021), 129.

35 *"singing 'Jesus Lover of My Soul' in her childish treble voice"*: Amy Louise Wood, *Lynching and Spectacle: Witnessing Racial Violence in America, 1890–1940* (Durham: University of North Carolina Press, 2009), 59.

35 *"the mad wantonness of gorilla ferocity"*: Giddings, *Ida*, 248.

35 *"vengeance of an outraged God . . . an innocent life"*: P. L. James, *The Facts in the Case of the Horrible Murder of Little Myrtle Vance and Its Fearful Expiation at Paris, Texas, February 1st, 1893, with Photographic Illustrations* (Paris, TX, 1893).

36 *"Two Murderous and Thieving Negroes . . . Indignant Farmers"*: Charles Seguin, "How Northern Newspapers Covered Lynchings," *New York Times*, June 11, 2018, https://www.nytimes .com/2018/06/11/opinion/northern-newspapers-lynchings .html.

36 *the* Atlanta Constitution *offered a $500 reward*: Richard Perloff, "The Press and Lynchings of African Americans," *Journal of Black Studies* 30, no. 3 (2000): 315–30.

36 *"If a Negro wants to escape . . . off white women"*: Rayford Whittingham Logan, *The Betrayal of the Negro, from Rutherford B. Hayes to Woodrow Wilson* (New York: Collier Books, 1954), 288.

37 *"See how my people . . . measures to prevent it"*: Cited in Amanda K. Frisken, "'A Song Without Words': Anti-Lynching Imagery in the African American Press, 1889–1898," *Journal of African American History* 97, no. 3 (2012): 240–69.

37 *"superior white men . . . reputed fathers of mulatto children"*:

Royster, *Southern Horrors and Other Writings*, 57. She is quoting a column by Albion W. Tourgée.

38   *"keep up the agitation . . . persecuted humanity":* Ida B. Wells, *Lynch Law in Georgia*, pamphlet (1899).

40   *"God and safety were synonymous":* James Baldwin, *The Fire Next Time* (New York: Vintage, 1992), 16.

40   *"I'm not just going to flex . . . from a street standpoint":* Maya Rao, "George Floyd's Search for Salvation," *Star Tribune*, December 27, 2020, https://www.startribune.com/george -floyd-hoped-moving-to-minnesota-would-save-him-what-he -faced-here-killed-him/573417181/.

40   *"to raise followers of Jesus for the city":* "Our Mission," Resurrection Houston, https://www.resurrectionhouston.org/about /our-mission.

42   *"I'll tell you why we came to Minnesota . . . white people here":* Howard Sinker, "Recalling Calvin Griffith's Bigoted Outburst in Southern Minnesota," *StribSports Upload* (blog), *Star Tribune*, April 29, 2014, https://www.startribune.com/recalling -ex-twins-owner-griffith-s-bigoted-outburst/257189521/.

42   *"inherent inferiority"* versus *"accidental inferiority":* Robert Penn Warren, "Race," *New York Review*, October 8, 1964, https://www.nybooks.com/articles/1964/10/08/race/.

43   *"the cultural history of Negroes . . . ever against a wall":* Ralph Ellison, *Shadow and Act* (New York: Knopf, 2011), 298.

44   *"well-mannered 'colored' boy . . . very good appearance":* John Nelson, "Fifty Years Later, ESPN Breaks New Ground on Robinson," Associated Press, February 27, 1997, https://apnews .com/article/4ec7e873c9442fd6681e53f37cd2bb24.

45   someone *"we would not tolerate in our houses":* Louis Menand, *The Metaphysical Club: A Story of Ideas in America* (New York: Farrar, Straus and Giroux, 2002).

45   *"We are a nation within a nation . . . British dominions":* Edward M. Stoeber, "Martin Delany's Advice to Ex-Slaves," http://www.columbia.edu/itc/history/foner/civil_war/linked _documents/delanys_advice.html.

46 *"literally burning my flesh to have it look like a white man's"*: Malcolm X, *The Autobiography of Malcolm X* (New York: Ballantine Books, 1964), 64.

46 *"It is a very grave matter . . . you do not exist"*: James Baldwin, *The Evidence of Things Not Seen* (New York: Henry Holt, 1985), 44.

46 *"invisible barbed wire fence of the restrictive covenants"*: St. Clair Drake and Horace R. Cayton, *Black Metropolis* (London: Jonathan Cape, 1946), 382.

47 *"the superior race to multiply rather than the inferior"*: William H. Pease and Jane H. Pease, "Antislavery Ambivalence: Immediatism, Expediency, Race," *American Quarterly* 17, no. 4 (Winter 1965): 682–95, https://www.jstor.org/stable/2711126.

47 *the arc of the moral universe . . . "bends toward justice"*: Theodore Parker, *Ten Sermons of Religion* (Miami: HardPress, 2018).

48 *a mere 7 percent . . . 20 percent is nonwhite:* US Census Bureau, "QuickFacts: Minnesota," July 1, 2021, accessed November 25, 2021, https://www.census.gov/quickfacts/MN.

51 *"desegregated lunch counter . . . freedom, justice, and equality"*: Malcolm X, "Message to the Grassroots," November 10, 1963, in George Breitman, ed., *Malcolm X Speaks: Selected Speeches and Statements* (New York: Grove Weidenfeld, 1965), 9.

51 *"culturally specific behavioral health services and training"*: Turning Point, "Mission & Vision," https://ourturningpoint.org/mission-vision/.

53 *"I've done drugs . . . as real as it gets"*: Robert Samuels, "Racism's Hidden Toll," *Washington Post*, October 22, 2020, https://www.washingtonpost.com/graphics/2020/national/george-floyd-america/health-care/.

54 *To keep himself steady, Floyd made to-do lists:* Ibid.

54 *By 2020, Floyd had two new roommates:* Tenzin Shakya, "George Floyd's Roommate: 'He Had to Give His Life for Every [One of] Us to Have Justice in a Different Way,'" ABC News,

June 11, 2020, https://abcnews.go.com/US/george-floyds
-roommate-give-life-us-justice/story?id=71201898.

56   *Floyd's encounter with the police outside Cup Foods in south
       Minneapolis:* Lydia Chebbine, "George Floyd Protests Across
       the U.S. and Beyond," *U.S. News & World Report*, June 1,
       2020, https://www.usnews.com/news/national-news/photos
       /2020/06/01/george-floyd-protests-spread-across-the-us-and
       -beyond.

56   *and in Paris . . . handcuffed and face to the ground:* Iman
       Amrani and Angelique Chrisafis, "Adama Traoré's Death
       in Police Custody Casts Long Shadow over French Society,"
       Guardian, February 17, 2017, https://www.theguardian.com
       /world/2017/feb/17/adama-traore-death-in-police-custody
       -casts-long-shadow-over-french-society.

CHAPTER 2: "YOU ABOUT TO LOSE YO' JOB"

60   *"You can't hear me? Then I'm going to sing it to you":* Cat
       Zhang, "How the Viral Protest Anthem 'Lose Yo Job' Came to
       Be," Pitchfork.com, June 9, 2020, https://pitchfork.com/the
       pitch/lose-yo-job-protest-anthem-interview/.

60   *"Okay IM NOT POSTING THIS TO BE FUNNY TOWARDS
       THIS SUBJECT!!!!":* Julia Reinstein, "The Woman in the 'Lose
       Yo Job' Video Told Us How It Changed Her Life," *BuzzFeed
       News*, June 8, 2020, https://www.buzzfeednews.com/article
       /juliareinstein/lose-yo-job-viral-video-woman-johnniqua
       -charles.

60   *The clip was picked up by DJ Suede and iMarkkeyz:* Ibid.

61   *Soon she was appearing on Instagram in a live stream:* https://
       www.instagram.com/tv/CBHVEJspOFx/?utm_source=ig
       _web_copy_link.

61   *A GoFundMe page followed, raising $55,386 for her:* https://
       www.gofundme.com/f/johnniqua-charles-quotlose-yo-jobquot.

61   *"I'm glad this video . . . all the love":* https://www.instagram
       .com/tv/CBHVEJspOFx/?utm_source=ig_web_copy_link.

61 *By election time, a new meme:* Jon Jackson, "'You About to Lose Yo Job': The Story Behind the Viral Hit Featuring Biden, Obama, and Other Dancing Dems," *Newsweek*, November 9, 2020, https://www.newsweek.com/democrats-biden-dancing -video-viral-lose-job-1546148. For a discussion of blackface and the use of memes and other methods to mock the Black poor, see Laur M. Jackson, "Memes and Misogynoir," TheAwl .com, August 28, 2014, https://www.theawl.com/2014/08 /memes-and-misogynoir/; and Spencer Kornhaber, "Defund the Police Gets Its Anthem," *Atlantic*, June 9, 2020, https:// www.theatlantic.com/culture/archive/2020/06/lose-yo-job -perfect-protest-song-today/612844/.

62 *her own GoFundMe page raising over half a million dollars:* https://www.gofundme.com/f/peace-and-healing-for-darnella.

62–63 *"It's been nights I stayed up apologizing . . . not saving his life":* Jeannie Suk Gersen, "The Vital Role of Bystanders in Convicting Derek Chauvin," *New Yorker*, April 21, 2021, https:// www.newyorker.com/news/our-columnists/the-vital-role-of -bystanders-in-convicting-derek-chauvin.

63 *She was there to accompany her nine-year-old cousin:* Darnella Frazier interview, *CBS This Morning*, June 15, 2020, https://www.youtube.com/watch?v=eoJQ5p9M1CQ.

64 *"thousands of Jewish corpses into nice photographic compositions":* Carole Naggar, *George Rodger: An Adventure in Photography, 1908–1995* (Syracuse, NY: Syracuse University Press, 2003).

65 *"Shots fired . . . grabbed my Taser":* Mark Berman, Wesley Lowery, and Kimberly Kindy, "South Carolina Police Office Charged with Murder After Shooting Man During Traffic Stop," *Washington Post*, April 7, 2015, https://www.washingtonpost.com /news/post-nation/wp/2015/04/07/south-carolina-police -officer-will-be-charged-with-murder-after-shooting/.

66 *the video goes on for nine minutes and twenty-nine seconds:* Eric Levenson, "Former Officer Knelt on George Floyd for 9 Minutes and 29 Seconds—Not the Infamous 8:46," CNN,

March 30, 2021, https://www.cnn.com/2021/03/29/us/george -floyd-timing-929-846/index.html.

67 *"Tank Man," as he came to be known:* Kyle Almond, "The Story Behind the Iconic 'Tank Man' Photo," CNN, https:// edition.cnn.com/interactive/2019/05/world/Tiananmen -square-tank-man-cnnphotos/; and Julie Makinen, "Tiananmen Square Mystery: Who Was 'Tank Man'?" *Los Angeles Times*, June 4, 2014, https://www.latimes.com/world/asia/la-fg-china -tiananmen-square-tank-man-20140603-story.html.

67 *Widener's shot, which he took from the sixth floor of a Beijing hotel:* Patrick Witty, "Behind the Scenes: Tank Man of Tiananmen," *Lens* (blog), *New York Times*, June 3, 2009, https:// lens.blogs.nytimes.com/2009/06/03/behind-the-scenes-tank -man-of-tiananmen/.

69 *thousands of people died in Tiananmen Square:* "Tiananmen Square Protest Death Toll 'Was 10,000,'" BBC News, December 23, 2017, https://www.bbc.com/news/world-asia -china-42465516. It's difficult to determine the precise number of deaths in the Tiananmen Square massacre; estimates have ranged from a few hundred to more than ten thousand.

72 *Filo was a twenty-one-year-old student at Kent State:* Patricia McCormick, "The Girl in the Kent State Photo," *Washington Post Magazine*, April 19, 2021, https://www.washingtonpost .com/magazine/2021/04/19/girl-kent-state-photo-lifelong -burden-being-national-symbol/.

72 *"Where are you going?" he said to himself:* "Photographer John Filo Discusses His Famous Kent State Photograph and the Events of May 4, 1970," CNN, May 4, 2000, http://www.cnn .com/COMMUNITY/transcripts/2000/5/4/filo/.

73 *"No one's going to believe . . . proof":* McCormick, "The Girl in the Kent State Photo."

73 *After getting his story, the reporter alerted authorities:* Ibid.

73 *"professional agitators . . . 'chicks up front' strategy":* Associated Press, "Kneeling with Death Haunted a Life," *New York Times*, May 6, 1990, https://www.nytimes.com/1990/05/06

/us/kneeling-with-death-haunted-a-life.html; and *Miami Herald*, May 26, 1970.

76 *"ikon of a boy in blue striking off... laughing in hope"*: Robert Penn Warren, *The Legacy of the Civil War* (Lincoln: University of Nebraska Press, 2015).

77 *the "overwhelming numbers and resources" that Robert E. Lee referenced:* Clifford Dowdey and Louis H. Manarin, *The Wartime Papers of R. E. Lee* (New York: Little, Brown, 1961), 934.

78 *The Myth of the Lost Cause served to explain the confounding elements of regional defeat:* "Myths," writes Paul Gaston, "are not polite euphemisms for falsehoods, but are combinations of images and symbols that reflect a people's way of perceiving truth. Organically related to a fundamental reality of life, they fuse the real and the imaginary into a blend that becomes a reality itself, a force in history." Paul M. Gaston, *The New South Creed: A Study in Southern Mythmaking* (Baton Rouge: Louisiana State University Press, 1970), 9.

78 *"genius and valor went down before brute force"*: Gary W. Gallagher, *The Myth of the Lost Cause and Civil War History* (Bloomington: Indiana University Press, 2010), 96–97. Gallagher is quoting an ex–Confederate soldier. Another declared that the South "had surrendered but was never whipped."

79 *Mississippi spent 20 percent of the state's revenue on the issuing of artificial limbs:* Eric Foner, *Reconstruction: America's Unfinished Revolution, 1863–1877*, updated edition (New York: HarperCollins, 2014).

80 *"If you call this Freedom ... what do you call Slavery?"*: Ibid.

80 *"negro equality ... still claim, and still assert"*: Edward A. Pollard, *The Lost Cause: A New Southern History of the War of the Confederates* (E. B. Treat, 1866), 752.

83 *On the subject of photography she appears to have been prescient:* Augusta Rohrbach, *Shadow and Substance: Sojourner Truth in Black and White* (Durham, NC: Duke University Press, 2012); and Maurice O. Wallace and Shawn Michelle Smith, *Pictures and Progress: Early Photography and the*

Making of African American Identity (Durham, NC: Duke University Press, 2012).

84　*The author of not one but three books of autobiography: Narrative of the Life of Frederick Douglass* (1845), *My Bondage and My Freedom* (1855), and *Life and Times of Frederick Douglass* (1881, revised in 1892).

85　*"the ends of the earth together . . . planet into a picture gallery"*: Celeste-Marie Bernier, John Stauffer, and Zoe Trodd, *Picturing Frederick Douglass: An Illustrated Biography of the Nineteenth Century's Most Photographed American* (New York: Liveright, 2015), 117.

85　*"a much more kindly and amiable expression . . . face of a fugitive slave"*: "A Tribute for the Negro," *North Star*, April 7, 1849, reprinted in Philip S. Foner, ed., *The Life and Writings of Frederick Douglass*, vol. 1 (New York: International Publishers, 1950), 380.

85　*"next to impossible for white men to take likenesses of black men"*: Bernier, Stauffer, and Trodd, *Picturing Frederick Douglass*, 148–49.

85–86　*"Mind is everywhere asserting . . . bonds of common brotherhood"*: Ibid., 145. The quote is taken from Douglass's 1862 speech "Age of Pictures," which appears in its entirety here. The authors speculate that it was in fact a revision of his 1861 speech "Life Pictures."

86　*mother was enslaved and whose father was, most likely, his mother's white slave master*: David W. Blight, *Frederick Douglass: Prophet of Freedom* (New York: Simon & Schuster, 2018).

86　*"if you teach . . . no value to his master"*: Frederick Douglass, *Narrative of the Life of Frederick Douglass*, illustrated edition (Mineola, NY: Dover, 2021), 41.

86　*In the end, Douglass would bring bits of bread with him*: Ibid., 45. "The plan which I adopted, and the one by which I was most successful, was that of making friends of all the little white boys whom I met in the street. As many of these as I could, I converted into teachers. With their kindly aid, obtained at different times and in different places, I finally succeeded in learning to read."

87   *"something about slavery . . . as I have felt it"*: Blight, *Frederick Douglass*, 109.

87   *"not a fugitive from slavery but a fugitive slave"*: Ibid., 103.

87–88 *"bloody whip, the chain . . . the blood-hound"*: Frederick Douglass, *My Bondage and My Freedom* (New Haven, CT: Yale University Press, 2014), 332.

88   *"filled the air with whines of compromise"*: Blight, *Frederick Douglass*, 332.

88–89 *"no man thinks of publishing . . . strive to look like the picture"*: Bernier, Stauffer, and Trodd, *Picturing Frederick Douglass*, 145.

89   *"It is perhaps . . . beautiful in heaven"*: Frederick Douglass, "Lecture on Pictures," December 3, 1861, quoted in Bernier, Stauffer, and Trodd, *Picturing Frederick Douglass*.

89–90 *"The dog fails . . . nations and individuals"*: Ibid.

90   *"the picture and the ballad . . . the other by the ear"*: Ibid., 254.

94   *two of Kueng's siblings joined the calls for arrests of the officers involved:* Kim Barker, "The Black Officer Who Detained George Floyd Had Pledged to Fix the Police," *New York Times*, June 27, 2020, https://www.nytimes.com/2020/06/27/us/min neapolis-police-officer-kueng.html.

96   *"You know you broke this man . . . You can't say nothing right now"*: "RAW: George Floyd Minneapolis police body camera footage," YouTube video, posted by 10 Tampa Bay, August 10, 2020, 1:05:08, https://www.youtube.com/watch?v=0gQYM BALDXc.

CHAPTER 3: THE "CAMPAIGN"

97   *security camera footage from a nearby home:* Bert Roughton Jr. and Brad Schrade, "Records Show a Neighborhood on Edge before Arbery's Final Run," *Atlanta Journal-Constitution*, May 17, 2020, https://www.ajc.com/news/crime—law/records

-show-neighborhood-edge-before-arbery-final-jog/P9shm
CoRGj9OXFWbKfApmJ/.

97   *about two miles from the Fancy Bluff home Arbery shared with
     his mother:* Roman Stubbs, "Ahmaud Arbery's Killing Was
     Met with Silence. His High School Football Coach Vowed to
     Find Justice," *Washington Post*, September 3, 2020, https://
     www.washingtonpost.com/sports/2020/09/03/jason-vaughn
     -ahmaud-arbery-coach/.

97   *Arbery's uncle, Paul Dix, told the* Brunswick News *that his
     nephew "loved to run":* Larry Hobbs, "Dispatcher: 'What Was
     He Doing Wrong?'" *Brunswick News*, April 29, 2020, https://
     thebrunswicknews.com/news/local_news/dispatcher-what
     -was-he-doing-wrong/article_fe51cdd4-3bb6-5815-9dec-dd
     cdc8f879f8.html.

98   *"And you said [he's] breaking . . . on the premises and not
     supposed to be?"* "Ahmaud Arbery shooting: 911 call made
     at 1.08pm – audio," YouTube video, Guardian News channel,
     May 7, 2020, https://www.youtube.com/watch?v=uFgy5ZT
     -1PA&t=4s.

99   *Notices had been posted to the community's Facebook page:*
     Roughton Jr. and Schrade, "Records Show a Neighborhood on
     Edge before Arbery's Final Run."

99   *"call [me] day or night when you get action on your camera":*
     Brad Schrade, "Police Enlisted Suspect's Help Months before
     Arbery Shooting," *Atlanta Journal-Constitution*, May 15,
     2020, https://www.ajc.com/news/crime—law/suspect-arbery
     -shooting-had-offered-help-police/gFMpkRpX0Zk5edjv
     XrE6sN/.

99   *"Y'all got him?" he called out before jumping into his own truck:*
     Bert Roughton Jr. and Hannah Knowles, "Newly Released
     Video Shows Police Didn't Immediately Help Ahmaud Arbery
     as He Lay Dying," *Washington Post*, December 18, 2020,
     https://www.washingtonpost.com/investigations/2020/12/17
     /ahmaud-arbery-body-camera-video/.

100 *Georgia, with 531, ranks second only to Mississippi in the*

number of lynchings: "History of Lynching in America," NAACP, https://naacp.org/find-resources/history-explained /history-lynching-america: "From 1882 to 1968, 4,743 lynchings occurred in the U.S. . . . The highest number of lynchings during that time period occurred in Mississippi, with 581 recorded. Georgia was second with 531, and Texas was third with 493." The Equal Justice Initiative, using a different time frame (1877–1950) counts 589 lynchings in the state of Georgia, second only to the 654 in the state of Mississippi; see "Lynching in America: Confronting the Legacy of Racial Terror," Equal Justice Initiative, https://lynchinginamerica.eji.org/report/. The number, however, is likely much higher, since the extralegal nature of the act makes it difficult to locate reliable statistics.

100 *In the 1890s alone, Glynn County was the site of three lynchings:* Wesley Lewis (1891), Henry Jackson (1891), and Robert Evarts (1894). See "Georgia Lynchings by County, 1880–1968," *Atlanta Journal-Constitution*, https://www.ajc.com/news /state--regional/map-georgia-lynchings-county-1880-1968 /VgES641NaOmfErITv6jnBN/. The map's statistics were drawn from Tuskegee University archives.

101 *Gregory McMichael later described him not simply as jogging but as "hauling ass":* "Read the Police Report on Ahmaud Arbery's Death," *Daily Mail*, May 7, 2020, https://www.daily mail.co.uk/news/fb-8297829/READ-POLICE-REPORT-AH MAUD-ARBERYS-DEATH.html.

101 *Gregory McMichael yelled at him, "Damn it, stop!" Then shots rang out:* Malachy Browne, Drew Jordan, Dmitriy Khavin, and Ainara Tiefenthäler, "Ahmaud Arbery's Final Minutes: What Videos and 911 Calls Show," *New York Times*, May 16, 2020, https://www.nytimes.com/video/us/100000007142853 /ahmaud-arbery-video-911-georgia.html.

102 *The first films, in turn, were "living photographs":* Optical Magical Lantern Journal, November 1896, as quoted in Charles Musser, *The Emergence of the Cinema: The American Screen to 1907* (New York: Charles Scribner & Sons, 1990), 15.

102   *the electrocution of a circus elephant called Topsy:* Edmund Morris, *Edison* (New York: Random House, 2019), 243.

103   *its nickname was "the Orphan Brigade":* Richard Schickel, *D. W. Griffith: An American Life* (Lanham, MD: Rowman & Littlefield, 2004), 20.

104   *In his autobiography . . . "returned home with him":* James Hart, ed., *The Man Who Invented Hollywood: The Autobiography of D. W. Griffith* (Louisville, KY: Touchstone Publishing, 1972), 29.

104   *One day, "Uncle Henry" gave one of David's brothers a haircut:* Ibid., 30.

105   *a twelve-reel, three-hour creation that played on large screens:* Melvyn Stokes, *D. W. Griffith's The Birth of a Nation: A History of "the Most Controversial Motion Picture of All Time"* (New York: Oxford University Press, 2007), 3.

105–6   *"became a living, human eye, peering into the faces of grief and joy":* Raymond Allen Cook, *Fire from the Flint: The Amazing Careers of Thomas Dixon* (Durham, NC: John F. Blair, 1968), 200.

107   *"like a company . . . along the moonlit roads":* "The Birth of a Nation: Film Version of Dixon's 'The Clansman' Presented at the Liberty," *New York Times,* March 4, 1915, https://timesmachine.nytimes.com/timesmachine/1915/03/04/issue.html.

109   *"anointed the white men of the south . . . shall be supreme":* Cook, *Fire from the Flint,* 140.

110   *"But, as Pontius Pilate said, 'Truth? What is the truth?'":* *Birth of a Movement,* directed by Bestor Cram and Susan Gray (Boston: Northern Light Productions, 2017), 10:10.

112   *"It is history . . . all so terribly true":* The quote appears in so many histories that it has, at the very least, to be acknowledged, but as Wilson's biographer A. Scott Berg wrote, "Wilson almost certainly never said it. The encomium does not even appear in the unpublished memoirs of the self-serving Thomas Dixon. The only firsthand record of Wilson's feelings about the film appears in a letter three years later, in which he wrote,

'I have always felt that this was a very unfortunate production and I wish most sincerely that its production might be avoided, particularly in communities where there are so many colored people.' There is no record of his sentiments beyond that." Berg notes that "another member of the audience that night reported that the President seemed lost in thought during the film and exited the East Room upon its completion without saying a word to anybody. The first sentence of the famous 'review' definitely captures the voice of a lyrical historian; the second, however, sounds more like Chief Justice Edward White, whom Dixon invited to another screening and who admitted to having shouldered a rifle as a Klansman in New Orleans. Whether the remark was a conflation of the two men's thoughts or a complete fabrication, the comment did not appear in print for more than two decades. In any case, word of a White House screening circulated, and that was tantamount to a Presidential endorsement." For more on Wilson, see A. Scott Berg, *Wilson* (New York: Penguin, 2013).

112 *The autopsy report on Ahmaud Arbery revealed:* Madeline Holcombe and Eliott C. McLaughlin, "As Autopsy Report Shows Ahmaud Arbery Was Shot Twice in the Chest, GBI Investigates Recused DAs," CNN, May 12, 2020, https://www.cnn.com/2020/05/12/us/ahmaud-arbery-video-william-bryan/index.html.

113 *Ware County prosecutor George E. Barnhill . . . insufficient cause:* District Attorney George E. Barnhill to Captain Tom Jump, Glynn County Police Department, https://int.nyt.com/data/documenthelper/6916-george-barnhill-letter-to-glyn/b52fa09cdc974b970b79/optimized/full.pdf?fbclid=IwAR2N7rUkU_9tPDOHOiNlFJcqvM03N1AZs_67Ur2Y_6TAjr16Y_E1Xwu4OtE#page=1.

114 *Barnhill's son also worked at the Brunswick District Attorney's office:* Stubbs, "Ahmaud Arbery's Killing Was Met with Silence."

115 *"Arbery's mental health . . . an armed man":* Richard Fausset,

"Two Weapons, a Chase, a Killing and No Charges," *New York Times*, November 24, 2021, https://www.nytimes.com/2020/04/26/us/ahmed-arbery-shooting-georgia.html.

115 *a shoplifting charge and a firearms possession charge:* Russ Bynum, "Judge Asked to OK Evidence of Ahmaud Arbery's Past Troubles," ABC News, May 13, 2021, https://abcnews.go.com/US/wireStory/judge-asked-evidence-ahmaud-arberys-past-troubles-77638053.

117 *"There is an aphorism . . . in our own time":* Andrew Delbanco, *The War Before the War: Fugitive Slaves and the Struggle for America's Soul from the Revolution to the Civil War* (New York: Penguin, 2018), 13.

117–18 *groups of men in Klan garb rode on horseback through the streets:* Bosley Crowther, *New York Times Magazine*, February 2, 1965.

118 *"men who once wore gray uniforms . . . shot up the screen":* Ibid.

118 *an advertisement for recruitment appeared adjacent to an advertisement for the movie:* John Hope Franklin, "'Birth of a Nation'—Propaganda as History," *Massachusetts Review* 20, no. 3 (Autumn 1979): 417–34, https://www.jstor.org/stable/25088973.

120 *"One could not find . . . tell some day our side of the story to the world":* Ibid.

120–21 *he converted his church into an auxiliary hospital and built a stockade for prisoners on its grounds:* Berg, *Wilson*, 34.

121 *the Bible does not "ask for equality . . . servitude on the other":* Joseph R. Wilson, "Mutual Relation of Masters and Slaves as Taught in the Bible: A Discourse Preached in the First Presbyterian Church, Augusta, Georgia, on Sabbath Morning, Jan. 6, 1861," Steam Press of Chronicle & Sentinel, 1861, https://archive.org/stream/mutualrelationof00wils/mutualrelationof00wils_djvu.txt.

121 *"a little less virile me":* Berg, *Wilson*, 294.

121 *"a veritable overthrow of civilization . . . protect the southern*

country": Woodrow Wilson, *A History of the American People*, vol. V (New York: Harper and Brothers, 1902), 48–60.

122 *In the meantime, "we must deal with it as practical men"*: Kathleen L. Wolgemuth, "Woodrow Wilson and Federal Segregation," *Journal of Negro History* 44, no. 2 (April 1959): 158–73, http://www.jstor.org/stable/2716036.

124 *"amused contempt and pity . . . revelation of the other world"*: W. E. B. Du Bois, *The Souls of Black Folk* (New York: Penguin Classics, 1989), 9.

124 *"The history of the American Negro . . . closed roughly in his face"*: Ibid., 5.

125 *"the Negro represented either as an ignorant fool . . . faithful but doddering idiot"*: W. E. B. Du Bois, quoted in David Levering Lewis, *W. E. B. Du Bois: Biography of a Race, 1868–1919* (New York: Henry Holt, 1994).

125–26 *"If Negroes and all their friends were free . . . color prejudice preclude this"*: W. E. B. Du Bois, writing in *Sixth Annual Report of the National Association for the Advancement of Colored People*, 1915, as quoted in Stephen Weinberger, "*The Birth of a Nation* and the Making of the NAACP," *Journal of American Studies* 45, no. 1 (February 2011): 77–93, https://www.jstor.org/stable/23016760.

126 *Briefly, Du Bois and the NAACP entered into negotiations for a film*: Stokes, *D. W. Griffith's The Birth of a Nation*, 166.

127 *"For every right, with all thy might"*: "Timeline of William Monroe Trotter's Life," Trotter Multicultural Center, University of Michigan, https://trotter.umich.edu/article/timeline-william-monroe-trotters-life.

128–29 *so enamored of Thomas Dixon that she converted one of his novels into a stage play*: Darden Asbury Pyron, *Southern Daughter: The Life of Margaret Mitchell and the Making of Gone with the Wind* (New York: Oxford University Press, 1991), 56–57.

129 *"that the Negroes come out decidedly on the right side of the ledger"*: Thomas Cripps, *Slow Fade to Black: The Negro in*

American Film, 1900–1942 (New York: Oxford University Press, 1977), 361.

130 *the actors paraded down Peachtree Street, bathed in klieg lights:* Taylor Branch, *Parting the Waters: America in the King Years, 1954–63* (New York: Simon & Schuster, 2007), 54.

130 *There, elite Atlantans dressed in crinoline petticoats mingled:* Ibid., 55.

130 *a "negro choir" entertained the white crowd . . . dressed as a slave child, singing along:* Matthew Bernstein, quoted in Associated Press, " 'Gone with the Wind' at 75: Premiere Highlighted Racial Tensions in 1939 Atlanta," AL.com, March 28, 2019, https://www.al.com/entertainment/2014/12/gone_with _the_wind_premiered_7.html.

130 *Gable threatened to boycott the premiere:* Sidney Blumenthal, "Romanticizing the Villains of the Civil War," *Atlantic*, July 22, 2013, https://www.theatlantic.com/national/archive/2013/07 /romanticizing-the-villains-of-the-civil-war/277969/.

131 *she rose from her seat at a segregated table:* Seth Abramovitch, "Oscar's First Black Winner Accepted Her Honor in a Segregated 'No Blacks' Hotel in L.A.," *Hollywood Reporter*, February 19, 2015, https://www.hollywoodreporter.com/movies /movie-news/oscars-first-black-winner-accepted-774335/.

132 *A whole generation of progressive scholars and policymakers emerged from Beard's influence:* Thomas J. Pressly, *Americans Interpret Their Civil War* (New York: Collier Books, 1962), 238.

133 *"wasn't two men with a Confederate flag . . . shooting a jogger in the back":* Sarah Mervosh, "Ahmaud Arbery Video Was Leaked by a Lawyer Who Consulted with Suspects," *New York Times*, May 8, 2020, https://www.nytimes.com/2020/05/08 /us/ahmaud-arbery-video-lawyer.html.

134 *where he referred to it as "a Monkey Parade":* "Explosive Texts Found on Phone of Suspect in Georgia Jogger Murder Case," CBS News, October 9, 2020, https://www.cbsnews.com/news /ahmaud-arbery-killing-text-messages-william-roddy-bryan -phone-48-hours/.

137 *murder charges . . . for Greg McMichael, Travis McMichael, and Roddie Bryan:* Richard Fausset, "2 Suspects Charged with Murder in Ahmaud Arbery Shooting," *New York Times*, May 7, 2020, https://www.nytimes.com/2020/05/07/us/ahmaud -arbery-shooting-arrest.html.

137 *a nearly unanimous repeal of the 1863 citizens' arrest law in the state of Georgia:* Maya T. Prabhu, "Overhaul of Citizen's Arrest Law Heads to Georgia Governor's Desk," *Atlanta Journal-Constitution*, March 31, 2021, https://www.ajc.com/politics /overhaul-of-citizens-arrest-law-heads-to-georgia-governors -desk/BSBFRMSKEBCTZHYNEVWH7ZPNUE/.

137 *"It's more likely that those in power . . . we are all watching":* Jesse Washington, "In Seeking Justice for Ahmaud Arbery, These Athletes Know the Work Has Just Begun," Undefeated, May 19, 2020, https://theundefeated.com/features/in-seeking -justice-for-ahmaud-arbery-these-athletes-know-the-work -has-just-begun/.

137 *The police had told Arbery's family that he had been shot and killed while in the act of a crime:* Jennifer Rae Taylor and Kayla Vinson, "Ahmaud Arbery and the Local Legacy of Lynching," Marshall Project, May 21, 2020, https://www.themarshall project.org/2020/05/21/ahmaud-arbery-and-the-local-legacy -of-lynching.

138 *There is even a point when the police appear to be consoling the men:* Bert Roughton Jr. and Hannah Knowles, "Body Cam Video in Ahmaud Arbery Shooting Raises Familiar Concerns about Unequal Police Treatment," *Washington Post*, December 17, 2020, https://www.washingtonpost.com/national/newly -released-video-shows-police-did-not-immediately-help-ah maud-arbery-as-he-lay-dying/2020/12/17/82fba128-4094-11eb -a402-fba110db3b42_story.html.

139 *"When they stop you . . . Make sure you got a video":* Browne, Jordan, Khavin, and Tiefenthäler, "Ahmaud Arbery's Final Minutes" (the quoted passage is at the 0:25 mark in the video).

139 *To explain these, McMichael referenced two heart attacks:* Greg McMichael personnel file, as published by the *Guardian*, May 14, 2020, https://drive.google.com/file/d/1Ncf0OyBr5Ih JR2IDrBToSoIZ7eHVbc1e/view.

140 *Even more disturbing . . . "Glynn County PD issued":* Jerry Lambe, "New Police Bodycam Footage Shows Travis McMichael Blaming Ahmaud Arbery After Shooting Him," LawandCrime .com, December 17, 2020, https://lawandcrime.com/high -profile/new-police-bodycam-footage-shows-travis-mcmichael -blaming-ahmaud-arbery-after-shooting-him/.

140 *Such assistance is allowed, but only if the person is disabled or illiterate:* Josie Duffy Rice, "How to Punish Voters," *New York Times*, October 31, 2018, https://www.nytimes.com/2018 /10/31/opinion/election-voting-rights-fraud-prosecutions .html; and Joel Anderson, "A Georgia Grandmother Faced Charges After She Helped a Black Voter," *BuzzFeed News*, April 4, 2017, https://www.buzzfeednews.com/article/joel anderson/this-is-what-happened-when-a-georgia-grand mother-went-on.

CHAPTER 4: THE "INFLUENCERS"

144 *His role was an unofficial one, part of a contingent of volunteer "guards":* About two hours before the first shooting, the pro- ducer of a video for the *Daily Caller* interviewed Kyle Ritten- house at the Kenosha vehicle dealership; see "Alleged Kenosha Shooter Spoke with Daily Caller before Fatal Incident," YouTube video, Daily Caller channel, August 26, 2020, https://www .youtube.com/watch?v=kYb7loD7RGg; and https://www .facebook.com/kristantharris/videos/10164052138640646 /?t=2. See also Haley Willis, Muyi Xiao, Christiaan Triebert, Christoph Koettl, Stella Cooper, David Botti, John Ismay, and Ainara Tiefenthäler, "Tracking the Suspect in the Fatal Keno- sha Shootings," *New York Times*, August 27, 2020, https://

www.nytimes.com/2020/08/27/us/kyle-rittenhouse-kenosha
-shooting-video.html for an *NYT* analysis of various related
videos.

144 *while the Kenosha police did not wear body cameras, a neighbor's cell phone had recorded it all:* Azi Paybarah and Marie Fazio, "Kenosha Police Shooting of Black Man Is Investigated by Wisconsin Authorities," *New York Times*, August 26, 2020, https://www.nytimes.com/2020/08/23/us/kenosha -police-shooting.html.

144 *"If there's somebody hurt . . . but I also have my med kit":* Rittenhouse interview with the *Daily Caller.*

145 *"I'm talking flames licking the sky":* David Aaro, "Kenosha Car Dealership Owner Says Nothing Done to Prevent Damage During Unrest," Fox News, August 31, 2020, https://www.fox news.com/us/kenosha-car-dealership-owner-says-nothing -done-prevent-damage-unrest.

145 *Roughly thirty businesses sustained damage:* Emily Witt, "The Streets of Kenosha and the National Stage," *New Yorker*, September 1, 2020, https://www.newyorker.com/news/dispatch/the -streets-of-kenosha-and-the-national-stage.

145 *civic buildings alone sustained $2 million worth of destruction:* Noreen Nasir and Michael Tarm, "Kenosha Unrest Causes $2M in Damage to City-Owned Property," ABC News, September 1, 2020, https://abcnews.go.com/US/wireStory /kenosha-unrest-2m-damage-city-owned-property-72747127.

145 *it was time to protect the city from "evil thugs":* Neil MacFarquhar, "When Armed Vigilantes Are Summoned with a Few Keystrokes," *New York Times*, October 17, 2020, https://www.ny times.com/2020/10/16/us/kenosha-guard-militia-kevin -mathewson.html.

145 *"thug" . . . had become the twenty-first-century equivalent of "brute":* Calvin John Smiley and David Fakunle, "From 'Brute' to 'Thug': The Demonization and Criminalization of Unarmed Black Male Victims in America," *Journal of Human Behavior*

in the Social Environment 26, nos. 3–4 (January 20, 2016): 350–66.

145–46 *plea spread from Facebook to Reddit . . . thousands responded:* MacFarquhar, "When Armed Vigilantes Are Summoned with a Few Keystrokes."

146 *"We appreciate you guys, we really do":* "Alleged Kenosha Shooter Spoke with Daily Caller before Fatal Incident" as excerpted in https://www.facebook.com/sam.wunderle/videos /10216501641126335/ (see 0:48-minute mark).

146 *Their numbers would eventually swell to two thousand, including many troops requested from nearby states:* Janet Loehrke, George Petras, and Ramon Padilla, "A Visual Timeline of Violence in Kenosha after Police Shooting of Jacob Blake," *USA Today,* August 27, 2020, //www.usatoday.com /in-depth/graphics/2020/08/27/jacob-blake-kenosha-police -shootishooting-two-killed/3442878001/.

146 *By then, the FBI and other federal personnel, two hundred in all:* Laurel White, "Gov. Tony Evers Doubles National Guard Presence in Kenosha," Wisconsin Public Radio, August 26, 2020, https://www.wpr.org/gov-tony-evers-doubles-national -guard-presence-kenosha.

147 *The protesters had formed into their own subsets:* John Eligon, " 'Enough Is Enough': New Racial Justice Leaders Rise in Kenosha," *New York Times,* September 10, 2020, https://www .nytimes.com/2020/08/29/us/29kenosha-march-protests .html?searchResultPosition=1.

147 *it was unclear whether there was any consistent identification among them:* Ali Swenson, "No Evidence 175 Arrested in Kenosha Identified as 'BLM-antifa,' " Associated Press, September 1, 2020, https://apnews.com/article/archive-fact -checking-9367990380.

147 *"The @NewYorker can sit behind a desk and arm chair QB while people like me risk their life":* Kristan T. Harris, Facebook post, https://www.facebook.com/kristantharris.

148   *a list that includes "liberty, police state, corruption, philosophy, technology":* "About," *Rundown Live,* https://therundown live.com/about.

149   *The livestream, when seen on YouTube:* "[EXHIBIT 18] Kristan T. Harris / The Rundown Live Livestream August 25 Kenosha," YouTube video, posted by Orcanut, May 12, 2021, 1:51:52, https://www.youtube.com/watch?v=PpkmYn7HzXM (henceforth referred to as KTH).

150   *"it looks like they're protecting their businesses, which is cool":* KTH, 4:40.

150   *Harris tells them that the police are enforcing a curfew:* KTH, 5:21.

151   *"BLM, that's what they do":* KTH, 9:40.

152   *Harris takes mild offense and tells the man that he, himself, identifies as libertarian:* KTH, 11:20.

152   *The "libertarian douchebag" that the man was trying to recall was in fact Garrett Foster:* Katie Hall and Danny Davis, "Videos: US Air Force Veteran, Protester Shot to Death during Downtown Austin Protest," American Military News, July 27, 2020, https://americanmilitarynews.com/2020/07/us-air -force-veteran-protester-shot-to-death-during-downtown -austin-protest/.

153   *"I've noticed . . . their car or whatever":* KTH, 16:40–17:02.

153–54   *you have to build the "muscle memory" that will allow you to react instinctively:* KTH, 21:30.

154   *"I mean, me, personally . . . And then, boom!":* KTH, 21:40.

154   *Rittenhouse, who has made his way back into Harris's shot, says that they're "mixing ammonia and gasoline":* KTH, 54:37.

155   "Rundown Live . . . *links to the Cash App and to PayPal":* KTH, 62:38.

165   *including what is now referred to as the "Pin Drop Speech":* "James Baldwin – Pin Drop Speech," YouTube video, posted by GLAZAR, July 26, 2017, https://www.youtube.com /watch?v=NUBh9GqFU3A.

165 *the fiery exchange he had with philosopher and Yale University professor Paul Weiss:* "Baldwin on Dick Cavett," YouTube video, posted by E Land, October 5, 2017, https://www.youtube.com/watch?v=_fZQQ7o16yQ.

165 *fascinating roundtable discussion undertaken on the day of the March on Washington:* "Hollywood Civil Rights Roundtable 1963 Harry Belafonte, Marlon Brando, Charlton Heston, Sidney Poitier, James Baldwin," Vimeo video, posted by Ira Gallen, June 1, 2020, https://vimeo.com/425001504.

166 *"the ugliest boy he had ever seen":* James Baldwin, *The Devil Finds Work* (New York: Vintage, 2013), 6.

167 *insisting that it was nothing more than a proper "white English" term:* David Adams Leeming, *James Baldwin: A Biography* (New York: Arcade, 2015), 511–12.

167 *"latest slave rebellion":* Baldwin used this term in a speech he delivered on January 15, 1979, at UC Berkeley's Wheeler Hall Auditorium; see Ivan Natividad, "The Time James Baldwin Told UC Berkeley That Black Lives Matter," *Berkeley News*, June 19, 2020, https://news.berkeley.edu/2020/06/19/the-time-james-baldwin-told-uc-berkeley-that-black-lives-matter/. You can watch the speech, which was titled "On Language, Race, and the Black Writer," here: https://www.c-span.org/video/?170651-1/james-baldwin-speech. The full text of the speech can be found in James Baldwin, *The Cross of Redemption: Uncollected Writings*, edited by Randall Kenan (New York: Vintage, 2010), 140–44. It also includes the following: "Well I know, in spite of the American Constitution, in spite of all born-again Christians, I know that my father was not a mule and not a thing. And that my sister was not born to be the plaything of idle white sheriffs."

167 *Baldwin was accused of demonstrating "intellectual inconsistencies":* Douglas Field, *All Those Strangers: The Art and Lives of James Baldwin* (New York: Oxford University Press, 2015), 53. Field refers to Harold Cruse, the Black academic and author of *The Crisis of the Negro Intellectual*, as using this phrase to

complain about Baldwin. The setting was the infamous meeting of Black leaders with Robert Kennedy at Kennedy's New York City apartment on May 24, 1963, which triggered, Field writes, federal "surveillance on the writer." Field goes on, "The ill-fated meeting with Kennedy illustrates Baldwin's willingness to get involved in civil rights issues, not just as a writer but as a participant or, to use his preferred term, 'witness.' For Harold Cruse, Baldwin's contribution to the Kennedy meeting was ineffectual, evincing the writer's 'intellectual inconsistencies,' and his refusal or inability to engage with 'sociology and economics jazz.' Cruse's harsh assessment of Baldwin may have been right in some ways: Baldwin was more interested in the moral complexity of politics than in the finer details."

167 *"a real writer . . . certain that he has achieved his intention"*: James Baldwin, *Nobody Knows My Name* (New York: Vintage, 2013), 149.

167–68 *"Poets (by which I mean all artists) . . . I don't know how long a time"*: Baldwin, *The Cross of Redemption*, 50–51.

168 race *"was the gate I had to unlock before I could hope to write about anything else"*: James Baldwin, *Notes of a Native Son* (Boston: Beacon Press, 2012), 27.

168 *"I didn't have to walk around . . . It's not my problem"*: Fern Marja Eckman, *The Furious Passage of James Baldwin* (Lanham, MD: M. Evans, 1966), 118.

170 *"an elaborate justification of mass murder"*: Baldwin, *The Devil Finds Work*, 47.

170 *"I could, simply, no longer sit around . . . time I went home and paid mine"*: James Baldwin, *No Name in the Street* (New York: Vintage, 2013), 50.

170 *"to everyone's astonishment . . . want to be treated like men"*: James Baldwin, "Fifth Avenue, Uptown," *Esquire*, July 1960, https://www.esquire.com/news-politics/a3638/fifth-avenue-uptown/.

170–71 *But it owes its surge in popularity to Twitter, especially the so-called Black Twitter:* Christian Roman, "Key Hashtags in

'Black Twitter' Activism," *New York Times*, August 13, 2014, https://www.nytimes.com/video/us/100000003053125/key -hashtags-in-black-twitter-activism.html?searchResult Position=1.

171 *"most-tweeted literary authority"*: William J. Maxwell, "Born-Again, Seen-Again James Baldwin: Post-Postracial Criticism and the Literary History of Black Lives Matter," *American Literary History* 28, no. 4 (Winter 2016): 812–27. Maxwell also writes, "Seen through Baldwin's eyes, the challenge of his time, and of BLM, is to accept that liberation can be won only 'if you will not be ashamed, if you will only not play it safe' (*Giovanni's Room*, 267)."

172 *"Not everything that is faced can be changed; but nothing can be changed until it is faced"*: James Baldwin, "As Much of the Truth as One Can Bear," *New York Times*, January 14, 1962, https://www.nytimes.com/1962/01/14/archives/as-much -truth-as-one-can-bear-to-speak-out-about-the-world-as-it -is.html.

172 *One researcher used reverse engineering to delineate "six subtly different Baldwins"*: Melanie Walsh, "Tweets of a Native Son: The Quotation and Recirculation of James Baldwin from Black Power to #BlackLivesMatter," *American Quarterly* 70, no. 3 (September 2018): 531–59, https://doi.org/10.1353/aq .2018.0034.

173 *"The purpose of art is to lay bare the questions that have been hidden by the answers"*: As we discuss with other Baldwin quotes, this one, often cited, is a paraphrase of what he actually wrote. See his essay "The Creative Process," as published in James Baldwin, *The Price of the Ticket: Collected Nonfiction, 1948–1985* (New York: St. Martin's Press, 1985), 321–24. There he writes: "The artist cannot and must not take anything for granted but must drive to the heart of every answer and expose the question the answer hides." See also this discussion of how the quote has evolved: "The Artist . . . Must Drive to the Heart of Every Answer and Expose the Question the Answer Hides,"

Quote Investigator, April 6, 2019, https://quoteinvestigator
.com/2019/04/06/hides/.

176 *"that what is really important . . . suffering of any person is
really universal":* James Baldwin, Emile Capouya, Lorraine
Hansberry, Nat Hentoff, Langston Hughes, and Alfred Kazin,
"The Negro in American Culture," *CrossCurrents* 11, no. 3 (Summer 1961): 205–24, https://www.jstor.org/stable/24456864.

177 *"Color . . . is a political reality":* Baldwin, *The Fire Next Time,*
104.

177 *"relations between Negroes and whites . . . we are all part of it":*
James Campbell, *Talking at the Gates: A Life of James Baldwin* (New York: Penguin, 1991), 38.

177 *Still, he understood how radical a proposition this was:* In *The
Fire Next Time,* Baldwin writes that "color is not a human or
personal reality; it is a political reality. But this is a distinction
so extremely hard to make that the West has not been able
to make it yet. And at the center of this dreadful storm, this
vast confusion, stand the black people of this nation, who must
now share the fate of a nation that has never accepted them,
to which they were brought in chains." Baldwin, *The Fire Next
Time,* 104.

177 *In an unpublished draft of his essay "The Price of the Ticket":*
Eddie S. Glaude Jr., *Begin Again: James Baldwin's America
and Its Urgent Lessons for Our Own* (New York: Crown, 2020),
154.

178 *"The problem in America . . . the result of what we've done":*
"James Baldwin – Pin Drop Speech," YouTube video.

179 *"Now this means very shortly . . . inadvertently stumble on this
corpse":* Baldwin, *Nobody Knows My Name,* 126.

180 *"deliver clarity in a world of confusion":* "About," Storyful,
https://storyful.com/about/.

180 *A few months after the events, Harris posted a longer, two-
and-a-half-hour assemblage from that night:* "[EXHIBIT 41]
(Version 3 - OLD) Tracking Kyle Rittenhouse - Kenosha 8/25
Protest Synchronized Videos," YouTube video, posted by Orca-

nut, November 26, 2020, https://www.youtube.com/watch?v=7
ferrn7Shyk.

180 *who suffered from bipolar disease and had only that afternoon
been released from a psychiatric hospital:* Robert Klemko and
Greg Jaffe, "A Mentally Ill Man, a Heavily Armed Teenager
and the Night Kenosha Burned," *Washington Post*, October 3,
2020, https://www.washingtonpost.com/nation/2020/10/03
/kenosha-shooting-victims/.

181 *At 23:48:44, a BLM protester fires a warning shot in the air:*
This was Joshua Ziminski, who also used the online pseu-
donym Alexander (or Alex) Blaine. According to a far-right
website, Wisconsin Right Now, court records show that
Ziminski has a lengthy criminal history in Wisconsin for carrying a concealed weapon and other offenses. He had an open
domestic-abuse criminal case at the time of the Rittenhouse
shooting. See Jim Piwowarczyk, "Joshua Ziminski: Charged
for Firing Gun Just Before Rittenhouse Shooting," Wisconsin Right Now, October 14, 2020, https://www.wisconsinright
now.com/2020/10/14/joshua-ziminski-alex-blaine/.

181 *"I just killed somebody!":* See Rittenhouse's lawyer's response
to the state of Wisconsin's motion to modify the conditions of
Rittenhouse's bond: https://www.wpr.org/sites/default/files
/rittenhouse_response_to_bond_motion_filed.pdf.

181 *Anthony Huber . . . throws his skateboard at Rittenhouse's
head:* Jessica Lee, "What's True and False About People Kyle
Rittenhouse Shot in Kenosha," Snopes.com, December 16,
2021, https://www.snopes.com/news/2020/09/11/rittenhouse
-victims-records/.

182 *"vaporized" his bicep:* Michael Tarm, Scott Bauer, and Amy
Forliti, "Shooting Victim Says He Was Pointing His Gun at
Rittenhouse," Associated Press, November 8, 2021, https://ap
news.com/article/kyle-rittenhouse-wisconsin-shootings-george
-floyd-homicide-cbd8653c42406417c2d3d8559632e3bb.

183 *He had heeded the call to come to Kenosha to protect "property":* Jemima McEvoy, "How Social Media Sleuths Found

the Suspected Kenosha Shooter 12 Hours Before His Arrest," *Forbes*, August 27, 2020, https://www.forbes.com/sites/jemima mcevoy/2020/08/27/how-social-media-sleuths-found-the -suspected-kenosha-shooter-12-hours-before-his-arrest/?sh =cb0614f327fa.

183 *He would eventually be charged with five felonies:* Here is the criminal complaint for Rittenhouse case: https://www .wpr.org/sites/default/files/rittenhouse_response_to_bond _motion_filed.pdf

186 *For a while, the Rittenhouse family even got in on the act, selling their own tees, hoodies, and hats:* Mark Guarino, "Kenosha Shooter Kyle Rittenhouse's New Merchandise Site Signals 'New Era' of Criminal Defense," *Washington Post*, December 22, 2020, https://www.washingtonpost.com/national/kyle-ritten house-website/2020/12/22/5d6fc122-445f-11eb-a277-49a6d 1f9dff1_story.html; and "Online Store Stops Selling Ritten-house Family's Merchandise," AP News, December 24, 2020, https://apnews.com/article/shootings-wisconsin-kenosha -00a31542096b7f46ddbc443c188f8efd.

186 *"law firm for the digital age . . . dedicated to the lost art of combat by trial":* Pierce Bainbridge Beck Price & Hecht, LLP, https://piercebainbridge.com/the-firm/.

187 *representing seventeen defendants in federal court despite never having tried a criminal case before:* "Notice Regarding Defense Counsel John M. Pierce, Esq.," https://storage.court listener.com/recap/gov.uscourts.dcd.229273/gov.uscourts .dcd.229273.23.0.pdf.

188 *caught "in the crosshairs of institutional forces that are much more powerful than him":* Jason Fechner, "Kyle Rittenhouse's Attorneys Claim Self-Defense in Kenosha Shootings," Spec-trum News 1, August 29, 2020, https://spectrumnews1.com /wi/milwaukee/news/2020/08/29/teen-s-attorneys-claim -self-defense-in-kenosha-shootings.

188 *they had rushed to judgment without performing an "in-depth review of the available video footage":* Ibid.

188 *his own edited video of the events of that night, "The Truth in Eleven Minutes":* "Kyle Rittenhouse - The Truth in 11 Minutes," YouTube video, #FightBack channel, September 22, 2020, 11:23, https://www.youtube.com/watch?v=E4dhPM99i4I.

189 *For the most part, the raw information that the narrator recites is true:* There are, nonetheless, some errors that are worth pointing out. The narration says that after shooting Rosenbaum, Rittenhouse called for help, when we know from the criminal complaint that he instead called his friend Dominick Black.

193 *"the visible reality hides a deeper one . . . all our action and achievement rest on things unseen":* Baldwin, *The Price of the Ticket,* 317.

193–94 *The old oppressive hierarchies would come tumbling down . . . "expand the horizons of freedom":* Larry Diamond, "Liberation Technology," *Journal of Democracy* 21, no 3 (July 2010): 69–83, https://doi.org/10.1353/jod.0.0190.

CHAPTER 5: ANOTHER CHANCE

198 *Jason Kessler, a Charlottesville local who was once a member of the Occupy movement:* Ian Shapira, "Inside Jason Kessler's Hate-Fueled Rise," *Washington Post,* August 11, 2018, https://www.washingtonpost.com/local/inside-jason-kesslers -hate-fueled-rise/2018/08/11/335eaf42-999e-11e8-b60b-1c897 f17e185_story.html.

198 *He now runs a blog called* Protect the West!*:* *Protect the West!* (blog), https://jasonkessler.us/.

198 *"You talk about black people . . . advocate for our rights as well":* "Charlottesville City Council Votes to Rename Lee, Jackson Parks," NBC29, June 19, 2017, https://web .archive.org/web/20170813144643/http://www.nbc29.com /story/35595559/charlottesville-city-council-votes-to-rename -lee-jackson-parks.

198 *drafted in response to a petition originating with a fifteen-*

year-old local high school girl: Theresa Vargas, "The Girl Who Brought Down a Statue," *Washington Post,* July 17, 2021, https://www.washingtonpost.com/local/zyahna-bryant-char lottesville-lee-statue/2021/07/17/9073933e-e688-11eb-b722 -89ea0dde7771_story.html.

198 *Lee's farewell address to the troops, officially General Order No. 9:* "General Order #9," National Park Service, https:// www.nps.gov/apco/general-order-9.htm.

199 *"virgin-birth theory of secession":* James M. McPherson, "Southern Comfort," *New York Review of Books,* April 12, 2001, https://www.nybooks.com/articles/2001/04/12/southern -comfort/.

199 *the Ku Klux Klan reached its peak membership nationwide, a number that ran somewhere in the millions:* The most recent history of the 1920s Klan is Linda Gordon's book *The Second Coming of the KKK: The Ku Klux Klan of the 1920s and the American Political Tradition* (New York: Liveright, 2017). Here, on page 217, is how she addresses membership numbers: "Reliable figures on the second Klan's membership are unavailable. Estimates of its size ranged from one million to ten million members. The lower figures are probably the most reliable, as both pro- and anti-Klan people exaggerated its size, and members left the Klan as often as new people joined."

200 *"hordes of the most undesirable people in Europe" arriving at its shores:* Kenneth L. Roberts, "Lest We Forget," *Saturday Evening Post,* April 28, 1923, 3.

200 *would be to "open the country to an African invasion":* Daniel Okrent, *The Guarded Gate: Bigotry, Eugenics, and the Law That Kept Two Generations of Jews, Italians, and Other European Immigrants Out of America* (New York: Scribner, 2019), 342. While not footnoted there, Okrent, in an email exchange with the authors, reported that he "found that quote in the Joseph Lee Papers, at the Massachusetts Historical Society . . . in a file memo Lee wrote March 12, 1924, about the Senate debate on Johnson-Reed." Joseph Lee was the founder and president of

the Massachusetts Civic League from 1897 to 1937 and an officer in the Immigration Restriction League from 1905 to 1937.

201 *"jumbled-up mass of undigested race material":* The quote is from white supremacist writer Madison Grant, as found in Okrent, *The Guarded Gate,* 331.

201 *"At one extreme . . . closer to the negro":* Carl C. Brigham, *A Study of American Intelligence* (Princeton, NJ: Princeton University Press, 1923).

202 *"regional defense, self-flattery and polemics":* C. Vann Woodward, *American Counterpoint: Slavery and Racism in the North-South Dialogue* (New York: Oxford University Press, 1971), 7.

203 *"For that matter . . . It is, of course, the Jews":* Eric K. Ward, "Skin in the Game: How Antisemitism Animates White Nationalism," Political Research Associates, June 29, 2017, https://www.politicalresearch.org/2017/06/29/skin-in-the-game-how-antisemitism-animates-white-nationalism#sthash.xyKGl7XX.s8lwywIo.dpbs.

203 *an impromptu gathering of around 250 of them shouted "Blood and Soil" and "White Lives Matter":* Matt Pearce, "Chanting 'Blood and Soil!' White Nationalists with Torches March on University of Virginia," *Los Angeles Times,* August 11, 2017, https://www.latimes.com/nation/la-na-white-virginia-rally-20170811-story.html.

204 *even as he, hypocritically, benefited from the work of four hundred slaves at Monticello, among them the mulatto Sally Hemings:* According to the museum site at Monticello, Jefferson had six hundred slaves over his lifetime. Four hundred were at Monticello; the other two hundred served at his other properties. Roughly 130 at a time served at Monticello. See "Slavery FAQs—Property," Monticello.org, https://www.monticello.org/slavery/slavery-faqs/property/.

205 *he viewed the end of bondage as an aspirational goal:* Joseph J. Ellis, *American Dialogue: The Founders and Us* (New York: Knopf, 2018), 23.

205–6 *"secrete less by the kidnies . . . not the effect merely of their condition of life"*: Thomas Jefferson, *Writings*, edited by Merrill D. Peterson (New York: Library of America Founders Collection, Penguin, 1984), "Notes on the State of Virginia."

206 *Lincoln showed interest in the idea. So did Harriet Beecher Stowe:* Josephine Donovan, "A Source for Stowe's Ideas on Race in *Uncle Tom's Cabin*," *NWSA Journal* 7, no. 3 (Autumn 1995): 24–34. Stowe later regretted her endorsement of colonization. For a discussion of Lincoln's interest in colonization, see Todd Brewster, *Lincoln's Gamble: The Tumultuous Six Months That Gave America the Emancipation Proclamation and Changed the Course of the Civil War* (New York: Scribner, 2014), chapter V, "Send Them Away."

207 *"a little rebellion . . . tree of liberty"*: Thomas Jefferson to William Stephens Smith, November 13, 1787, in Jefferson, *Writings*, 911.

207 *better to "be exercised when wrong . . . than not to be exercised at all"*: Thomas Jefferson to Abigail Adams, February 22, 1787, in Jefferson, *Writings*, 890.

208 *Madison, wisely, disagreed:* Drew R. McCoy, *The Last of the Fathers: James Madison and the Republican Legacy* (Cambridge, UK: Cambridge University Press, 1989), 45–61.

208 *a tribute to Jefferson's support for religious freedom:* "God Is in the Details," *University of Virginia Magazine*, Fall 2014, https://uvamagazine.org/articles/god_is_in_the_details.

209 *"and prove to the world that if we did not succeed in our struggle, we were worthy of success"*: Samantha Baskind, "Moses Jacob Ezekiel's *Religious Liberty* (1876) and the Nineteenth-Century Jewish American Experience," in Michelle Facos, ed., *A Companion to Nineteenth Century Art* (Hoboken, NJ: Wiley-Blackwell, 2018).

210 *"This is where the magic happened"*: Michael Edison Hayden, "Charlottesville Murder Suspect's Teacher: 'He Thought Nazis Were Pretty Cool Guys,'" Yahoo! News, August 13, 2017, https://www.yahoo.com/gma/charlottesville-murder

-suspects-teacher-thought-nazis-were-pretty-210804600—
abc-news-topstories.html.

210 *After high school, he enrolled in the army but was discharged
after just five months:* Alan Blinder, "Suspect in Charlottesville
Attack Had Displayed Troubling Behavior," *New York Times,*
August 13, 2017, https://www.nytimes.com/2017/08/13/us
/suspect-in-charlottesville-attack-had-displayed-troubling
-behavior.html.

210 *"We're not the one [sic] who need to be careful," he responded:*
Kristine Phillips, " 'We're Not the One Who Need to Be
Careful,' James A. Fields Jr. Texted Mother before Charlottesville Rally," *Washington Post,* December 4, 2018,
https://www.washingtonpost.com/local/public-safety/were
-not-the-one-who-need-to-be-careful-james-a-fields-texted
-mother-before-charlottesville-rally/2018/12/04/c69e63e4
-f752-11e8-863c-9e2f864d47e7_story.html.

210 *Fields was seen dressed in a white polo shirt and khaki pants:*
Nedra Rhone, "Khaki Pants and Polos the New Look for White
Supremacists," *Atlanta Journal-Constitution,* August 18, 2017,
https://www.ajc.com/blog/talk-town/khaki-pants-and-polos
-the-new-look-for-white-supremacists/MmiGOURZjbpK
YkZg0ntf3O/.

210 *sentimental, almost mystical connection between "racial
purity" and the "homeland":* Susan Neiman, *Learning from
the Germans: Race and the Memory of Evil* (New York: Farrar,
Straus and Giroux, 2019), 29.

210 *Fields was not a member of their group and had only picked
up a shield when offered one at the rally:* Justin Wm. Moyer
and Lindsey Bever, "Vanguard America, a White Supremacist
Group, Denies Charlottesville Ramming Suspect Was a Member," *Washington Post,* August 15, 2017, https://www.washington
post.com/local/vanguard-america-a-white-supremacist-group
-denies-charlottesville-attacker-was-a-member/2017/08/15
/2ec897c6-810e-11e7-8072-73e1718c524d_story.html.

211 *the company "is not associated in any way with the events*

that took place in Charlottesville": Aaron Smith, "Tiki Torch Company: We Have Nothing to Do with White Nationalism," CNN, August 14, 2017, https://money.cnn.com/2017/08/14 /news/companies/tiki-torches-charlottesville/index.html.

211 *"never seen so many white people standing up for Black people":* David Brennan, "Charlottesville Unite the Right Attacker Did Not Brake as He Drove into Crowd, Witness Says," *Newsweek*, December 1, 2018, https://www.newsweek.com /charlottesville-unite-right-attacker-did-not-brake-he-drove -crowd-witness-1240083.

212 *"That's what someone's eyes look like when they're dead":* "Ohio Man Sentenced to Life in Prison for Federal Hate Crimes Related to August 2017 Car Attack at Rally in Charlottesville, Virginia," press release, US Department of Justice, June 28, 2019, https://www.justice.gov/opa/pr/ohio-man-sentenced -life-prison-federal-hate-crimes-related-august-2017-car -attack-rally; and Samantha Baars, "Day 5: More Victim and Police Testimony in James Fields' Trial," C-Ville, November 30, 2018, https://www.c-ville.com/day-5/.

212 *a cartoon meme . . . adopted by the alt-right:* Holly Swinyard, "Pepe the Frog Creator Wins $15,000 Settlement against Infowars," *Guardian*, June 13, 2019, https://www.theguard ian.com/books/2019/jun/13/pepe-the-frog-creator-wins -15000-settlement-against-infowars.

213 *"You have the Right to Protest . . . But I'm Late for Work":* Jasmine Turner, "Fields' Instagram Posts Depicting Car Running into Crowd to Be Shown," NBC12, November 30, 2018, https://www.nbc12.com/2018/11/30/fields-instagram-posts -depicting-car-running-into-crowd-allowed-trial/; and Claudia Koerner and Cora Lewis, "Here's What We Know About the Man Accused of Killing a Woman at a White Supremacist Rally," *BuzzFeed News*, August 14, 2017, https://www.buzz feednews.com/article/claudiakoerner/what-we-know-about -james-alex-fields-charlottesville-crash.

216 *"The basic building block . . . real estate out in the void":*

Michael Moynihan, *The Coming American Renaissance: How to Benefit from America's Economic Resurgence* (New York: Simon & Schuster, 1996), 193–96.

221   *in effect, "two constitutions":* Don E. Fehrenbacher, *Slavery, Law, and Politics: The Dred Scott Case in Historical Perspective* (Oxford, UK: Oxford University Press, 1981), 15.

221–22   *in America the laying of track was by itself the founding act in the conquering of the wilderness:* Wolfgang Schivelbusch, *The Railway Journey: The Industrialization of Time and Space in the Nineteenth Century* (New York: Urizen Books, 1980).

222   *the "black cylindric body . . . power-pulse of the continent":* Walt Whitman, "To a Locomotive in Winter," in *The Works of Walt Whitman*, vol. I (Farrar, Straus and Giroux, 1968), 407.

222   *"lap the Miles . . . At its own stable door":* Emily Dickinson, "I like to see it lap the Miles," in *Poems by Emily Dickinson, Three Series, Complete* (Seattle: Amazon.com Services LLC, 2012), 62–63.

224   *But the Court found against him:* Roger B. Taney, "The Dred Scott Decision," 1857, reproduced on the Digital History website, https://www.digitalhistory.uh.edu/disp_textbook.cfm?smtID=3&psid=293.

224–25   *would have "burned into his very soul the brand of inferiority":* Blight, *Frederick Douglass*, 290.

229   *Donald Trump, responding to the story, praised Robert E. Lee and declared that there were "very fine people on both sides":* Angie Drobnic Holan, "In Context: Donald Trump's 'Very Fine People on Both Sides' Remarks (Transcript)," Politifact, April 26, 2019, https://www.politifact.com/article/2019/apr/26/context-trumps-very-fine-people-both-sides-remarks/.

230   *Within days, Cole White, a cook at Top Dog . . . was outed:* Maura Judkis, "Charlottesville White Nationalist Demonstrator Loses Job at Libertarian Hot Dog Shop," *Washington Post*, August 14, 2017, https://www.washingtonpost.com/news/food/wp/2017/08/14/charlottesville-white-nationalist-demonstrator-fired-from-libertarian-hot-dog-shop/.

231 *University of Nevada at Reno (UNR) student Peter Cvjeta-novic was also identified:* "Student/Employee in March Won't Be Expelled or Fired," KOLO8, August 13, 2017, https://www.kolotv.com/content/news/UNR-student-in-viral--440205643.html.

232–33 *"I have got to that condition . . . without winking my eyes":* Gary W. Gallagher and Alan T. Nolan, eds., *The Myth of the Lost Cause and Civil War History* (Bloomington: Indiana University Press, 2000), 37.

233 *The measure was only repealed in 2014:* Teo Armus, "Door by Door, a Push to Rename Confederate Streets for George Floyd and Breonna Taylor," *Washington Post*, October 17, 2021, https://www.washingtonpost.com/dc-md-va/2021/10/17/alexandria-confederate-streets-floyd-renaming/.

233 *"a damned nigger regiment" is how Forrest described them:* Jay Winik, *April 1865: The Month That Saved America* (New York: HarperCollins, 2001), 280–81.

234 *thirty thousand people—about a third of the city—attended the ceremony:* Court Carney, "The Contested Image of Nathan Bedford Forrest," *Journal of Southern History* 67, no. 3 (August 2001): 601–30. Memphis's population in 1900 was 102,320; today it is 633,104.

235 *without a two-thirds vote of approval from the Tennessee Historical Commission:* The law can be found here: https://law.justia.com/codes/tennessee/2016/title-4/chapter-1/part-4/section-4-1-412/. See also Holly Meyer, "Why Removing Confederate Monuments in Tennessee Is Not an Easy Process," *Tennessean*, August 17, 2017, https://www.tennessean.com/story/news/2017/08/17/why-removing-confederate-monuments-tennessee-not-easy-process/573067001/; and David A. Graham, "Memphis's Novel Strategy for Tearing Down Confederate Statues," *Atlantic*, December 21, 2017, https://www.theatlantic.com/politics/archive/2017/12/memphis-confederate-statues/548990/.

236 *the only acknowledgment of Forrest's brutal past is to say that*

he is "a controversial figure": "Nathan Bedford Forrest State Park," Tennessee State Parks, https://tnstateparks.com/parks /info/nathan-bedford-forrest.

238 *He compared his project favorably to the unrealized dreams of Alexander the Great:* Simon Schama, *Landscape and Memory* (New York: Vintage, 1996), 401.

238 *he had been the original sculptor for the Confederate carving at Stone Mountain:* John Taliaferro, *Great White Fathers: The Story of the Obsessive Quest to Create Mount Rushmore* (New York: Public Affairs, 2002), 55.

239 *Immigrants were "slippered assassins":* Ibid., 192–93.

241 *"almost . . . to the point of fetishism":* Elizabeth Mitchell, *Liberty's Torch: The Great Adventure to Build the Statue of Liberty* (New York: Grove Atlantic, 2014), 38.

242 *the white southerner's fascination with protecting the fragile sex and, implicitly, the threat posed to her by the Black race:* Tyler Stovall, *White Freedom: The Racial History of an Idea* (Princeton, NJ: Princeton University Press, 2021), 79.

244 *"free yourself, free the Panther 21, free the streets . . .":* "Free yourself, free the Panther 21, free the streets, free food, free housing, free medicine, free Bobby Seale, free education . . . ," Library of Congress, https://www.loc.gov/item/2015649390/.

245 *"as a blurred grayish something . . . ravaged by natural disaster":* John Edgar Wideman, "Looking at Emmett Till," in Lee Gutkind, ed., *In Fact: The Best of Creative Nonfiction* (New York: W. W. Norton & Company, 2005), 24.

246 *"His mother had done a bold thing":* Muhammad Ali, *The Greatest: My Own Story* (New York: Mayflower Books Ltd, 1976), 39–40.

249 *"What, then, is the American . . . this new man?":* J. Hector St. John de Crèvecoeur, *Letters from an American Farmer and Sketches of Eighteenth-Century America* (New York: Penguin, 1981), 69.

249 *"all his ancient prejudices and manners" are left behind:* Ibid., 70.

249–50 *"nature opens her broad lap to receive the perpetual acces-sion of new-comers"*: Ibid., 42–43.

250 *"persons they know not, and who have no other power over them than that of violence"*: Ibid., 169.

250–51 *"I shudder . . . covered with a multitude of wounds"*: Ibid., 177–79.

Index

Index

Index